Global Vision

Global Vision

Building New Models for the Corporation of the Future

John L. Daniels
Dr. N. Caroline Daniels

McGraw-Hill, Inc.

New York   San Francisco   Washington, D.C.   Auckland   Bogotá
Caracas   Lisbon   London   Madrid   Mexico City   Milan
Montreal   New Delhi   San Juan   Singapore
Sydney   Tokyo   Toronto

Library of Congress Cataloging-in-Publication Data

Daniels, John L.
    Global vision : building new models for the corporation of the
future / John L. Daniels, N. Caroline Daniels.
        p.   cm.
    Includes index.
    ISBN 0-07-015350-7
    1. International business enterprises.   2. International business
enterprises—Management.   I. Daniels, Caroline.   II. Title.
HD2755.5.D35   1993
658.8'48—dc20   93-30294
                                                                      CIP

1 2 3 4 5 6 7 8 9 0   DOC/DOC   9 9 8 7 6 5 4 3

ISBN 0-07-015350-7

*The sponsoring editor for this book was Betsy Brown. It was set in New
Baskerville by North Market Street Graphics.*

Printed and bound by R. R. Donnelley & Sons Company.

To Reuel and Wilder, Justin and Carrie,
Christopher and Jeffrey, Allen and Taylor,
and Douglas: future global executives

Contents

5. Building Global Teams and Individuals   105

6. Global I.T.: Connecting the World   125

Foreword

One gets easily tired of globalization. The concept has been around for quite a while, enough certainly to become commonplace, a cliché. It is vague enough to be broadly applicable: three offices around the world and you have a global firm . . . It is appealing enough to generate adhesion at first sight: opposing globalization would be like being against the environment! And the ultimate synthesis, proof of our consensus, has already been created: any speech on international business must feature terms such as "glocal," which for some unknown reason is systematically preferred to "lobal."

Is it therefore time to put aside globalization and move to the next topic in business strategy and business academia? No, we should resist this temptation, for three reasons. First, the globalization phenomenon is significant enough to deserve precision in its definition and analysis, and a set of tools to measure it. Second, as most international firms claim to be global, we wish some clarity. What does it require to be ahead in this game, who is, and why? Third, as most every firm eventually wishes to be global rather than local, how does one get there? How does one translate the vague concept into crisp strategic objectives, what are the steps to achieve them, and how does one manage such an ambitious undertaking?

To these questions, the book of John and Caroline Daniels brings, just in time, substantial answers. It reflects real research, namely intensive practical work with the actors of globalization, the managers of larger and smaller world corporations. As executives struggle to expand all too often parochial and seemingly contradictory experiences, the authors have extracted concepts and frameworks which are an order of magnitude more precise, and therefore fruitful, than the usual "globalization talk." For example, their views on the centralization/decentralization dilemma will delight many executives attempting to untie this knot of knots . . .

Their work would be useful if it stopped there. But these academic virtues are coupled with an orientation towards action which the very dimension of the topic could have discouraged. Based on the progress recorded by some of the most enlightened businesses, they propose a way to assess the degree of globalization achieved by a company, and to define the essential milestones of an action plan giving the right world dimensions to the business strategy.

At the end of the book, one cannot help but feel that it carries an overwhelming message: the globalization process might just be starting!

For corporations, even large, international ones, which are at the trailing edge of globalization and must compete with worldwide firms, the task is stunning because so many aspects of their business strategy stand to be revolutionized by a true global vision. How will they muster the required intellectual and economical muscles? Even more critically, how will they buy time, as the process does not suffer improvisation? And will they be creative enough to invent their own form of globalization, to avoid suffering from a long-lasting competitive disadvantage?

Even for the most advanced corporations on the global trail, the evolution of large economic entities raises issues which one hoped to have closed, such as how to reconcile downsizing and globalization. For example, can one afford, in the trend towards smaller entities, an information technology strategy favoring global integration? More than one worldwide database may now look unwieldy, yet it epitomized a certain form of globalization just a couple of years back.

For all firms, the evolution of the markets constantly reopens globalization issues. For example, what happens if, as a result of microsegmentation, markets are worldwide, but so narrowly defined that their multiplication changes the links among them and the way the corporation organizes around them? How can one move from a worldwide product line to a worldwide line of services, in which products play the role of subordinated carriers, as the information industry experiences now?

In a flourishing economic situation, the pursuit of globalization requires a single-minded determination stretching over years. In today's environment of worldwide stagnation or, at best, slow growth, maybe the greatest test of the company aspiring to become global is to protect the investments for its grand design against the short-term economic pressures. How?

As if these business challenges were not enough, the evolution of the social environment will question at least one of the basic assumptions of globalization, the ability to optimize on a global scale: can the reduction of the company's employment in a given country be justified by a global view?

Will governments tolerate decisions which are entirely justified in terms of global business, but carry national political liabilities? Will the global firm become a victim of the general increase in regional conflicts?

All these interrogations lead to the inescapable conclusion that globalization will be with us into the next millennium. John and Caroline Daniels deserve our gratitude for giving the topic a new focus and a deeper understanding. And the reader will no doubt share the hope that they will keep working on it, marrying theory and practice to help executives explore all of these questions.

Pierre Hessler

Preface

In 1990, *Forbes** stated that globalization was the number one concern of top executives. Since then, the level of this concern has increased at a rapid pace. The decade of the 1990s will be referred to in the next century as the decade in which the leading global corporate players created the fundamental strategies that brought them market leadership. The winners of the next century are clarifying their global strategies today.

Although the models for effective global corporations will be evident in the next century, they remain somewhat a mystery for executives today. Today, these models are in their formative stages. As we tackle the issues of globalization with executives, certain things are becoming abundantly clear:

- Executives believe not only that becoming global is necessary for corporate survival, but also that the innovators and leaders will have an enormous advantage over their rivals. This advantage will be far greater than the advantage created in the past by merely introducing a new set of products or services ahead of competitors. The differentiating factor of this innovation will result in a new way of doing business, nothing less than the restructuring of international business and changing the ways companies compete transnationally. Globalization of business requires a fundamental structural change in business practices.

- Companies are starting from different places as they attempt to become global corporations due to their regional structural evolution. These dif-

---

* Listing ten themes of concerns for future business, CEOs stated that globalization would be the most important strategic theme for the future. "What I Learned in the Eighties," *Forbes*, January 8, 1990, pp. 100–114.

ferent structures are the multinational (primarily U.S. firms); the multi-local (European firms); and the global exporter (Japanese firms). These different organizational structures, having supported the nascent stages of the internationalization of business on a regional basis, must change fundamentally to be successful in the global arena. Aspects of each model of how business is being conducted today are holding companies back from becoming global.

- Articulating the attributes of global business is difficult, if not impossible, without a change in the way executives and managers view the fundamental assumptions of international business. Attributes of the global corporation are different in scope than those of earlier international business models.

As the regional markets of the world progress through trial and error to achieve integration, companies are attempting to address regional changes to their businesses while expanding their global reach. Executives and managers seldom have time to observe how changes are taking place in multiple markets.

Since we are constantly working with a number of companies across many industries, we have been involved with pragmatic globalization issues from a variety of perspectives. We decided to write this book to form a collection of corporate experiences and to organize their presentation as a practical guide for executives and managers to help their organizations become global.

The Global Information Technology Dimension

We started our research very much from an information technology perspective. This proved to be our first bit of string in the global business riddle, yet the more we pulled on this string in attempting to assist companies in developing global information technology, the more we realized that the root of the issues were in the business practices themselves.

The development of transnational* systems didn't appear to be working very well in a variety of companies. The way the systems had been built actu-

---

* We decided not to use the term "transnational" in preference to global since Professor John Stopford of the London Business School informed us that his research showed that the term had been invented in the 1960's by the United Nations to move away from using the term "multinational." At that time, the term "multinational" had negative connotations to developing countries in so far as the question of who benefitted from a multinational's relationship with a developing country had been raised for the first time by the developing countries themselves. "Multinational" at that time was associated with exploitation in many peoples' minds. The U.N. created the term in an effort to progress constructive negotiations between developing countries and businesses.

The term also emphasizes the existence of borders in international business and does not go far enough in emphasizing the borderless, holistic or systemic nature of global companies.

ally inhibited companies' abilities to do business across borders. We saw that companies had built a set of disparate systems over a decade in different countries and, as they tried to get their business processes to work more homogeneously across national borders, their systems were viewed as major inhibitors. For example, systems built for the United Kingdom would be exported to France or to Germany where they weren't working anywhere near as well as they were in the United Kingdom. This story was repeated over and again as companies attempted to export systems from one country to others. We began to attack the question of how companies could get systems in different countries to better support international business growth.

The most significant problems were caused by the lack of a global vision to guide the design of business practices across national borders. We wondered how global systems would work when companies insisted on having business processes that were different across national boundaries. We discovered that there were many other business issues that needed to be addressed, in addition to addressing the systems issues.

Companies like Ford of Europe were trying to sell products and services in 15 countries across Europe. They wanted to be able to order cars with one common ordering system for Europe, but over the years had developed one order processing system for each country. The problem with having 15 different systems for order processing is that the passing of information delays the delivery of the product and delays the operation of the business cycles (inventory turns, etc.). Ford of Europe wanted a PanEuropean view of the number of cars that were on order, but with 15 separate systems, managers couldn't integrate the management of orders. We found simple discrepancies in basic business definitions within the company; for example, parts had different order numbers in different countries. We then began to look for these same problems in other companies, and found them much more often than not.

In our work with Apple Computer, Inc. in 1987, we began to identify the essential attributes of becoming global. One of the things we discovered at Apple was that their general ledger and order entry systems were very different in different countries in Europe than in the United States. Developing a common I.T. system for financial reporting worldwide became a very tall order.

We traveled around the world to ask managers, "What is it that you have to do to become global?" We discovered it was much easier for them to articulate what they considered *not* to be global than what they considered as global. With perseverance and the help of many executives and managers around the world, we built definitions of global attributes. These attributes include: a business concept of globalization, an ability to do business regardless of location, in an integrated way, with low boundaries, networks of trust among employees, ensuring cultural fit, with managers acting as coordinators and connectors, capturing economies of scale and scope, great communications and a long-term view.

Taking these ten attributes to many companies helped us to identify key aspects of becoming global that executives considered important. The attributes framework is helpful in getting executives to articulate how they are attempting to change their corporations to become global.

We wanted to go further; what we were trying to do was find a way to be more prescriptive. This led us to thinking about the starting points for corporations. Fundamentally we found that there were three different models for international business for companies: multilocal, multinational, or global exporter.

We tested the attributes and the issues with many companies representing each of the starting points and discovered that each starting point embodies a different attribute profile. No matter which starting point a company was starting from, it would still be wrestling with a similar set of issues that we discovered and will be highlighting in this book.

We discovered a fundamental dichotomy between the hopes of executives attempting to build global corporations and the conventional management wisdom of the 1980s. Michael Porter and others taught us that a company can't be both low cost and offer highly differentiated products and services to the market at the same time. What the aspiring global companies we visited were telling us, however, was exactly that: "We have to be low cost and market differentiated to compete successfully in the global marketplace." The leading corporate visions of globalization we encountered all emphasized this duality of capability: being able to respond to local customer needs in all of these different geographies at a low cost. Examining and chronicling how international businesses were trying to achieve this helped us to build a pragmatic methodology for globalization.

We continued asking companies, "What do you have to do well to become global?" When we stepped back and looked at the breadth of comments, we found descriptions of 15 or 20 essential activities taken toward becoming global corporations.

Executives at Canon emphasized the need for product and service localization, at the same time saying that they have to operate the company as one integrated system. Managers in companies such as Electrolux that were very local in a number of countries were saying that they had to operate more as one integrated system. They thought that their plants should be focused on a logical plant structure, supporting products for the world, as opposed to having one plant in every country for every product that they had. They still wanted to maintain their localness because it achieved an advantage. Many managers were attempting to deal with the dichotomy of being both global and local. They wanted to achieve both, and not be forced to make tradeoffs any more.

One of the companies that came to us interested in our project to understand globalization was IBM. Pierre Hessler, Director of Operations in Europe, articulated the interest.

"The reason we are very interested in this topic is that we have identified 454 companies as being international accounts that do significant business with us in multiple countries. One of the things we've seen is that the volume of business they are doing outside their home countries is growing faster than the volumes of business in their home countries.

"We are very interested in the topic, but what we don't know is if this concept is just a fad, an idea that is the flavour du jour, or an idea that's going to be a topic of concern on the minds of CEOs in the coming years."

In positioning IBM's business for the future, the company wanted to know what global services companies will want.

In essence, what IBM wanted to know is what many leading companies want to know: is globalization just a fashionable concept or is there something that is fundamentally different in doing business globally? The second thing leading companies want to know is, if companies are truly trying to become global, what is it that they will be trying to do tomorrow that is different from what they were trying to do today? The third thing executives want to know about companies attempting to become global is if they thought they would be able to do all of this by themselves, or if they would need service partners, and, if they were going to need service partners, what kind of services were they looking for? Ultimately, is it possible to determine what the product and service requirements will be of companies attempting to become global?

This book is our attempt to answer these questions. Before beginning this journey, let us look briefly at the root causes and recent trends leading to globalization.

Globalization: Recent Trends

Since the 1970s, waves of change have been rolling over business. First, there was downsizing, followed by the wave of quality. Next came the wave of customer focus, and today the wave of cycle-time compression as a competitive factor is cresting.

But the wave that is building is the wave of globalism and globalization.

As we have seen, those who do not find the wave and engage it early—those who do not, to use the surfer's term, get into the curl of the wave, where the best ride lies—are bound to falter as the wave crashes around them.

This stormy period of the last 20 or so years is indicative of a much larger transformation that is occurring throughout the world. These massive waves, coming one after another, are marking the end of the industrial economy and the beginning of the information economy. This can be seen in Figure P-1.

That is not to say that there will not be any more industrial companies, for they are the producers of real goods that real people use every day. It is

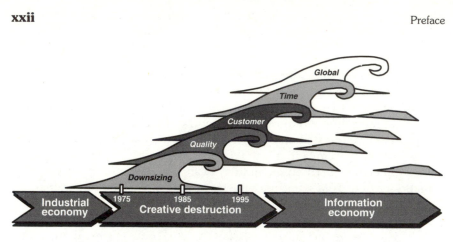

Each wave builds upon and incorporates its predecessors.

Figure P-1. Transformation has been accompanied by waves of change.

to say, however, that the forces that shape every company—industrial, service, and financial—will be of an information nature; the competitive advantage will go to those who can make best use of the information they have or can find, those who can distribute information and knowledge most freely throughout the executive, managerial, technical, and product/service-making workforce, and those who deliver the fruits of this knowledge to customers throughout the world.

The prerequisites for getting on the global wave successfully will include initial mastery of downsizing, improving quality, having the ability to satisfy customers, and reducing cycle times. Many other business books have been written on these topics. Our book is about the additional requirements imposed by the desire to do these all well on a global basis. The truly global company will have an advantage because it will be more flexible and responsive than its predecessors. As we have seen in other periods when business has undergone massive change, the winners will be those that capture the perspective of the new age.

Just as the nineteenth century transition from an agrarian to an industrial economy transformed the lives of people throughout the world, so too the current transformation from an industrial to an information economy is transforming our lives.

The first lesson we learn, if we study this transformation, is that these very big, real changes in the way we work and live are driven by changes in our base technologies. New technologies allow us to envision new ways to break through previously impenetrable barriers.

Then, once the potentials of a technology become more apparent as applications are invented, a supportive infrastructure, essential to wider adoption, emerges. Business and society become transformed as the infrastructure supporting the adoption of new technologies begins to be set in place.

For example, the development of the railroad steam engine, a base technology of the industrial age, awaited the establishment of an extensive network of track and maintenance facilities with standard-sized parts and tools to promote its widespread use. By the turn of the twentieth century, with this infrastructure in place, you could get almost anywhere by train.

Similarly, the automobile and truck awaited an infrastructure of paved roads and service stations. Modern container ships required new and larger ports, with more sophisticated equipment to handle loading and unloading. Airplanes required a network of airports, navigation aids, and ground controllers before they affected our daily business lives.

The systematic development of these transportation infrastructures allowed companies to get their products to further and further distances. But the products, by and large, were conceived of, developed in, and manufactured in a limited number of places.

Today, these constraints no longer exist. The reduced cost of transportation allows for goods to be produced almost anywhere. And, increasingly, as the information and communications infrastructure becomes more widespread, companies can truly have global aspirations. This communications' infrastructure includes satellites and fiber optics, television and teleconferencing, personal computers and multi-media workstations, local area networks and wide area networks, on-line databases, compact discs with read-only memory (CD-ROM), electronic mail and voice mail, and facsimile (fax) machines, to name just a few developments of the last quarter of the twentieth century. By the beginning of the twenty-first century, the world will truly be wired.

Globalization represents the next major stage in an evolutionary sequence that first saw domestic companies develop from exporters into either multidomestic or multinational companies (depending on the company's penchant for decentralization or centralization). But today, despite the rapid developments in the communications infrastructure, companies are only beginning to exhibit some global characteristics.

Why this lack of progress?

We believe businesses misunderstand the whole concept of globalization. Many managers do not yet realize that globalization is important and urgent. And, even when they grasp the concept and its importance, businesses do not know "how to become" global. The purpose of this book is to provide a guided tour of what globalization is, why it is important, and some of the first steps to getting there.

What Is Globalization?

Globalization is more than just doing business in a number of countries around the world. Globalization involves doing business around the world in a new way, balancing the global qualities of your product or service and the unique needs of various local customer bases. It involves breaking down the culturally hidebound ethnocentric qualities most businesses have, whatever their nationality. Globalization involves, as one corporate executive has said, "recognizing the particular genius" of employees from the company's operations anywhere in the world, whatever the employees' nationality, and rewarding employees for their genius and their efforts at creating a seamless company.

Doing business with this scope involves determining who the "global consumers" or "global customers" are for your products and services. These global consumers may be large customers with operations in many countries who want global contracts for sales and service or they may be individuals around the world who, through their access to the global information infrastructure, have come to desire the same products wherever they live (the global traveler, for example).

As company after company is finding, certain consumers in Manhattan have far more in common with certain consumers in Tokyo, Paris, or Rio de Janeiro than they do with consumers in Queens, the Bronx, Brooklyn, or Staten Island.

The Importance of Becoming Global

Becoming global allows businesses to:

- keep up with the competition
- keep abreast of new trends in technology
- create and take advantage of developing business opportunities

Keep Up with the Competition

The global marketplace has three key economies that can afford to develop these global customers: the United States and Canada, Europe (predominantly Western Europe), and the Far East, centered around Japan. Kenichi Ohmae has called these economies the Triad.*

Most successful companies—small and entrepreneurial, medium-sized and growing, or large and worldwide—are going after these continuously expanding global markets. Many of these companies are your customers, and they want to do business with you wherever they are located. You can rest assured that, if you are not in a market where your customers are, a

* Ohmae, Kenichi, *Triad Power,* New York: The Free Press, A Division of Macmillan, Inc., 1985.

competitor is or soon will be. The competition may be using geographic markets you are not serving not only for revenue, but also to determine how to penetrate the markets you are serving.

In the early 1960s, Komatsu, which was much smaller than Caterpillar, had a global strategic intent. The company's slogan was "Maru-C," which, translated, was company shorthand for "encircle Caterpillar." Caterpillar's strategic intent, on the other hand, was to defend its market leadership through domestic dominance, even though it had operations in multiple markets.

It took Komatsu more than 15 years to create a global capability, but the company caught Caterpillar napping. In the late 1970s and into the early 1980s, Caterpillar was simply not in a position to retaliate in Komatsu's profit sanctuary. Since then, of course, Caterpillar has made remarkable progress in thinking globally, and in using technology to enhance human creativity and work.

In 1989, Caterpillar earned $497 million profit on $11.1 billion in sales. The company has 32 manufacturing plants around the world, and is in the process of developing what it calls the "Plant With a Future," a worldwide, integrated, order-driven manufacturing process. Donald Fites, Caterpillar's chairman, describes the system this way:

"Orders received will set all the machinery in motion to build the product. All of our manufacturing drawings will be done electronically. Not only will that have a great benefit in terms of speed, but we will be able to transmit repair information to our dealers and customers instantly. We envision the time when we'll be able to ask any Caterpillar machine in the world how it is. You will be able to enter the serial number of a tractor working in Kenya; the information will go up to a satellite and tell us whether there are impurities in the oil, what temperature it's running, whether it's generating full power, things like that."*

The same strategic global intent Komatsu had could be seen in Japanese car manufacturers. Honda was talking about being a global force back in the 1950s when it was a repair shop with 50 employees. Since General Motors, Ford, and Chrysler chose to ignore the Japanese market, they never saw the competition coming when Honda decided to push into the North American market.

The automobile industry has not been the same since. In 1990 General Motors and Ford both earned more money in Europe than in the United States. Toyota now manufactures more Camrys in the United States for sale in North America than it exports from Japan. United States car manufacturers have all formed important alliances with Asian as well as European companies—GM with Toyota and Saab, Ford with Mazda and Jaguar.

---

* *Technology Management Review*, Sloan School, Massachusetts Institute of Technology, Cambridge, Massachusetts, Spring 1990.

Chrysler has developed a partnership with Mitsubishi, and has made attempts to form alliances with a number of European car makers. Many analysts of the auto industry believe the terms export and import will be nearly meaningless by the end of the twentieth century; they believe there will be a handful of global automobile companies manufacturing for distribution and sale around the world.

Keep Abreast of New Trends in Technology

In almost every industry, technology is evolving at different speeds in different places. Companies attempting to become global are arbitraging and combining technology capability.

For instance, in the computer industry we see basic computer technology, including chip sets, being most advanced in the United States, while the Japanese are ahead in peripherals (especially imaging), magnetics, and display technology. The Europeans at the same time have the greatest interest in the integration of telecommunications with computers (ISDN and OSI).

In financial services, as the world increasingly becomes one marketplace, capital-market products are developed in different areas of the world, using intelligent workstations, and then become available on a global basis.

Regardless of your industry, to be at the forefront you must recognize and act on emerging ideas before your competitors "blind side" you. No one can afford to develop or source strategic technologies from one origin. It is critical to understand where all aspects of the technologies that are important to your business are headed.

Only if you understand where the technology is going will your perspective on where your business can go be as broad as possible and provide the greatest potential.

To be at the forefront, a business's pure research must occur at those places most advanced in the key technologies, so it can leverage emerging technological expertise and resources.

In the pharmaceutical industry SmithKline Beecham's emergence from an "also-ran" position to a major player in the United States was a direct result of its development of Tagamet in its research and development (R&D) labs located in the United Kingdom. Tagamet, the world's first $1 billion-generating pharmaceutical product, resulted after SmithKline decided to locate an R&D lab near London, where leading-edge gastrointestinal researchers were located.

For his work on Tagamet, and previous work he did on beta blockers at Imperial Chemicals, Sir James Black, M.D., was awarded the 1988 Nobel Prize for medicine.

Similarly, IBM's three Nobel prize winners in the late 1980s were all Europeans, two of whom worked on superconductivity in IBM's lab in Zurich, and one of whom, Benoit Mandelbroit, worked on fractal geometry in a U.S. lab.

This search for genius around the world has led to the creation of "centers of excellence" in R&D and to locating various forms of R&D or worldwide marketing efforts in locations where market conditions are receptive.

For example, IBM decided in 1991 to move its 150-person strong headquarters for its Communications Systems line of business from New York to London, closer to continental Europe, which is both the center of OSI and ISDN research and the dominant market for integrated systems. Even though there is more technology development in the United States, there is much more market receptivity in Europe, partly because the formerly government controlled post, telegraph and telephone (PTT) organizations, are usually the only party to have rights to bring voice and data transmissions into homes, while in North America those rights are more fragmented among telephone companies, cable television companies, and others.

On the R&D front, German pharmaceutical companies have been partnering with or acquiring American biotechnology companies throughout the 1980s, partly because German laws forbid biotechnology research in the country. The Japanese have also been partnering with or acquiring these companies in an effort to capture the unique genius of U.S. biotech researchers and their entrepreneurial spirit.

To Create and Take Advantage of Developing Business Opportunities

The political/economic/technical environment is changing the way the world does business, as well as opening up the global marketplace. Developing at a faster and faster rate, this global marketplace offers incredible opportunities for growth and profit.

Getting an adequate return on your international investment, however, requires a global perspective, developed from the company's global vision and architecture.

Being a global-market player helps you recover your costs in this time of shortening product life cycles and increasing product-development costs. Beyond lengthening the life of products, access to local resources and global communications enables the company to leverage resources, thereby creating new synergies and minimizing the replication of resources.

Being global enables you to create or capture a new market well ahead of your competitors. Being global allows you to serve your global customers.

As globalization increases, these global customers will want to feel that they are dealing with the same company everywhere they do business with you. This will require internally consistent systems and cooperation. Further, this coordination will have to strike a balance between global consistency and local look and feel.

Being in the global environment can help to counterbalance against cyclical swings by spreading risk during individual market economic downturns and helping to hedge against foreign-exchange fluctuations. Fickle markets require a company to know how to deploy quickly. Being global means that you are fast and flexible.

How to Become Global: The First Five Years

We have been tracking the formation of the global wave since the mid-1980s, and much of our consulting work with companies has been in getting executives and managers to think about globalization, what it means for them, and how they can begin to take advantage of new technologies to create their own global information architecture.

In 1990 we joined with a group from IBM in a study of 10 large companies that operate on a worldwide basis; we set out to determine the competitive forces driving globalization, and how these 10 companies are responding to these forces. These companies are Banque Nationale de Paris (BNP), Canon, a U.S.-based manufacturing company, CSX, Electrolux, JCB, Pirelli, Royal Trust, TNT Express Worldwide, and Waste Management, Inc. We presented the companies with some of our theoretical constructs about globalism and globalization and asked for their reactions. These constructs are laid out in Chapter 1.

What we found was almost universal acceptance that we had framed the big, long-term issues surrounding globalization correctly. What we got from these companies was a wealth of detail and concrete examples of how they are coming to grips with the day-to-day realities involved in grappling with this issue.

Clearly, a sample of 10 in no way constitutes a statistically valid study population. Then again, as a leading executive is fond of saying, "One doesn't need to see too many people swimming across the Thames before we know that we should build a bridge." The anecdotal information these companies provided is highly indicative of the forces affecting all companies.

These companies come from the ranks of manufacturing, services, and financial services. Four are headquartered in North America, three in Europe, and three in the Far East.

The executives we visited were all clear in their own minds about what globalization represents to their industries and their companies. From their discussions, some generalizations about the "definition" of a global company emerge.

1. Global is a business concept. To be global means that you have a global strategy and you have a worldwide plan in terms of your products, marketing, manufacturing, logistics, and R&D. These activities need to be

looked at holistically; they all need to be thought of and treated as being driven by the mindset of a global system. These mission-critical activities need to be undertaken wherever it makes sense.

2. A global company has no boundaries. Where a global company has its headquarters should be transparent to the market or individual customer. Being global means extending a company's reach and presence within its sphere of influence, to be broader in scope than only where it has facilities. A global company knows where its customers and its customers' customers are going with respect to becoming global themselves.

3. Not only does a global company serve its global customers with excellence, but a global company has a delivery system that is highly sensitive to local customer needs. In order to prosper, to succeed in the long term, a global company must be perceived wherever it does business as a respected member of society. A global company adjusts its business to the countries it is in. It takes a basic set of values, business principles, and systems, then tailors them to the areas in which it does business. Being global requires a high degree of cultural diversity and understanding.

4. A global company balances those aspects of the company that must be viewed and planned as a global system with those aspects that must be highly sensitive to local requirements. This means striving to be more accommodating to the local environment, while simultaneously striving to act as an integrated global system.

All of the executives who participated recognize that becoming truly global will be a long-term activity. Some had put down a five-year strategy, but even they acknowledged that this is only a first step on what may be a ten-year or even a twenty-five-year process.

From the commonalities in responses by the participants in this study as to the first steps that need to be taken to become a truly global company, we have created six global strategic imperatives that we believe can reasonably be undertaken by a company in a five-year time frame. These six imperatives will be more fully described in this book.

Global Strategic Imperative 1:
Create a Clarity of Vision and Mindset

Every company going global must clearly articulate and widely disseminate its global vision and aspirations to all employees. Creating a global business vision will require a disciplined process of three phases: discovery, which entails validating and internalizing the rationale for undertaking the globalization process; visualization, which involves describing the shared concepts upon which the global vision can be built; and actualization, in which a global vision statement is created and driven through the organization.

A global vision has to go beyond powerful words and slogans; it has to create a shared mindset in all employees and guide employee decision making and actions. (See Chapter 1 for a complete discussion.)

Global Strategic Imperative 2:
Know Your Global Customer

Every company going global should be conducting extensive market research on the product, information, and service requirements of its global customers. Some of these global customers will be companies that do business around the world, and want to create more efficient supplier/customer relationships. Others will be individual consumers (a global consumer type) who have similar lifestyles wherever they live, and want the same kinds of products and services. (See Chapter 3.)

Global Strategic Imperative 3:
Understand the Global-Local
Balance and Constantly Adjust It

Every company going global needs to develop a means to better balance global and local activities. This may mean significantly restructuring the management of operations outside the home country, creating new business processes, and rethinking resource allocation. Companies need to identify which aspects need to be planned for and managed on a worldwide basis, develop business blueprints of how these processes should be carried out, and how local processes should interact with global processes. (See Chapter 4.)

Global Strategic Imperative 4:
Move from Isolation to Partnership

Every company going global should have a process to identify and develop key supporting alliances. The effort of going global demands that companies look to partner with others who have competencies and strengths that complement the company's own. Management must be educated on the potential role of partners, and the environment must reward synergistic activities with partners. (See Chapter 4.)

Global Strategic Imperative 5:
Nurture Global Employees

A global company will need to find, train, and develop employees who are comfortable working in the global framework. They will need to create a strong, nurturing global culture that accepts input from employees who possess strong local and regional ties, yet have a global mindset. Performance measurements, and reward systems must foster a global outlook, information and knowledge sharing, and global teamwork. (See Chapter 5.)

Global Strategic Imperative 6:
Key on I.T.

Information technology is the key to globalization. Every company going global needs to develop a global I.T. plan. Companies must understand the linkage of I.T. to business strategy. They must create and manage global I.T. portfolios (product-support systems, process-support systems, knowledge-support systems, and coordination/control systems). They need to understand the difference between global and local I.T. infrastructure requirements, and balance them. (See Chapters 6 and 7.)

These are the six strategic imperatives that apply to all companies, regardless of where they are when they begin their journey toward the global ideal. (In Chapter 2 we'll describe the three starting points most companies find themselves in, that of global exporter, multinational, or multilocal.)

Depending on which of the three starting points a company finds itself at, it will have other imperatives it must undertake during the first five years of the journey to globalism. In addition, each company will find that it has its own set of imperatives because of its industry and its competitive position. But this book will stress these six universal global strategic imperatives.

It is important to understand at the outset that these six strategic imperatives are inextricably linked. Therefore, if a company fails to address even one of these six strategic imperatives, it imperils its entire effort at globalization. Also, balanced progress is necessary; if a company gets too far ahead in dealing with one imperative, or allows another to lag too far behind the general progress, it also may flirt with failure.

To facilitate this process, we wish to add two pragmatic steps to the six imperatives: (1) measuring today's global position and establishing priorities, and (2) taking steps to accelerate the globalization process. Measuring today's global position and establishing priorities at the beginning of the journey helps give executives and managers a perspective of where they are going and how far they have to go in clear, measurable terms. Identifying steps to accelerate the process offers a number of first measures the company can take in the beginning to start the journey off well, with immediate benefits.

Together these six strategic imperatives and two action steps represent eight fundamental stages or steps toward globalization. We've chosen this set of issues as the organizing principle of the book. Figure P-2 illustrates some of the questions addressed in each chapter and serves as a high-level

	Yes	No
1.0 Developing a global vision and mindset		
Does your company have a clearly stated vision to be global?		
Are you satisfied that the vision has been effectively communicated to all employees worldwide?		
Do your employees have performance measurements and reward systems that encourage global behavior?		
2.0 Measuring today's global position and establishing priorities		
Has your management defined the gap between being global and where it is today?		
Has your management defined an action strategy that will allow it to close the gap?		
Can your company outpace your competition in the race to become global?		
3.0 Understanding your global customer's demands and needs		
Will global customers generate a significant proportion of your future revenue stream?		
Do your customers view you as a global supplier?		
Do your employees understand the information and service requirements of customers on a worldwide basis?		
4.0 Balancing global/local activities		
Does your management understand which aspects of the company have to be managed on a local basis?		
Does your management understand which aspects of the company have to be managed on a worldwide basis?		
Does your management system allow you the capability to find the optimum balance between the two?		
Does your company have strategic partners who extend your global reach?		
Does your company have strategic partners which complement your core competencies?		
Does your company have an efficient process to locate and select strategic partners?		

	Yes	No
5.0 Building global teams and individuals		
Do the performance measures of the company support global cooperation?		
Does your company source ideas from around the world?		
Does your management allow individuals, who need to know, access to global business performance information on a frequent basis?		
6.0 Developing the global I.T. plan		
Does your organization have a global I.T. plan?		
Does your organization have a supportive global I.T. infrastructure?		
Are you able to leverage knowledge contained in any part of the organization in any other part of the organization (on a worldwide basis)?		
7.0 Implementing global I.T.		
Does your company have access to the skill mix required?		
Are the implementation programs linked clearly with the strategic initiatives in the global vision?		
Do people working on the projects understand what it is they have to do and how their actions link to others'?		
8.0 Accelerating the globalization process		
Has management clearly articulated action programs associated with the global vision?		
Has the executive team established clear priorities for action?		
Is the leadership of the firm actively involved in the global projects?		
Are incentive programs in place for every employee?		

Figure P-2. A global strategic ingredients checklist.

checklist for executives and managers about how companies are becoming global.

The road to true globalism is fraught with danger; however, for companies to turn their backs on the inevitability of globalization is even more dangerous. Executives and managers that come to grips now with the fundamental issues of globalization will have an advantage in meeting the challenges of the global marketplace.

John L. Daniels
Dr. N. Caroline Daniels

Acknowledgments

We both began living "abroad" in the late 1970s. Our experiences, especially in Europe, working as consultants to a wide variety of companies in different countries, has given us a heightened sense of awareness to both differences and similarities in the way companies operate. We are grateful to the managers of all those companies who have shaped our view of the world. These include Banco Nationale del Lavoro, Chartham Paper Mills, Courtaulds, E. I. DuPont de Nemeurs, Financiere Credit Suisse First Boston, Heineken, Lex Service Group, Lloyds of London, Merrill Lynch, Merloni, Sinclair, Swiss Bank Corporation, and Whitbread.

We owe a deep debt to Murray Reichenstein and Graham Gooding at Ford of Europe, who gave us the opportunity to work in 15 countries across Europe designing a variety of pan-European business systems, and Alan Loren and Michael Spindler of Apple Computer, who sent us to 19 countries on 4 continents as part of our first "global vision" study in 1987. These two experiences gave us first hand insights into the effect of cultural differences on shared values and business processes, as well as proved to us, beyond a doubt, that becoming global was a strategic imperative for many companies.

Most importantly we would like to thank Pierre Hessler, Gordon Venters, and Wally Seymour of International Business Machines Corp., who engaged us to run global vision workshops in 10 IBM customer headquarters in 1990. The conclusions from that engagement confirmed our views and deeply influenced the structure of this book. More recently our ideas have been profoundly influenced by Bob Howe, Joe Movizzo, Scott Oldach, and Paul Lewis in the newly formed IBM Consulting Group.

At Nolan, Norton & Co., where we were consultants until 1991, we had the great fortune of working closely with and being mentored by Professor Richard L. Nolan and Dr. David P. Norton. They provided us a powerful lens through which to view the world with their "stages theory" and constant striving for new ideas and frameworks to simplify the complex task of managing information technology. They encouraged us to begin writing this book and without their advice and support we never would have stayed the course. They also created an environment that attracted a wonderful set of colleagues which influenced a number of ideas found in this book and whose advice we value: Eugene Lockhart, Bruce and Winnie Rogow, Thomas H. Johnson, Stuart Richards, Robert Hanson, Barbara Lind, David McKay, Paulo Mariotti, Sergio Fabris, Donald St. Clair, and Douglas Brockway.

We would also like to thank KPMG Peat Marwick, especially Barry Mundt and Richard Worrall for their great support when it looked like we might not be able to finish this project.

Betsy Brown, our editor, has been a delight to work with and extraordinarily patient. Jon Zonderman was very helpful working with us on the book during one of its several iterations. Mathy Mergian and Debbie La Femina helped us in countless ways as we neared production. Troy Van Marter and the IBM Consulting Group's graphics team in White Plains combined talents with Lisa Carr at North Market Street Graphics to get us to the goal post. Mary Rose Greenough has been helpful in ensuring that the media gets the message.

Finally, we would like to thank Elizabeth and John Daniels, Lorraine and Donald Pitts, Sybil Baker, Althea Howe, Hunt and Lucy Breed, Dr. Diane Wilson, Caroline Raby, Melody Flaxman, and Carolyn White for their wonderful support and encouragement.

John L. Daniels
Dr. N. Caroline Daniels

1

Develop a Global Vision and Mindset

The globalization of the marketplace is a complex phenomenon. The process of becoming a truly global company will be no less complex. Only through the cross-pollination of ideas from different geographic and functional areas of a company will globalization occur.

Why is Global Vision Crucial?

Companies going global need a powerful global vision to lead the organization and every employee into the future. An effective global vision offers inspiration and is a powerful intangible that can create powerfully tangible results. Equally, the lack of a powerful vision can divide companies' efforts.

"Change in business starts with a vision," says Arch McGill, the former president of AT&T Advanced Information Systems. "We need to create an exciting outlook that engages people on a daily basis: something that they feel good about giving themselves to; something that will catalyze their inherent desire to make a fundamental difference in the world.

"An effective vision must be simple and compelling, but concrete. It must be uplifting enough for people to consider it worthy of their time and their energy. It is the kind of thing they want to talk to their friends about, brag that they are participating in. Simply put, it must inspire almost religiously an exciting day-by-day, minute-by-minute focus."* Richard Feynman, the late physicist and a member of the president's commission that investigated the space

---

* Arch McGill, "Vision: The Executive Perspective," *Stage by Stage* 7, no. 3 (Lexington, Mass.: Nolan, Norton & Co., May–June 1987).

1

shuttle Challenger's explosion, provided dramatic insight into the role of a vision in any endeavor. He observed the value of a vision and the cost of the absence of a vision in his experience as a scientist.

"I have this idea because I worked at Los Alamos, and I experienced the tension and the pressure of everybody working together to make the atomic bomb. When somebody's having a problem—say, with the detonator— everybody knows that it's a big problem; they're thinking of ways to beat it, they're making suggestions, and when they hear about the solution they are excited, because that means their work is now useful.

"I figured the same thing had gone on at NASA in the early days. When NASA was trying to go to the moon, there was a great deal of enthusiasm: it was a goal everyone was anxious to achieve. They didn't know if they could do it, but they were all working together. If the space suit didn't work, they couldn't go to the moon. So everybody's interested in everybody else's problems. But then, when the moon project was over, NASA had all these people together . . . there seemed to be some reason why guys at the lower level didn't bring problems up to the next level."*

A good global vision supports good communication among the people who are making the effort. People understand the overall mission, and how their part fits in as a necessary and useful ingredient. Conversely, when there isn't a powerful vision operating to energize the workforce, then that vital problem-solving attitude, the openness and willingness to face realistic business issues, and the camaraderie developed to make the impossible possible, is muffled by management's concern for running a smooth organization with no waves.

A good global vision expresses purpose, action, and feeling. It should be expressed clearly, capturing people's imaginations and inspiring everyone toward a common purpose. Expressing the essence of a company's position in the marketplace, a global vision provides the rationale for a company's style and organizational approach. It provides the basis for shared beliefs and values, raising the level of awareness about the need for change, while at the same time diffusing fear. An effective global vision appeals to one's intuition through the use of stories, models, metaphors, and shared symbols.

While different types of themes emerge in global vision statements, they reflect global trends which transcend geographic borders, reaching for a broader perspective.

Headquartered in Japan, Matsushita emphasizes fundamental human values when it says, "Our global strategic goal is to contribute to the betterment of human life."

* Richard P. Feynman, *What Do You Care What Other People Think?* (New York: Bantam Books, 1988), 213–215.

In Europe, ICI strikes the same chord with, "By developing and applying its technological skills, ICI aims to make the world a better place during our lifetimes, and the lifetimes of our children."

Similarly, in the United States, Merck says, "The primary goal of our research is to benefit people everywhere by finding new ways to protect health, save lives, and ease suffering."

Another common global theme is to be a world-class company or to have world-class products. Sony aims at "building a worldwide reputation as a pacesetter in the electronic equipment industry." British Telecom's goal is to be recognized by its customers as "the most successful worldwide telecommunications group." GE says, "We are creating a company consisting of only world-class global business that can compete and win in the 1990s and beyond."

Delighting customers is another dominant theme. Nissan claims that, "By placing the customer first, Nissan has won acclaim for its state-of-the-art, top-quality products that appeal to customers in all markets." Pilkington, a British manufacturer of glass and related products, says that it "plans to build on its powerful position in world markets to improve by anticipating the changing needs of customers." And IBM says, "We compete in a global marketplace, and IBM is uniquely positioned to bring worldwide resources to bear on solving customers' specific problems and achieving individual goals."

The global visioning process is the skill of piecing together a variety of notions of value that have never been combined in quite the same way before. The viability of global vision statements rests on these shared concepts, embodying such ideas as:

Basis of Global Competition: The definition of the company's franchise, how it will compete, how it will build and maintain a competitive advantage, why a customer will choose the company, and how each employee contributes to the differentiating advantage.

Global Operating Mode: How the company will create value, generate revenue, and make profit. Many global visions are influenced by operating problems a company has faced, but all global visions incorporate new directions for world-class companies.

Global Structural Approach: The way a company measures performance and rewards effort is a clear indicator of the value a company places on the consistency of its global structure.

Shareholder Value: How and why the company will be a good investment for its stakeholders.

Place to Work: How employees will feel about working at the company, how they will be treated, and how the company will behave as a corporate citizen.

It's hard to make global progress without a global vision. While strategies address sets of actions to meet explicit objectives, visions guide the company through both tangible and intangible experiences. Global visions provide guidance against which individuals can measure their own intuitions when they are faced with situations in which they have to exercise judgment.

Global visions offer a compelling and concise description of the long-term core or essence of a company's beliefs. Global visions help companies embrace change. Global visions serve as a powerful magnet to attract the eyes of the company to the future.

A New Global Mindset: 10 Critical Attributes

Working with large companies around the world over a number of years to explore and apply the global business potentials offered by information technology, we have discovered 10 global attributes that help us understand the essence of the global vision, and what it is to be global. These global attributes can all be seen in juxtaposition with current ways of operating.

These 10 global attributes make up the core of the global vision and, more importantly, the mindset that each individual working in a global corporation must have. It is one thing for corporate leadership to go off into the stratosphere and return with a "vision" of what the company could and should be. But it is far different for every employee to be able to incorporate the components of that vision into the corporate mindset and corporate culture.

The corporate executives who speak about how they are actively working on making these components part of the company's mindset say a lot about the difficulty of such an endeavor.

The 10 components are listed here and represent a move from an industrial perspective to a global, information age perspective of doing business:

1. From a geographic concept (where I do business) to a business concept (how I do business)

2. From a focus on centralization versus decentralization to business "anyplace"

3. From a mechanistic view (the whole of the business equals the sum of its parts) to a holistic view of business (the whole is greater than the sum of its parts)

4. From isolationism to low or nonexistent boundaries

5. From "not invented here" to networks of trust

6. From mere physical geographic presence to acceptance by the local culture

7. From centralized controllers to core management

8. From duplication of resources to taking advantage of economies of scale

9. From vertical "stovepipe" communications to communication networks

10. From a solely short-term focus to including a long-term view.

During a discussion with an executive team of the Parts and Services Division of a U.S.-based manufacturing company, the following description of being global emerged:

"Being global is to extend your reach and presence, to be broader in scope than only where you have facilities. It means promoting anybody without regard to their country of origin. Being global is trying to adjust your business to the countries you are in. It means taking a basic set of values and business principles and basic systems and tailoring them to the area you're doing business in. It means trying to be more accommodating to the local environment—and still simplify. You need to accommodate and you need to identify the basic needs while you stay with some basic values/principles/systems and still have economies of scale. To be really global, you need to understand the values/principles/systems of every place in the world."

Jacques Henri Wahl, President and COO of Banque Nationale de Paris talks about the difficulty of taking a vision of what being global is and communicating it with others in his organization.

"Being global means that you have a global strategy, that you plan worldwide in terms of your products. If you are global, your strategy is global. I'd like to share objectives and goals, be integrated by strategy, by strategic organizational procedural links. Currently, there is not enough participation from our foreign staff. In so many countries the top staff is not international enough. There is not enough foreign talent in the senior management team. It's not a lack of will on our part, it's because people are not responsive enough."

From a Geographic Concept (Where I Do Business) to a Business Concept (How I Do Business)

Many companies confuse the term "global" with "multinational" or "worldwide." But global is a business concept (how you do business) rather than a geographic concept (where you do business).

A company that has a global way of doing business has a "sphere of influence" that includes all its potential business relationships. A global company looks at its suppliers, owners, alliance partners, and competitors and asks the question, "What situations and relationships can be leveraged to create a global advantage?"

While many companies operate in a number of locations to earn revenue, source material, or distribute goods, a global company stretches beyond its operations to areas of influence such as exploring potential relationships with third parties, or supporting the efforts of a supplier to enter a market that has little to do with the company now, but may be of strategic importance later.

Rather than view the actions of business as an "input→ process→ output" flow, the global business manager views global business as a process of influencing parties for a desired outcome.

In answering the question, "How is your company attempting to become global?" many executives recite geographic statistics. "We operate in 117 countries worldwide," usually means that the company has people physically located in those countries operating on its behalf in functions ranging from research and development to manufacturing to selling and servicing.

Sometimes these executives describe such geographic performance measurements as the level and nature of physical asset investment in each country, the number of employees in each country, and the revenues or profits generated in each country. But as we will show, geographic thinking often encourages the creation of barriers; by dwelling on geography the more intangible and sometimes more important influences of global business are often overlooked.

We do not know from these geographic descriptors, for example, how the company acts; what the nature of relationships with customers, countries, suppliers, business partnerships, or alliances is; or how frequently and directly the company communicates and bidirectionally shares knowledge across borders and company functions.

In a global business, relationships with suppliers, distributors, and customers are leveraged cross-functionally and cross-geographically. In any particular business system, there may be a number of cross relationships; a business partner may be a customer for one product or service and a coprovider of another.

For example, Canon supplies chips, print engines, and other products to many high-tech companies in the United States and Europe. The company also acts as distributor for many of these companies in Japan. Canon expands its activities with any one company by sharing the knowledge of its relationships with that company cross-functionally.

Canon's first Global Corporation Plan, launched in 1988, focused on the company's approach to forming relationships with consumers, joint venturers, and technology exchanges in order to move "toward greater equilibrium," by cross-functionally sharing the knowledge gained from its relationships with customers. Canon is expanding its activities and converting these customers into successful alliance partners.

In 1993, Canon is entering the second phase of its globalization program. The company uses the word *kyosei* as its cultural philosophic watchword: it means "mutually rewarding coexistence." The ideograph suggests relationships between people/people, people/machines, and people/nature. The company crystallizes the global vision in words that describe its operations: "technology for people," "unity in diversity," "borderless contributions," "thinking globally, acting locally," and "across town—or oceans." In their 1992 efforts, Chairman Ryuzaburo Kaku and President Keizo Yamajii stated that as well as maintaining the focus on earnings as a primary challenge for the company, "Equally, important . . . will be developing products with longer life cycles—a key to lowering demands on the planet's natural resources. . . . We are planning to strengthen our worldwide sales and service system, with moves such as setting up a company for computer sales in the U.S., extending our network in Asia, and developing such untapped markets as Eastern Europe. . . . We are preparing to expand our overall imports, with increased use of semiconductors for overseas manufacturers. Tie-ups with companies abroad can also play a significant role in raising imports of parts and products. And we can look to our overseas research laboratories to develop unique products that reflect the character and requirements of their locales."

Just as Canon is exploring its sphere of influence by cultivating relationships in a globally balanced way, other businesses, attempting to become global, are examining who is involved in the flow of goods and services, and how these relationships can be leveraged globally.

This is being done by formulating answers to such questions as:

- How many companies—customers, suppliers, distributors, research-and-development alliances, and others—do you have relationships with?
- What is the nature of these relationships?
- Are there any other dimensions to these relationships that can be leveraged?

In producing world-class products with dependent technologies developing in different parts of the world, it is especially important to organize around the context of a whole-world system, rather than to organize around the function of geography. We have found that activities that combine a cross-functional, cross-geographic approach, leveraging the company's sphere of influence, produce benefits to the global corporation that are not normally found in the typical multinational corporation.

A senior executive of Pirelli, in Milan, Italy, puts it this way: "We need to move from being fully responsible managers for our own country into becoming players on a larger team. What is important is not country market share so much as comprehensive share. It makes less and less sense to talk about local share."

A company's global presence is defined by the perception of the participants in the company's sphere of influence. These perceptions, held by the company's customers, business partners, regulatory bodies, and employees, affect the company's ability to carry out business.

Customers and business partners are concerned with the quality of operations, the company's image, and the products and services.

Employees and regulatory bodies are concerned with the commitment to the long-term viability of business activity, how the company shares management activities and experience, and the effect a company has on the environment and culture as a whole.

Mats Agurren, Senior Vice President of Administration at AB Electrolux, talks about the need to be "good citizens in the countries where we work and return profits to localities. Globalization raises some problems. For example, 97 percent of the Swedish workforce is unionized. At the same time, Electrolux is dealing with other countries, like the U.S., where unionism is not as strong. By managing via local requirements, Electrolux may be subject to criticism at home."

Adhering to or surpassing environmental standards is increasingly important for global companies. Many companies set a global excellence objective by stating that they will adhere everywhere to the highest standards set anywhere in the world. These companies are considering the environmental affect of their strategies and visions early in their direction setting processes.

"Depth of presence" in the multinational form is most often talked about in terms of how much manufacturing capability is located in the region in which a company is selling, or in terms of the number of physical assets and people employed in a particular place. Depth of presence in the global corporation is generated by viewing the world as one market, one source of resources, and a fabric of relationships. We are looking not only at where a company manufactures, but also at how a company's ideas originate and grow.

The global perspective of business is wider and more sensible than other forms of organization because it begins with the notion of the company's global sphere of influence, which addresses the company's intangible assets as well as the tangible. These intangibles—such as research and development, good will, computer software, serviceability, quality, design, and influence on various players in the global community—more and more often determine the difference between profitability and lack of profitability, between success in global business and failure.

From a Focus on Centralization versus Decentralization to Business Anyplace

Globalization is the ability to do business anyplace, as opposed to being obsessed with which functions are centralized and which are decentralized. In order to become an "anyplace" company, it is necessary to be able to communicate efficiently and effectively. Today's information technology makes it possible to wire the world for any company, to allow members of the company to connect with anyone else in the company, as well as anyone outside the company who can add value. For example:

- We've seen Digital Equipment Company engineers in Augusta, Maine, call up a computer-aided design (CAD) drawing on their terminals from a database in Reading, England, update it, and send it back, in less than five minutes.

- We've watched Ford engineers in Cologne, West Germany, examine and discuss a failed engine part with a Ford engineering team in Essex, England, using video-teleconferencing, an electronic blackboard, and a fax machine. One of the three video cameras was movable, in order to provide close-up views of the engine from all angles.

- Club Med, the worldwide travel and holiday accommodation company, has built stand-alone interactive multimedia stations that allow customers to view video tapes on holiday locations, ask questions about sports and interest activities, select travel arrangements and accommodations, and authorize payment of the holiday. The tickets for the complete package are delivered wherever the customer requests.

These are everyday occurrences.

Increasingly, your customers and business partners will want products and services delivered, negotiated for, and even designed at a place that is convenient for them. They will not care whether or not you make your decisions centrally, or whether you share knowledge cross-functionally or cross-geographically. What will matter to them will be your ability to answer their questions and to deliver your products and services where they require them.

An executive with U.S.-headquartered CSX Corporation, a transportation company, believes that "today, global companies have no boundaries. A global company is one that undertakes its mission-critical activities wherever it makes the most sense; its research and development can occur wherever the skill or talent for performing it physically resides. We are trying to achieve globalization by making connections between assets across countries without putting assets on the ground in a particular country."

The fundamental shift in the balance of world economies over the past two decades—away from U.S. dominance and toward equilibrium among the Triad groupings—means that the number of global customers has increased exponentially in that time. And the trend continues; with the collapse of Communism in Eastern Europe, the possibilities for greater distribution of wealth in the Middle East, the growth of the younger capitalist economies in the Pacific Rim, and vibrant economies in South America. A generation from now, global customers will be doing business all over the world and may be headquartered anywhere.

IBM's recognition of this trend was one of the driving forces behind its decision to join with us in the study of 10 global businesses we conducted in 1990. IBM found that in 1990 20 percent of its worldwide revenue stream was generated by 454 international customers. IBM's total customer base is about 5 million, but one-fifth of the company's revenue was generated by less than one-hundredth of one percent of the customer base. And the percent of revenue created by this tiny customer base was growing through the late 1980s and into the 1990s faster than the revenue growth in any "domestic" (single-country) market IBM had.

When IBM developed the Kanji workstation, it thought it was aiming at a domestic—Japanese—market. But when it went to sell the product, it found that Japanese companies needed the product sold, supported, and serviced in Detroit, where a number of subcontractors to Japanese auto companies are located.

Executives of one company told us that its products, which are advertised at some international sporting events, are now being seen in parts of the world that are able to watch the races on satellite television, but where the company does not sell its product, and therefore has no ability to satisfy the consumer demand generated by its advertising.

At TNT Express Worldwide, a Dutch-based company we spent time with, salespeople used to bid on business in a country by country way but were increasingly being required by its largest customers to submit pan European and occasionally worldwide bids.

A European consumer-durables executive we met told us that she has categorized all individuals who live in industrialized countries as having one of four global lifestyles, and has determined that those of us who are urban or suburban professionals and who live in the Boston area have more in common with urban or suburban professionals in Paris or Tokyo than we do with people who may live only a few miles from us. The company has begun to revolutionize its business in order to cater to a global market segment rather than people with national characteristics.

Finally, the companies we studied all told us of the information intensity required to satisfy the "anyplace" demands of business.

Even a company whose business is disposing of industrial waste is being encouraged by its global customers to maintain detailed records of what was dumped, where, and when, on their behalf.

A prime example of the global consumer and a provider creating the ability to meet the global consumer's needs is the demand for news and information and the case of the Cable News Network (CNN).

For years, the rap against CNN in the United States has been that "it's the same thing over and over"—the same headlines, the same features, the same videos, for hours and hours. And, if one sits in front of the television and watches CNN for hours at a time, that is often true.

But the goal of CNN and its 24-hour news format is not to provide something new and different all the time to the person sitting in one location. The goal is to provide one product for any person anywhere at any time.

The penetration of CNN around the world, which began running on a number of U.S. cable systems in 1980, has been driven by the U.S. business traveler, who, beginning in the mid-1980s, was able to watch a half hour of U.S.-oriented "international" news in his or her hotel room, in the morning or evening, before or after work, or just before going to bed, exactly as he or she does at home. This is all made possible by the same satellites that allow television to broadcast live pictures from anywhere around the world.

The anyplace consumer population for any-time news continues to grow. Like the European consumer-goods company that now makes washing machines and stoves for a target customer of urban and urbane professionals, CNN has found a growing audience in English-speaking consumers of news around the world with the financial wherewithal to purchase a satellite receiving dish. Some viewers who do not speak English watch the images to keep informed.

During the U.S. military invasion of Panama in late 1989, viewers around the world listened to a wealthy Panamanian who called CNN to report what was going on because he watched CNN. Its correspondents were on the line live telling the world that the hotel they were in had not been secured by U.S. forces, and that "dignity battalions" were coming from room to room rounding up journalists. The Panamanian man continued watching CNN as he spoke to its anchor people in Atlanta and Washington, narrating for them scenes their cameramen were videotaping in his neighborhood.

And its reach continues to grow. CNN's around-the-clock, around-the-world coverage of the war in the Persian Gulf in early 1991 was so riveting (its correspondents reported the first night of the bombing of Baghdad live via portable satellite telephone after all other broadcasters were put off the air when the Iraqi telephone exchanges were bombed) that all around the world news consumers asked their governments to allow CNN a place on the national television dial so it is available to all households.

And while the three major U.S. networks, ABC, NBC, and CBS, all bemoaned the loss of revenue during the Persian Gulf war, and all cut back on their news operations after the war, CNN immediately announced that it would seize the day and expand its worldwide capabilities, adding bureaus and personnel. Politicians around the world stay current with up to the minute reporting and tracking of events. The CNN crews have called this "telediplomacy."

Around the same time, Ted Turner, founder and principle owner of CNN, decreed that the word "foreign" would no longer be used by CNN anchors or correspondents because of its ethnocentric connotations; when you have a global audience no one is foreign.

From Mechanistic (The Whole of the Business Equals the Sum of Its Parts) to Holistic (The Whole Is Greater than the Sum of Its Parts)

A global business acts as an organic whole, rather than as one with a number of disconnected elements moving in different directions. Making progress toward becoming a global business means moving from a mechanistic organization, where the whole of the business equals the sum of its parts, to a holistic organization, where any part of the business reflects its "genetic code," and where the whole is greater than the sum of its parts.

Monsieur Wahl at BNP put it best when he said, "A corporation is global like a human, living structure. In one cell is all the description of the whole. The cell allows the corporation to reconstitute the whole being."

For employees, global holism means the organization has shared beliefs, attitudes, and values. This creates a consistency in the way you treat customers, vendors, other business partners, and each other, wherever business is being done.

As John Mullen, CEO of TNT Express Worldwide, says, "We try to project a corporate culture worldwide. Managing Directors travel widely, and each middle manager is driven by a similar set of requirements and a short-term focus on results. They all talk the same language. We move managers around a lot. We use profit incentives—all parties benefit from an international deal."

Holism also defines the way the functional pieces of a global company fit together. Rather than seeing things as sequential, or "happening somewhere else," the global company sees all of its internal functions as a closely choreographed operation. An executive with CSX says, "It makes sense to look at manufacturing, marketing, and logistics holistically and think of them and treat them as a single system or entity. Sourcing may be worldwide but driven by the mindset of a global system."

And an executive of an American service company chides his organization for its lack of such ability: "We still react to requests as though there are other parts of the company who take care of such things; we don't have the holistic feeling or approach to universally handling a customer's needs on a universal basis. Our attitude is that we have made the introduction, now it is someone else's problem. In other words, the barrier we have to going global is how to work together."

Whether you offer the same or different products in different countries, customers carry a holistic expectation of the quality of your products and services, and an idea of your company wherever they go. Whether you are organized as an integrated global company or a set of distinct multidomestic enterprises, your customers' experiences are holistic. The effect of how any one part of the company operates has an effect on the company's global image.

We like our American Express and VISA cards because we travel constantly. We have the convenience of needing local currency in small amounts only for cab fare and tips, because every hotel, restaurant, and major store we visit accepts our anyplace plastic. We realize that we sometimes get a better rate of exchange from the cards than we do by converting cash at local banks. And at the end of each month, all of the charges from around the world have been pulled together on one statement.

For American Express, global holism means that we and its other customers can expect a certain quality of convenience and service wherever we travel. American Express cards and travelers checks provide customers with convenience and standard methods of payment anywhere in the world, while their offices provide worldwide and local travel information and services, as well as a place to convert local currency.

American Express realizes that the customer has a global, integrated view of its business—that if you have a bad experience with the company in Brisbane or Brussels, you are likely to switch providers when you get home, wherever home may be. American Express personnel around the world must have a similar level of expertise and set of standards for treating customers.

The same is true for the environmental services company we studied, Waste Management, Inc. It has created a standard for the management of wastes around the world, and tries to maintain that standard at the level of the highest government standard anywhere it does business. This is to protect not only its image, but also the image of the companies it serves in many locales.

From Isolation to Low
or Nonexistent Boundaries

To be global is to have the ability to act as if boundaries are low or do not exist at all. It means eliminating the isolationism that precludes sharing. Barriers between functions, divisions, or locations of your company are powerful impediments to process effectiveness, innovation, and flexibility. A global company eliminates the isolationism that gets in the way of sharing.

To believe that, if a company stays home and sticks to its knitting, business will go well just doesn't fit the way the world works.

The truth is, if a company has a good product in a healthy market with good margins, someone else will want to introduce a product in that market and get at those margins. The other company may figure out how the product is made and make it better, or more efficiently, or more precisely tailored to the customer. Or the other company may come up with a new idea that addresses the market in a way that makes the first company's product obsolete. With global competition, these things happen every day.

When the Berlin Wall fell in late 1989, most people on both sides of the wall were astonished. They had not conceived that what they had so recently regarded as a "permanent" barrier to trade and human interchange could give way so easily.

East Germans brought down the wall because they finally woke up to the reality that their economic system could not work in isolation from their close neighbors to the west. They wanted the goods and services, as well as the jobs, that they could see just over the frontier.

Western business perspectives about the possibilities of doing business in Eastern Europe changed almost over night. Well-laid business strategies went out the window as companies rethought basic principles and scrambled their resources to adapt to the expanding European market which went from 160 million people to over 350 million with the addition of the Eastern European countries.

As the world economy opens into a broader playing field, and more and more companies are able to offer global products and services, the value of physical barriers, such as the Berlin Wall, and conceptual barriers, such as protectionist "local-content" practices, will have less and less meaning.

From "Not Invented Here"
to Networks of Trust

Being global means creating relationships built on trust.

By trusting other managers to act as reliable entities in a corporate organization, you can reduce the amount of time and effort required to accomplish anything. If someone trusts you, you don't have to spend all of your time getting "buy-in" from that person.

Global companies gain trust by focusing on similarities rather than differences. By sharing the responsibility for the development of ideas wherever they come from, global companies create a powerful global advantage. To move flexibly and quickly, therefore, your business must have a well-woven fabric of mutual trust upon which it can depend.

Many companies hold worldwide management meetings at least once a year, for all levels of management. During these meetings, team-building exercises are run to create bonds among the group, and to encourage people to share expertise. Groups are arranged to solve particular issues the company will face in the coming year.

Solutions must consist of global-action programs that management is willing to engage in. Not only does the company gain powerful insights into issues from many perspectives, but also the individuals gain contacts within the company. They learn alternative ways to solve problems by sharing process issues. Many companies, holding these meetings in exotic places, say that the return from such sessions can be exponential.

From Mere Physical Geographic Presence to Acceptance by the Local Culture

Globalization means more than merely having a geographic presence in a country or region. It means the local customers and business partners recognize your company and perceive you as appealing. Further, it means that your company and your products and services are accepted by the culture, and perhaps are identified as part of the culture. This usually means that you are a "good citizen" in those countries where you do business, and that your global products and services reflect the local culture and tastes.

Yatsutaka Obayashi, Deputy Senior General Manager of Corporate Strategy and Development at Canon in Tokyo, put it this way: "In order to prosper, to succeed long term, we must be perceived wherever we do business as a good member of society, accepted as a good, respected manufacturing company. This requires our being a total company, a complete company, wherever we do business."

"Local look and feel" describes your company's products, services, and presence when they are tailored to achieve cultural fit. The most obvious example of local look and feel is the ability to speak your customer's language.

Apple Computer reaps benefits by providing different keyboards, as well as software packages in many languages, for its globally consistent personal computer processors. Operating with a "local face," by providing local languages, has increased the ease of use and diffusion of Apple products in many countries.

As Michael Spindler, Chief Executive Officer of Apple Computer, Inc., says, "The concept of global business does not allow for a company that is based in one country or location to look at the rest of the world as one big market. It must have a truly international perspective."

"The new global company starts with a clear vision behind a product and then adjusts or adapts that idea to products uniquely suited to each country or market. It not only manufactures and markets worldwide, it interacts culturally in a dynamic way so that the original idea or product becomes part of the local society."

In the process of setting a new course, companies need to consistently tinker with their global/local balance, reevaluating which elements of their business have to be the same so that all other elements can be different as they create a proper balance between global economies of scale and local responsiveness.

As companies enter countries, often the initial impressions formed are the most long-lasting. Local good citizenship can ease the tension of entry or expansion.

As Dr. Diane Wilson, a researcher on strategic alliances and investment in information technology at the Massachusetts Institute of Technology, states, "Cultural fit is all about realizing that there will be conflict with the local culture, planning for it, and taking some form of action that demonstrates a long-term interest in the community."*

An executive with Waste Management put it slightly differently when he said, "The global company must learn to deal with the issues of unity (being one company) and disparity (being many companies). Regarding disparity we need to learn how to respond to local needs. This is very important in a service company. We need to learn how to be an Italian company in Italy.

"We have to be 'local' wherever we do business. We have to have business processes that allow that behavior. We have to internalize and adapt to/in our processes everything going on in local markets served with regard to competitive behavior and translate that into our behavior."

Turning conflict into accord, diversity into strengths, is a necessary concern for the global corporation.

---

* Dr. Diane Wilson (researcher, Sloan School of Management, Massachusetts Institute of Technology), interview with author, 1992.

From Centralized Controllers to Core Management

In a global business, the management core of the organization functions as connectors of the many operational areas, as well as amplifiers and interpreters of the communications among those groups. This is in marked contrast to the center functioning as the controller of the entire network of operations.

Core connectors recognize a responsibility to solve problems rather than merely asserting status by being remote from the work.

In knowledge-worker dominated industries, where technical expertise is as valued as management expertise, management acts more and more as coordinators and connectors.

At the IBM Consulting Group, the senior partners act as connectors to the local practices by providing information about engagement results and industry expertise being developed in different parts of the globe. Local practice managers are responsible for the running of their unit, as well as connecting the people within the unit.

On the shop floor at Nissan Motors plants, management joins in on the assembly line when there is a problem. They see their job as managing the contingencies, assisting the line with problem-solving resources. Connecting the shop floor to the resources for solution is one of their primary duties, and their attitude reflects that.

Bill Harker, Chief Operating Officer of Royal Trust, in Toronto, sees the need for the whole organization to become connected in how it goes after business, and in how individuals are rewarded for group success. "Mutuality of interest is a key global value. The firm seeks to build this mutuality of interest by exchanging shares of stock. This gives everyone a stake in the game. Executive bonuses are issued in stock. Decisions are therefore made with the long-term impact on stock price and customer service in mind, not this year's objectives. This builds and sustains the company network worldwide. We have given up control to get control. It is the common understanding of where we are going and how we will get there that keeps it working."

From Duplication of Resources to Taking Advantage of Economies of Scale

Global companies take advantage of economies of scale without overly replicating resources. And increasingly, knowledge is the source of many of these economies of scale.

Individuals are responsible for sharing relevant information with others who will benefit from knowing it, without creating so much "clutter" that everyone constantly has information overload. Individuals can't be passive receptors of other people's communications. This is part of the shared trust that makes it possible for global companies to function efficiently.

A chemical company we studied is a good example. "Having access to a central pool of skills and knowledge is key," says one executive. "For example, we had a disaster in Taiwan. A typhoon came through and virtually wiped out the operation. We were able to fly in operational and technical specialists as well as staff for a period of four to six months in order to get the situation restored. They had no problem working together or working in that local environment as they shared the same values and knowledge base."

More than 20 years ago IBM created the RETAIN system, a knowledge repository that gives customer-service engineers anywhere access to vital information about how to fix especially difficult hardware and systems-software problems. Over the years engineers have built the database of problems they have encountered and solutions they found or created. Over the years the system has been upgraded to make it easier for customer-service representatives to get into the database and find the useful information.

At Bain & Company, a consulting firm, "librarians" travel from project to project to document progress and create a database of the company's experiences.

Without good mechanisms for keeping others informed of what work is being done, redundancies such as the following can happen. A team of financial-markets dealers in London, was, unknowingly, competing with a team from their own company in California to make an offer to a Japanese client. By studying the patterns of purchases and other client behavior, both teams were trying to develop the most attractive combination of global financial instruments to offer. Because of their limited view of the client's holdings, neither team felt that it had a great chance of winning.

In the initial stage of the deal, the California team had a database of only the client's equity positions, while the London team had access to a database of the client's debt-instrument positions.

When a senior company executive discovered the fact that the two teams were competing, he urged them to work together. They readily agreed, but it took the back-office staff much time to find a way to link the two databases so the teams could share information, ideas, and solutions to the client's needs.

In the area of waste disposal, with a company becoming global by acquisition, there are unique problems and opportunities. An executive at Waste Management says, "Since most of the costs of doing business are incurred locally, we can't see how to achieve global economies. However, there are some good examples of how we can achieve global synergy if we consider some of the technologies we export. Our big advantage is that we know how we can move the knowledge and technical know-how to the local operator. We need to drive the company to where it is a local company for one global customer."

From Stovepipes*
to Communications Networks

Being global means having anyplace, anytime communications with anyone in the organization, not communicating vertically up stovepipes within specific organizational functions.

Field forces at most companies are well aware of the lag time predicament in hierarchical decision making. What field force has not taken an action, deciding to deal with the consequences later, rather than send the request up the stovepipe and wait for it to come back down again?

You cannot be truly global without being connected.

In fifteenth century Spain and Portugal, this meant having fast ships. Today it means having great telecommunications facilities, knowledge repositories, and windows into those repositories in the form of microprocessor-based workstations and other information-processing tools.

Jacques Henri Wahl of BNP explains, "To accomplish the strategic imperative of privileging our relationships with customers with global needs we have to have the highest amount of information on our customers. Information systems are central to our vision."

It also means having an organizational culture that permits direct communication from any person to any other person in the organization, a culture that calls for true communication and not merely following a chain of command.

A global business does not have one center, but multiple centers, located around expertise and competence. Communications need to be outbound and node-to-node as well as inbound; they need to be from anyone to anyone.

An executive with Pirelli sees one of his company's chief objectives as "taking a global perspective in designing products and positioning brand names." To do this, the company must "develop the means to update drawings and coordinate design, engineering, and manufacturing activities in real-time; increase headquarters knowledge of market trends within and across countries to help it track the development of, and changes in, global lifestyles."

---

* A stovepipe is a chimney stack and represents vertical communications within functional hierarchies.

We've seen this concept in operation, as bond traders in London, Tokyo, and New York, all watching multiple digital and video inputs on their desks and talking on multiple phone lines to clients, at the same time monitor a shared internal "hoot and holler"* system that allows them to stay in touch.

Communications are also of utmost importance in how global customers interact with the company. "We need to start with information closer to what the customer really wants," says an executive with CSX. "Moreover, we need to provide a common interface for linking electronically to the customer throughout the domain of where they do business."

And executives with a U.S.-based manufacturer say that to "accommodate customer requirements in developing prime products we will need, among other things, to be able to automatically translate documents and training materials into at least eight primary languages. This will open doors to customers, make it easier and less expensive to do business with us, shorten the cycle time of product roll out, protect our premium pricing position, increase our accuracy, and reduce customer liability."

From Short-term Focus Only to Long-term View

You can't become global without adding a long-term financial view to a short-term focus. To do this, you need to understand the worldwide economics of your business, including geographic and competitive forces and opportunities. Effective tradeoffs can only be made if there is sufficient information available to make global decisions.

Adding a long-term view can only be accomplished if there is full commitment to and acceptance of your global business vision. To enter a new market, for example, it may be necessary to use cross-subsidies from other parts of the business, rather than looking for a one-year return on investment. A business will handle different parts of the business in different stages of development in ways that are appropriate to the situation, and will enable them to effectively grow their resources.

An executive with one U.S. service company says, "Our goal is to make money everywhere. But we may have to do business where we will not be making money to be able to do business someplace else."

Taking a long-term view does not mean formulating an extensive strategy and set of implementation plans that can not be changed in the future. On the contrary, long-term means putting a stake in the ground as to the iden-

---

* An internal, informal system of communication. This particular reference refers to a voice-activated intercom that connects multiple traders across multiple offices around the world.

tity of your company, around which your customers, business partners, and employees can act.

Royal Trust's Bill Harker describes how his company has become more global over time. "Our operations are around the world, but quite independent. The way we got into each country was different. Management did not think of it as an attack on the globe. Product niche has been the main focus, as opposed to geographic concern. In the future our configuration is likely to contain more nodes in the galaxy . . . and it is a galaxy, not a pyramid. There will be more focus on building the core values by design, rather than by accident."

Summary

Companies going global need a powerful global vision to lead the organization into the future. A good global vision addresses such issues as how the company will serve customers, compete, create value, and reward effort on a global basis. Ten key attributes differentiate global visions. Fundamentally, globalization is a business concept (how you do business), not a geographic concept. Global companies design to operate as an organic whole with a clarity of business process that is readily understood by customers, employees, and business partners.

Action Checklist

1. Has your company's management team articulated its global vision and broadly disseminated it across the organization?

2. Do you explore your company's sphere of influence and search for ways to leverage relationships?

3. Do you understand which parts of your company have to be the same so everything else can be different?

4. Do you allow parts of your company to erect walls which isolate their activities from the rest of the business?

5. Do you have programs across the organization which nurture the development of relationships based on trust?

6. Are you accepted as a "local" company wherever you do business?

7. Does your company constantly seek out ways to better share its intellectual capital?

8. Is your company's global vision supported by a long-term investment program?

2
How Is Your Company Positioned Today? Three Approaches to International Business

The ideal global company is both a low-cost producer and customer driven. It balances global consistency with local diversity. It has a flexible product and service architecture that allows for a high level of customization. It has a highly coordinated value chain that utilizes multiple centers of excellence distributed throughout the world in the most appropriate locations.

The global company can support both global and local customers with balanced global/local sales and support channels. It operates like a geodesic network that enables and encourages its employees to communicate point-to-point rather than through the hierarchical chain of command.

These attributes may seem too good to be true. Certainly, no one company has come close to realizing all of them. But many companies have already implemented some of these ideas. If we were to assemble an all-star company out of exemplary global practices of companies around the world, we could create a single entity pretty close to our target.

The Starting Point

Companies are attempting to cross the global frontier from three very different starting positions, that of a global exporter, a company with a multilocal form of operation, or a company with a multinational form. Understanding where your company is, in terms of its current business form and global characteristics, is an important first step in the process of aligning and focusing a company's development as it moves up the global learning curve. It is also a place to start when creating a global vision.

Figure 2-1 shows where these three types of companies—global exporter, multilocal, multinational—fall on a two-dimensional model, with the ideal being a position at the high end of customer responsiveness and at the low end of cost.

The box in which your company currently sits determines the course it will have to plot to reach the global ideal. Of course, these boxes are generalizations, and you may feel that your company straddles boxes, or, especially in large multidivisional companies, that parts of the company fall in one box and parts in another. For such companies, the key to global progress is an understanding that no single approach will work for the entire company's trip up the global ladder. In fact, for some large multidivisional companies, an argument might be made that certain divisions do not even need to "go global," at least not yet.

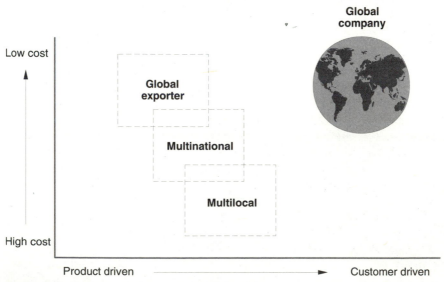

Figure 2-1. Positioning a company in a global context.

At the heart of the question of business models is the question of whether or not the company can grow into the future with its current mindset, configuration of resources, and management practices. Clearly, we believe not.

The goal of any business on its quest for globalism is to reconfigure itself, working from its platform of current capabilities and adding to those capabilities to face the business requirements of tomorrow. Unless a business is at least taking its first steps today on the road toward becoming truly global, moving from one of the current, somewhat rigid, constructs, toward the fluidity and flexibility of a globally run business, that business will face difficult challenges in the twenty-first century.

The process of becoming a truly global company will take years. Changing not only the paper structure of a company, but also the organizational atmosphere and the mindset of leadership will probably take a full generation; not until those who have been doing business "the old way" for so long retire and a new generation of global-thinking leaders comes into being will a company make the complete transition. However, there are concrete steps a company can take in the first five years of planning for and working toward a global company.

With that in mind, it is useful to take a more detailed look at the three operating structures today's internationally active companies take.

Three Approaches to International Business

The Global Exporter— The Japanese Model

Companies are motivated to begin international activities when they realize that a market for their products and/or services extends beyond the geographic borders of their country. This expanded perception of the market carries with it the attraction of increased revenues and profits. Companies expand into the international marketplace by pushing domestic products through an expanded distribution channel.

Key initial responsibilities include increasing domestic production capacity and finding suitable distribution agents.

Exporters usually develop local sales capacity in new markets by finding trading partners to act as their agents in selling, distributing, and servicing their goods. The initial investment, depending on the choice of a local agent, might be very small, while the return is increased sales. Sources of suggestions for suitable partners can come from overseas acquaintances, customers, industry colleagues, or trade departments of the countries in which the company wants to do business or of its own country.

As business develops, the responsibilities of the agent grow as products and services penetrate the market. Ultimately, the reputation of the exporter is in the hands of its trading partner. The partner's ability to manage the local distribution system must keep pace with the increased market.

It is difficult for a company to sustain whatever initial market advantages it has as an exporter in a foreign market. The market typically conspires against exporters to increase the aggregate costs to the customers: the distribution system is not under the exporter's direct control, and its agents often demand a larger cut of the pie; countries express concern about lack of local content; protective tariffs are raised; or local competition, suddenly aware of a market opportunity, emerges.

Characteristics of the exporting company include a product-push view of foreign markets, with maintenance of most if not all value-chain activities, except sales and service, in the home country, run by home-country nationals, and with complete home-country control in management. As Figure 2-1 suggests, the exporter gets its advantage by being a low-cost producer, and has great difficulty being highly responsive to the customer.

Examples of successful exporting companies, like Hyundai in the late 1980s, are easy to find for short periods of time. But over the long haul the export approach is seldom sustainable.

Exporters often find that success is dependent on expanding local activities early. Companies most often do this in one of two ways. They either increase the human element, by locating expatriate company representatives in the country to act as sales and marketing agents, or they add value to the product itself and make it more attractive to the local market by means of minor modifications or features to fit the local environment.

We call companies that engage in such value-enhancing local modifications "global exporters." They often make extensive forays outside of their home countries to capture knowledge about market and customer requirements. They also study competitors' operations around the world to increase their management knowledge base. While they gather and analyze this market intelligence information from other countries, however, they still run most company operations from home.

As global exporters begin to set their sights on globalization, they gradually bow to local pressures and initially deploy local manufacturing activity to support local sales presence. Eventually, perhaps reluctantly, they deploy product-development in selected locations. By doing so, they begin to take on the structural appearances of a multinational.

As Figure 2-2 shows, global exporters tend to treat the world more from a geographic perspective than a business perspective. They do well at managing their company as a world business system.

On the other hand, they are very reluctant to move any core activities outside of their home country.

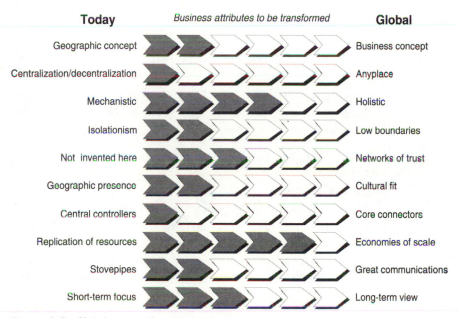

Today	Business attributes to be transformed	Global
Geographic concept		Business concept
Centralization/decentralization		Anyplace
Mechanistic		Holistic
Isolationism		Low boundaries
Not invented here		Networks of trust
Geographic presence		Cultural fit
Central controllers		Core connectors
Replication of resources		Economies of scale
Stovepipes		Great communications
Short-term focus		Long-term view

Figure 2-2. Global exporter business attributes.

Global exporters are not configured to do anyplace business because most of their trusted personnel and talent are concentrated in the home country or major business centers, and they rely on agents and partners to support customers in most outlying regions.

Global exporters are highly integrated, work in multidisciplinary teams, and share a strong common culture, which gets them high marks in holism. The home country is like a high-walled citadel, but barriers in national organizations are permeable, primarily because the national organizations are weak and run by expatriate home-country managers. Global exporters rely very heavily on these home-country nationals for all major decision making, which reflects little trust in foreign employees.

Global exporters produce products that seek to find the lowest common denominators in product appeal, so as little customization as possible has to be done locally. These homogeneous, or "global" products, are primarily successful when they are extremely high quality, because service and support can be a real challenge for the global exporter.

Global exporters rely on very strong control and directives from home-country headquarters. Because of their highly integrated world business systems, they have little overlap of resources, and consequently get high economies of scale. Outside the home country, global exporting companies communicate very efficiently through formal organizational stovepipes.

Global exporters are very patient, and prepared to take a long-term view of such investment decisions as subsidizing a start-up operation in a new country.

But while they do a number of things well, more often than not global exporters find themselves bound by their strongly nationalistic exporter mindsets, and they have difficulty developing sufficient appreciation and sensitivity to the required openness of a global mindset, which makes them globally shortsighted.

The Multinational—
The United States' Model

Being multinational is another option.

Most multinationals were once global exporters, and most global exporters will probably have to pass through a multinational phase on the road across the frontier to true globalism. However, that doesn't mean that the trip across the frontier to globalism will be any easier for the entrenched multinational.

The trick for the global exporter will be to pass through the multinational phase as quickly as possible, without losing the strong attributes of the global exporter and picking up the bad habits of the multinational.

Multinationalism usually begins with the creation of national sales and service organizations, often followed soon after by national manufacturing organizations. Research and development is almost certainly the last function to be moved out from the home country. And basic—or fundamental—research often never leaves the home country and the centralized organization, while product development is distributed to prime regional market areas. Significant innovations, however, can be rapidly transferred from headquarters to the rest of the world.

The multinational develops relatively homogeneous products or services for the world. Manufacturing is distributed around the world to exploit economies of scale and vault barriers to entry. The multinational tries to maximize the use of resources through strong central coordination, rather than flexibly integrating resources to distributed competence centers. By physically moving closer to its customers and taking advantage of scale economies, the multinational is able to deliver fairly low-cost products to most customers.

In a multinational company, headquarters plays a strong role in setting strategies and policies and establishing standards. While a matrix management structure may be in place to handle the complexity of product/service offerings in individual locations, major decisions are made by headquarters and communicated via outbound directives. Sales and delivery channels tend to be regionally controlled with some level of autonomy from corporate headquarters, provided fairly rigid revenue and profit guidelines are met. This concern creates a bias toward the further development of home-country and major markets, since markets are often judged by profit-generating measures.

The multinational, then, still offers a primarily product-push set of strategies, while capturing economies of scale. By locating some operations in countries for cost or entry reasons, the company gathers some intelligence about local customers, and is more open to innovation than global exporters.

Multinational companies have a very different profile of global attributes than global exporters, as shown in Figure 2-3.

With a much more distributed value chain outside of the home country, they find it a more complex task than the global exporter to manage their company as a world business system. The greater deployment of their value chain gives them more cultures and technical resources to draw upon, which tends to make the multinational a more open and innovative company. This deployment of resources also means that the multinational is much better positioned to do business anyplace than the global exporter.

Multinationals are less holistic than global exporters, because they tend to be more bureaucratic and functionally specialized. They decentralize much more power into regional and national organizations, and they spend a lot of energy trying to create multigeographic teamwork. While national barriers are still severe impediments, multinationals are better

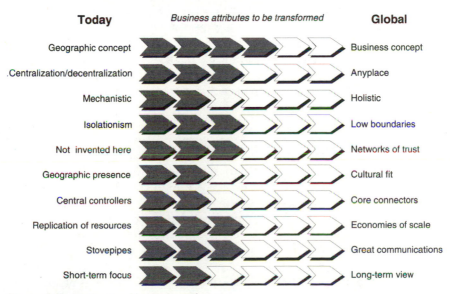

Figure 2-3. Multinational business attributes.

positioned than global exporters; while they have a long way to go on building trust, they are similarly better positioned on this attribute.

Multinationals, like global exporters, produce homogeneous products for world markets, and they also produce tailored products for specific markets. Because they have much broader geographic presence than global exporters, they acculturate better.

Multinationals have a strong control mentality, but more decision making is decentralized than in the global exporter. Given their less integrated way of working, their communications are less efficient; while many multinationals have the technology installed for point-to-point geodesic communications, they are frequently held back by their regional "hub and spoke" business-operating philosophy.

The Multilocal—
The European Model

Once a company expands its frontiers beyond export, management sometimes decides to develop markets with less of a strong, centralized approach and go to the other extreme, laissez-faire. This approach allows management to focus on local-customer expectations.

Customers increasingly want customization of some aspects of products and services. The multilocal specializes in local customization to meet local-customer requirements. It is through customization that companies add value to commodity goods. Local sales and delivery offer customized products.

The multilocal is focused on and responsive to its customers and flexible to local requirements. The balance of power is with the national organization. These strong national organizations operate as a set of independently operating, self-reliant, and geographically dispersed units. While fostering independence and initiative, the sharing of management knowledge across boundaries is minimal, and such an approach forces unit managers to go up steep learning curves as they continuously reinvent knowledge on how to carry out the business.

The multilocal company tends to duplicate a large portion of the value chain in each country where it does business, and sacrifices economies of scale in an attempt to meet local-market requirements.

The aggregate worldwide customer pays a high cost for this, as does the global customer. The global customer has to deal with several separate operating units of the same company, and at times has to sort out its own account administration. In multilocal companies, there is often no assurance of consistency in company policy across borders with regard to price and quality.

Any effort to create synergy by integrating ideas of processes at any great depth encounters high barriers. Since headquarters measures each unit or country on return on investment, or profit, cross-measures are not set and synergistic targets are only achieved with great difficulty. Newer markets may not get the investment earlier markets received, since they are expected to "stand on their own."

Multilocals take a very different approach to managing themselves, and have a very different profile from global exporters and multinationals, as seen in Figure 2-4.

Multilocals do not approach the world as one business system, but rather as a set of individual markets, each to be approached separately. Because this leads to many separate and distinct sets of operating procedures, the multilocal has more difficulty than the multinational in supporting any-place business, although it has an edge on global exporters because of the broader geographic scope. It also means that multilocals are much more mechanistic than either global exporters or multinationals.

Multilocals have to contend with high walls built around each country, as well as the strongest case of "not invented here" syndrome. On the other hand, multilocals have a strong advantage over the other current forms in terms of cultural fit, often leading to high-value differentiated services.

Multilocals are much less focused on formal control systems and rigid policies and procedures; corporate headquarters' role is often oriented to connecting different pieces in the organization through personal relationships. There is much less point-to-point communication, however, among

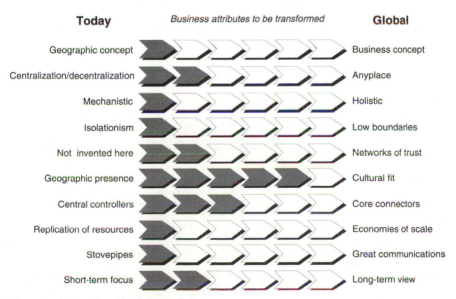

Figure 2-4. Multilocal business attributes.

operations in different countries than in other forms, and much less likelihood a physical wide-area telecommunications network exists.

Multilocals are long-term oriented in local or regional markets, but have shown little interest to date in taking a long-term investment position in doing business globally.

Wherever You Are, Take Global Aim

Figure 2-5 shows comparisons in attributes between the three types of organizations. As you can clearly see, each structure has some attributes closer to those of a truly global company than the others. The key to becoming global is, in effect, to cherry pick these attributes to form a single entity with all of the strong points, while divesting the company of the kind of attributes that hold it back.

One might say that a quick way to think of the global company would be to think of a company that combines (1) the holistic approach and ability to take advantage of economies of scale of a global exporter, (2) the strong business concept and decentralization of knowledge and decision making found in the multinational, and (3) the rigorous attention to cultural fit of the multilocal.

One could assign the business forms described here to a majority of companies working internationally from the economic triad areas of the world —Japan and the Pacific Rim, Western Europe, and North America.

Characteristic	Global exporter	Multinational	Multilocal	Global
Products and services	Homogeneous	Homogeneous; some customized	Customized; some homogeneous	Flexible architecture allowing for mass customization
Value chain activities	Highly concentrated in home country	Distributed, but highly controlled by home country	Highly duplicated in each country	Highly networked and distributed around the globe
Basis of competition	Economies of scale in production	Sharing innovations outbound from H.Q.	Local responsiveness	EOS of production and knowledge; low cost/customer driven
Organization	Home-country nationals	H.Q. controls national companies	Strong national organizations; H.Q. plays primarily financial role	Decisions made at centers of competence
Customers	Global and local customers get the same treatment	Local customers supported by national sales companies; global customers supported with difficulty	Local-customer focus; global customers supported only with great difficulty	Supports global and local customers

Figure 2-5. Business characteristics of global exporter, multinational, multilocal, and global companies.

By and large, the global exporter model is one we typically see in Japanese companies; the multinational organization is an American phenomenon; and the multilocal format is one favored by Western European companies.

The results of our joint study with IBM reinforce this; what we found when we did this detailed study of 10 companies, their current global positions, and their thinking about how to become global in the future, adhered for the most part to this pattern. It is, however, notable that we found a Canadian company that fit what one might call the European model. Figure 2-6 shows the position of the 10 companies who participated in the study on the global chart.

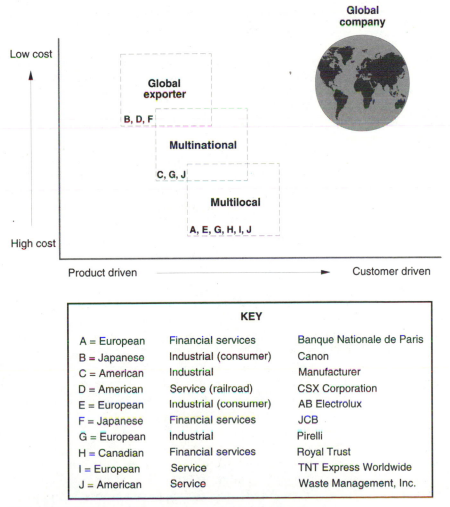

KEY

A = European	Financial services	Banque Nationale de Paris
B = Japanese	Industrial (consumer)	Canon
C = American	Industrial	Manufacturer
D = American	Service (railroad)	CSX Corporation
E = European	Industrial (consumer)	AB Electrolux
F = Japanese	Financial services	JCB
G = European	Industrial	Pirelli
H = Canadian	Financial services	Royal Trust
I = European	Service	TNT Express Worldwide
J = American	Service	Waste Management, Inc.

Figure 2-6. Positions of 10 companies on the global matrix.

Note: It is interesting that Pirelli was classified as being in two different positions at the same time. The Cable Division of the company had a multilocal approach, while the Tire Division more closely resembled the multinational model. As a Pirelli executive explains, "In the Tire Sector, vehicle manufacturers are becoming global. The industry is concentrated, competition takes place on an international basis, and innovation occurs in many places around the world. The Cable Sector, on the other hand, has developed products and services to cope with different national specifications from country to country. Customers are happy with their local specifications and care less about globalization. And yet the cable product is everywhere."

Figure 2-7 shows how companies 1, 2, and 3 answered the broad question, "What are the first-line imperatives you see to becoming a truly global company?

Each of these companies is starting from a different point on our global-position map; company 1 is multilocal; company 2 is a global exporter; company 3 is multinational. The 13 headings use nine different words or notions: balance, market, system, people, information, organization, service, customer, mindset. These words symbolize the companies' attempt toward globalization.

The simple fact is that it does not matter where your company—or each part of your company—falls precisely on this map. At the end of the day every company will have to undertake the same set of basic tasks in order to get through the first set of hurdles on the way to becoming global.

Developing your company's capability to operate and compete in the global business arena requires an ongoing program of change focused on realizing your company's global vision. That vision is not static; it lives and is kept alive by constant reshaping to reflect the dynamics of the changing business environment.

As your company prepares its global vision, management must take stock of where the company is in its current global development. The company's current position influences the options it can take to create global strategic initiatives that build global processes and programs, and to align the company's global efforts. Figure 2-8 offers a calibration for assessing your company's positioning on the global learning curve. We recommend that management use this set of position attributes to assess not only your company's position, but also that of your competitors.

By understanding where your company is positioned today, management can make more effective decisions to build a sustainable program to capture the global payoff. In moving through the global frontier, and ultimately capturing the global payoff, management must first take stock of the company's current and future position and identify leading global processes and projects. Then it must align the company with globalization stages.

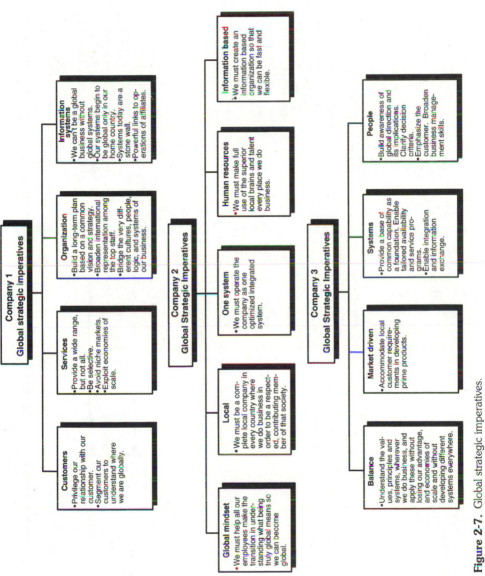

Figure 2-7. Global strategic imperatives.

Global position attributes	Scale	Description
Exploring	Never ←——→ Always	Managers think of the world as one operating environment, exploring the company's depth of presence, business opportunities, and threats.
Committing to global vision	Never ←——→ Always	All employees are aware of global vision and are thinking globally in the carrying out of both their present and future-oriented (e.g., planning) work.
Building global strategic initiatives	Not at all ←——→ Throughout the company	Multidisciplinary teams are actively involved in carrying out global strategic programs based on global strategic imperatives of the company.
Appealing to customers worldwide	Never ←——→ Always	The company understands the global/local spectrum of demand and is able to meet the needs of global customers, customize offerings, and achieve cultural fit.
Building globally scalable resources	Never ←——→ Always	The company is deliberately designing resources to be scalable by sharing knowledge, cultivating positive attitudes toward work, and creating synergies.
Managing the connections	Never ←——→ Always	Managers are managing in cultural contexts sensitively, developing global corporate culture, and connecting and empowering knowledge workers.
Developing global leaders, teams, and individuals	Never ←——→ Always	Global values are permeating the culture, compensation schemes are linked to global behavior, and leaders place importance on globalization.
Leveraging I.T. to build global capability	Not at all ←——→ Throughout the company	Point to point communications systems and portfolios of systems addressing the global process, customer, and product exist and are running effectively.
Capturing global benefits	Never ←——→ Always	Resources are aligned to global stages and investment returns are realized which support global/local balance.

Figure 2-8. Estimating your company's global position.

Benchmarking Your Company's Global Progress

Initially, exploring the global frontier involves finding out just how much discussion is currently going on in a company about the globalization of business, and creating forums for further discussion. Concerns about globalization will bubble up in different ways from different functional and geographic areas.

Marketing may be concerned about serving global customers and the lack of integration in serving these clients; manufacturing may be concerned about integrating worldwide capacity for production; and research and development may be concerned that there are various parts of the world that are developing competing technologies faster than one or two centers can keep up with.

By integrating a few of these concerns around a common issue—such as examining the state of world-class competition, tracking global trends in new technologies, and/or finding the company's emerging global business opportunities—management may find that there are several people who already have ideas about how to become global. By pulling together these various people and parts of the company that are already concerned with global issues, management can develop the roots of global change already occurring in the company's culture and cultivate the process more organically.

Focussing discussion around the 10 global business attributes is one way to further develop ideas within the company. By exploring the forces driving your company and others to become global, the management team can generate a set of global themes.

At a heavy-equipment manufacturer, for example, an executive team discusses the difference between isolationism and low boundaries; the team determines that functional barriers are an important global issue to the company. While the company possesses strong functional expertise in its managers, there is a lack of cross-functional, multicultural business perspective. Assigning accountability is done on a functional basis, creating roadblocks to multidisciplinary objectives. Serving global customers will become more and more difficult if these functional barriers remain intact.

The company's managers have to learn to think more globally. The company has to invest in developing managers who are more aware of the company's global direction and its implications.

By discussing the forms of international business—global exporter, multinational, and multilocal—and the pros and cons of each type within a forum, management can determine what type the company currently is, as well as key strengths and weaknesses of the company in its current business form and what must be done to become truly global. Management may learn that many of the perceived obstacles to becoming global can be overcome in the short run by sharing existing knowledge across organizational and national boundaries, while other issues must be addressed in long-term efforts.

Developing a shared global vision and a set of global strategic initiatives adds depth to current global thinking.

Creating a global vision and mandate involves going through three phases. The initial phase is discovery—creating the right team and mandate, developing a vocabulary to discuss problems, and identifying major issues and themes. The next phase involves making the global vision as tangible as possible—visualizing the global objectives, adding flesh to the bones, and coalescing the issues and themes into direct action of value statements about the company's attitudes and beliefs in becoming global. The third phase involves the actualization of the global vision—developing a call for action and commitment throughout the company and "passing the torch" to the rest of the organization.

The global vision and global strategic initiative processes ultimately must involve all levels of the organization. Crafting global strategy takes advantage of the experiences of many members in the company to make decisions to cope with a global environment of discontinuous change. By constantly revisiting the global vision and global strategic initiatives to keep them current, management steers a course for the global company.

Creating Global Strategic Action Programs

Global strategic initiatives are action-oriented programs, addressing the issues management feels are most important. Some examples are: appealing to customers of the world; creating globally scalable resources; managing organizational connections; developing global leaders, teams, and individuals; and leveraging information technologies to build global capabilities.

Scanning the environment and gathering intelligence on the activities in the company's sphere of influence develops management's global frame of reference. Deciding what the company absolutely must do well to fulfill the global vision focuses efforts on key global strategic initiatives and integrates various multidisciplinary activities around global processes.

Well-formulated global strategic initiatives are well-defined plans of global action. Understanding how strategic efforts converge with the process of forming the global strategic initiatives ensures that everyone in the company is prepared to share a common global mission and synchronized global strategic efforts. Without this understanding, senior management may be unwilling to give up its own agenda, or be unwilling to combine efforts to forge the global initiatives. To create powerful initiatives, the company's best minds should be focused on the effort.

As in the global-visioning process, the right players must be involved in the global strategic initiative formation process, so commitment to the resulting initiatives is high. These people will most often be heads of business and geographic units, key global thinkers, key stakeholders, such as designers of new products or company representatives of customer interests, and multidisciplinary, multigeographic managers who will be instrumental in carrying out global strategic programs.

We have found from experience that the more the major geographic and functional constituencies are given the opportunity to provide input into the process, the more they will feel like they have crafted the result and feel responsible for it, and the more easily it will spread to the rest of the company. While this level of involvement up front is often viewed as expensive and time consuming, it is miniscule compared with the quality and cost of the result. If a company doesn't involve the right people up front, it will discover that it is much more expensive and time consuming later on to get the whole organization committed and moving favorably on the initiatives.

Setting the company's global strategic initiatives involves deciding what must be done well on at least five dimensions to reach the vision*; those five dimensions are:

- the global strategic objective
- global macro performance measures
- global pressure points
- global success measures
- the time horizon

A *global strategic objective* is a statement of strategic intent, a translation of a generic vision into a set of more specific objectives. It is a stake in the ground the company plants to focus the company's efforts on. An example might be "to dramatically improve relationships with global customers." The global strategic objective sets the attitude of the initiative, positioning its importance in the company's value system. When a company's objective states, "We will serve global customers with the same responsiveness wherever they are located," employees are getting the signal to focus on global customers.

This global strategic objective begs the question, "How, and to what extent?"

To answer this question we need *global macro performance measures,* which establish the link between the organization's strategic objective and the economic baseline or performance measures. Every objective, if accomplished, will have an impact on the macroeconomics of the organization.

* David P. Norton, Renaissance Strategy Group, Lincoln, Mass.

An example would be "increasing world market share by three percent." The global performance measure provides an indicator of the benefits the company wants to achieve by reaching its objectives. The measures must be stated as clearly as possible.

The macro performance measures beg the question, "Who will be accountable to do this?"

The answer is the *global pressure point,* which is the area of the organization that has the greatest ability to have an impact on accomplishing the objective. The pressure point identifies the programs' targets, i.e., to provide globally consistent and profitable prepurchase and postpurchase support on a local basis. The pressure point also identifies who will apply the energy to the activity to get the job done.

The pressure point, in turn, begs the question, "How will we know this work has been successful?"

The *global success measure* answers that; it is a measure of the impact the pressure point has had on the strategic objectives. It provides a means of quantifying the results of actions and investments being made to influence the pressure point, such as "improving global-customer satisfaction survey results by 25 percent." This measure should be directly linked to the macro performance measure, i.e., "If the quality survey improves we should see an increase in market share."

This, of course, begs the question, "In what time frame?"

The *time horizon* is the time associated with accomplishing the global strategic initiative. It is of little value to set clear targets if the timing is ambiguous. When John Kennedy committed the United States to "put a man on the moon by the end of the decade," he not only established a clear, focused objective, but also added a sense of urgency. Global business objectives must also be established in clear, focused terms with a sense of urgency.

This schema is powerful when put into practice. Global strategic initiatives provide the focus for actions, set up a process for review of the required actions, and give each person an understanding of how his or her performance relates to the overall global objectives.

Most companies launch a set of three to five global initiatives to lead the company's global effort. The initial projects in support of the initiatives should be designed in a coordinated fashion. Strong participation should come from people involved in developing the global vision and other aspects of the globalization process. As well, others should be brought in who are new to the process. Bringing more and more people into the process as the global projects spin out will gradually draw the majority of employees' efforts into the global domain, until everyone is involved.

Sponsorship of the global strategic initiatives is the job of the top management team. Having shaped the global vision and translated it into global strategic initiatives, the executives' role shifts. They then define and assign accountability to a network of multidisciplinary, multigeographic individuals empowered to develop and implement programs that will accomplish the global strategic initiatives.

When a well-known retail company in the United Kingdom was in the process of expanding to international markets in Europe and North America, the CEO said, "I have a vision of our international undertaking that builds from our strength here in the U.K. and rapidly broadens our global frame of reference. The overall objective is to remain one of the leading retailers in the U.K. while becoming one of the top five in several European countries and in Canada."

With this as a starting point for the global visioning exercise, management continued to develop the global strategic initiatives. They revised the global vision to a mission statement that read, "We will be the top retailer in our major product markets in the U.K., while developing a 25 percent market share in Sweden, France, Holland, and Canada within five years. This means we will control 25 percent of the jobber-delivered shelf space dedicated to the three brand-name products we sell. In addition, we will launch a new product line to examine how product design can be used to best advantage in serving these markets."

The statement then went on to place this initial international step within a framework for overall globalization of sourcing and forming alliances and ventures in other markets. Management was delighted with this refinement. The original statement communicated strategic intent, while the refined mission statement accomplished such specifics as:

- Focusing the objectives on the areas of priority (jobbers)

- Defining a measurable target (shelf space)

- Setting a stretch objective (shelf space was between five and nine percent in these countries)

- Establishing a time horizon (five years)

By further defining the global strategic initiative the management team was able to form multidisciplinary teams to address global programs to improve global business practices and products. Keeping in mind that business conditions change, management developed a process to create an ongoing understanding of how the company adds value on a global/local basis to track the effect of the initiatives.

Let's look closely for a moment at some of the global processes a company must look at when creating its global course of attack.

Appealing to Customers of the World

Appealing to customers of the world entails:

1. Exploring the concentrations of customer demand ranging from global to local preferences
2. Blending the company's consistent and diverse competencies to develop quality products and deliver in a competitive and timely fashion
3. Designing the global/local, product/service architecture
4. Appealing to customers in a cultural context

A worldwide, multimodal transportation company identified opportunities to establish one-step, point-to-point service for its customers. The opportunities, focused on creating a network of hardware, software, and data, allow salespeople to offer a range of integrated transportation and logistics services. They also help customer-service personnel in tracking and managing those transportation- and logistics-management services to assure total customer satisfaction.

Identification of the best opportunities for the company to attract and build relationships with customers on the global/local spectrum will lead to designs of global customer programs, the capability to manage global/local customers consistently with diverse customization, and the ability to act as a good corporate citizen.

Creating Globally Scalable Resources

Creating globally scalable resources involves:

1. Creating a means to transfer knowledge to develop flexible resources and capture economies of scale
2. Promoting creativity and problem solving to develop global resources
3. Sharing breakthroughs and lessons learned to break down barriers created by a centralization/decentralization methodology
4. Seeking knowledge in the company's entire sphere of influence to reap economies of scale and to figure out the process flow of the business
5. Creating synergies and capturing the benefits by integrating internal processes

A high-technology manufacturer identified opportunities to cut its product-development cycle in half, including linking its worldwide R&D facilities through a network of shared data and engineering diagrams, linking its prototype-manufacturing facilities and product-development teams with a video-teleconferencing system, and coordinating the work of its product-development teams through a network of shared product-management databases.

A leading chemical company identified opportunities to improve the management of its production operations by identifying procedures and information systems aimed at linking the market demand forecasts of its globally dispersed product/market teams to better manage its worldwide refinery capacity, materials procurement, and product-outsourcing activities.

Global companies can ensure the scalability of global resources by developing a process orientation—to the business and the integration of global resources, to the flow of multidirectional ideas and knowledge, and to the use of joint ventures and other alliances. The global company deliberately designs resources to be scalable by sharing knowledge, cultivating positive attitudes toward work, and creating synergies.

Managing the Connections

Managers in global companies must learn how to manage the organizational connections. This involves:

1. Learning how to manage in a cultural context
2. Tying the organization together with a shared culture
3. Changing management roles from controllers to facilitators
4. Empowering knowledge workers
5. Constantly positioning the company along its strategic vectors for employees

Many companies try to organize according to one dominant management dimension, such as product or line of business, geography, or function. They have a hard time managing business this way because they have not found the consistent qualities of their resources, nor have they figured out how to organize those resources. They cannot operate as global companies because they hold onto their hierarchical bureaucratic way of doing business.

The hierarchic organization developed as a response to a functional business world. Form followed function. But today—and especially tomorrow—organizations develop as a response to a process-driven business world. Form follows process.

In a global company, managers act as connectors, global learning is supported, knowledge workers are empowered and connected, and top management has international experience. Building the commitment to the company's global purpose with constant and current communications fosters a thriving global culture.

Developing a global inventory of ideas, skills, and employee assets allows for a greater development of global resources. The global perspective is greater than a local view and greater than a mere aggregate of local perspectives.

Developing Global Leaders, Teams, and Individuals

Global leaders, teams, and individuals need to understand the global challenges facing leaders across many industries. The changes taking place in any particular industry will change all competing organizations. How a company balances global consistency with local look and feel will be different than the way its competitors do, because of the difference in corporate culture.

Global leaders issue global mandates to teams and individuals, reward them for global behavior, build a worldwide perspective among their management teams, help set global management policies and actions, support the dissemination of shared experiences, and pay careful attention to permeating the culture with global values. They ensure that compensation schemes are linked to global behavior by demonstrating that they, as leaders, place great importance on being a global individual. Global leaders recognize that the role for global teams is growing in importance and value. Teamwork can yield more flexible business planning, stronger commitment to achieving demanding worldwide goals, and closer collaboration in carrying out strategic change.

Leveraging I.T. to Build Global Capability

The global company is dependent on employees' capabilities to learn. Of primary importance is the global individual's, team's, and leader's capacity to relate to new technologies. Information technology, in particular, is key to a global company's performance.

Installing a global information technology architecture involves:

1. Using the global planning frameworks to understand the linkage of I.T. to business strategy

2. Recognizing the fundamental differences among global I.T. application portfolios

3. Understanding the role of global and local I.T. infrastructure

4. Understanding the value of having a global I.T. architecture process and beginning to apply its concepts

5. Developing global I.T. resource allocation and deployment frameworks

A global design of I.T. architecture will give your company great point-to-point communications, a sound global infrastructure, and differentiated global portfolios addressing global processes, customers, products, and services.

Aligning the Company with Globalization Stages

Companies go up the global learning curve at varied rates, depending on their inclination and ability to change.

For instance, global exporters are realizing that homogeneous products sold worldwide do not make a company global. As world competition increases, creating pressure for greater integration of resources and customized marketing, these companies are trying to develop global capabilities. Many of these companies want to become global without going through the stage of either being multinational or multilocal.

Many multinational and multilocal companies are caught in a structural dilemma, vacillating between "multi" states. The multinational attempts to develop more of a local focus by creating more local resources—becoming more multilocal. At the same time, the multilocal company tries to gain economies of scale by spreading resources over many countries' operations by centralizing certain functions—becoming more multinational. What each is missing is a sense of developing a global/local balance among capabilities and resources.

Most companies trying to become global Ping-Pong back and forth between the multinational and multilocal forms of business. This is time consuming and expensive. Many companies have parts of their organization in different states, vacillating in opposite directions, trying to be both low cost and customer driven.

Some say that a company cannot be both low cost and highly differentiated at the same time, but their conclusions are based on looking at the wake of companies' historical data, as opposed to looking forward at requirements for the success of companies in the future. Figure 2-9 illustrates the efforts of many companies to become global.

For progress to be made toward becoming global, low cost, customer driven, and scalable, two fundamental processes must be established, carried out, and followed through on a continuous basis.

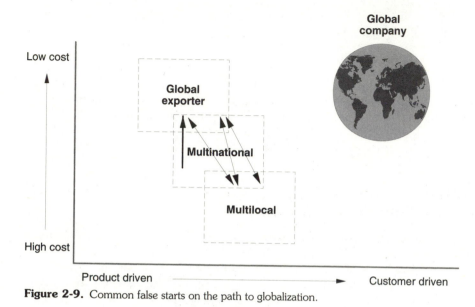

Figure 2-9. Common false starts on the path to globalization.

The first is that management must experience a change in mindset to becoming more global; global experience must be shared. For the global exporter hoping to avoid the "multi" stage, this is perhaps the most important directive to follow, to create a cadre of global managers. This cadre will build a corps of globally minded workers and build global processes. They will share learning experiences to move up the learning curve quickly and effectively. By building the trust inherently required to form this cadre, the company can establish a number of ambassadors who will energize the development of the global company. They will infuse the organization with global values, share perspectives, and solve problems with a balanced view. They will thrive on the mutual interests they establish.

Secondly, milestones need to be established to see how well the company is doing vis-a-vis achieving its global strategies and opportunities. Although significant returns may take years to achieve, progress should be measured and communicated. Milestones serve as steppingstones. Benefits should be accrued at each milestone. Measurements relate the business activities to the global vision, the global strategic initiatives, and the milestones.

Establishing a global system of measuring performance allows alignment of global stages in the company so that any given individual employee knows at any given point in time how his/her performance is contributing to the global business objectives and strategy.

Developing global performance measures involves designing the essential performance indicators for the business because, while all business will not be global, all business—including global business—will need to measure up to the same standards. The organization of the future must give equal emphasis to measuring the factors that create financial value, such as quality, service, and response time, rather than simply measuring financial value itself.*

Because the future corporate structure will be radically different, performance measurement systems will need to reflect this, incorporating such features as cross-functional integration, customer/supplier linkage, global scale, and continuous improvement. Finally, the performance measurement system will need to be linked to a new accountability/reward system that is based more heavily on team performance. The ultimate success or failure of new performance measurement systems will be determined by the ability to develop and administer the executive information system that reflects these principles.

The performance measurement system of the future must be a balanced scorecard[†]; companies need a balanced scorecard that monitors the factors whose performance today will create shareholder value in the future.

Management's mission is to create value for its shareholders. Traditional financial measures such as return on equity and return on investment distort performance measurement and encourage a dysfunctional short-term focus. New financial measurement techniques, such as "shareholder value," are needed to motivate the effective use of assets in the creation of value.

Shareholder value must be measured by measuring the determinants of that value. Shareholder value can only be enhanced by satisfying customers. Quality, cycle time, and service are the determinants of customer satisfaction and, ultimately, of shareholder value.

These performance measures must be driven from the top, directly linked to the organization's strategy and vision. The ability of the organization to continuously change and improve is strategic. Measurement of the rate of change in performance is more important than the absolute level of performance itself.

---

* In 1990, the research group of the Nolan Norton Institute, led by David P. Norton and Winnie Rogow and supported by professionals from KPMG Peat Marwick and leading experts from industry and academia, spent the year with a dozen Fortune 500 companies to design a management framework for measuring performance in the organization of the future.

The study was based on the assertion that current approaches to performance measurement are based on an obsolete organizational model, and are interfering with companies' ability to move into the future.

† David P. Norton and Robert S. Kaplan, "The Balanced Scorecard—Measures that Drive Performance," *Harvard Business Review* (Jan.-Feb. 1992).

Finally, this vision and rate of change must be reflected in the work of each individual within the organization. In order to satisfy—indeed, to delight—customers, individuals within the organization must be allowed to influence their work and to relate their performance to the overall corporate vision.

Summary

Companies are attempting to become global from three fundamentally different starting positions. Global exporters get their advantage from being low-cost producers and have great difficulty being highly responsive to local customer differences. Multilocals get their advantage from being highly responsive to the local customers, but pay a penalty by having more costly products. Multinationals rely on strong central coordination to share innovations across their distributed manufacturing, sales, and service organizations. They are positioned between the global exporter and multilocal in both cost and responsiveness. Regardless of the starting position, most companies today aspire to being global (both low-cost and highly customer responsive). Well-formulated global strategic initiatives help companies move from today's position toward their global aspirations.

Action Checklist

1. Have you defined how each of your company's major lines of business (LOBs) are positioned on the globalization matrix?

2. Have you developed benchmarks of progress towards your globalization goals?

3. Have you defined global strategic initiatives (for each LOB) which focus the company on achieving its global vision?

4. Are your global strategic initiatives founded upon a thorough understanding of your global customer requirements?

5. Have you defined global performance measures to encourage global behavior?

3

Understanding Your Global Customer's Demands and Needs

Every company that sells its products or services on a worldwide basis has a growing and increasingly powerful customer segment—the global customer.

For businesses that sell to other businesses, this global customer is the customer who creates then sells its product or service around the world. For consumer-products companies this global customer is really a global customer type, the person in Manhattan, Milan, or Marakesh who has the same purchasing habits, appreciates the same styles, works in the same industry, and travels to the same vacation destinations.

Many industrial companies,—large, medium, and small—in all industries, headquartered all around the world, are finding that an increasing amount of revenue is being derived from a tiny fraction of customers who purchase goods and services around the world and want a consistency of service and product performance. Many want consolidation of information and billing, even if they make their purchasing decisions on a distributed, individualized basis. The role of "relationships managers" overseeing the work of account managers is becoming more commonplace.

For years, IBM worked very successfully in a decentralized international mode, with strong national organizations managed as independent subsidiaries with their own revenues and expenses. This worked fine when major customers made separate purchasing decisions. But increasingly, IBM's global customers—the 454 companies that provide IBM with nearly 20 percent of its revenues worldwide—are demanding a more integrated approach.

IBM calls these 454 companies "select international accounts" (SIAs), and has assigned a worldwide account coordinator for each of these. The SIA-1 account manager works out of the IBM office in the customer's home country—often its home city. Since introducing this system in the late 1980s, IBM has gradually vested more authority in these SIA-1 managers, allowing them to influence worldwide decisions for their account, including discounting and service agreements.

While this approach has cut down greatly on the "around the world" sub-optimization that had been occurring—such as account managers in one country undercutting account managers in other countries to make sales to a global customer buying in both countries—it has caused the company to think hard about how its employees' performance is measured and rewarded.

Since the beginning of the 1990s, IBM has been gradually introducing into its performance appraisal—beginning with senior executives at the national level and eventually getting to the account executives and systems engineers in local offices—a measure of their global cooperation with other IBM employees to sell to and to service and provide timely information for the company's global customers, in the manner in which the customer wants that sales, service, and information—ranging from centralized buying and contracting to completely independent buying and contracting.

Other companies are finding that a worldwide clientele can transform a niche market into global reach. No longer are companies merely extending their domestic products and services to overseas markets, but worldwide customers are driving products and services. A Sony Walkman is as appreciated in Toronto as it is in Tokyo, and a McDonalds' hamburger can be found in New Delhi as easily as in New York. In some instances, global customers are attracted to the universality of products, while at other times the cultural distinctiveness of a product is a major selling point; the French hotel chain Sofitel has found that travelers from around the world, traveling anywhere in the world, enjoy staying at their small, relatively inexpensive hotels that remind them of the French countryside.

Unfortunately, most companies know precious little about their global customers: who they are, what they want, what they need, why they choose to do business with a particular company, how to attract more of them, and how to retain the ones they have.

Some companies know who their global customers are, but others can still only guess at their characteristics. Even when companies become adept at identifying their global customers, they sometimes have little understanding of how to support these customers, or more fundamentally, what these customers' expectations are.

To better understand the current and future requirements of this global customer segment, to better anticipate demand, and to better develop and deploy leading-edge products and services, companies need to conduct some rigorous market research, then develop global-customer action strategies.

An executive of a European financial-services company, trying to put his finger on who his global customers are and how to better service them, puts it this way:

"Some of our products have more globalization logic than others. It depends on how a customer looks at his/her needs. It's important to know which customer needs us to be global and which does not. It's important to be driven by the customer first, then products, then geography. It's important to focus—where to be global and where to be selectively global.

"With regard to customers, the greatest source of profits over the next ten years will come in global services and products. I expect more growth from those of our businesses which require a global approach. You cannot survive on one product. In order to have a global approach to customers, you need a wide range of products. You can take a local customer and make them global if you can offer them the right products and services."

Make no mistake, however. The global customer demands of a company customization of product and localization of services in each locality in which that customer buys products and receives services. Products and services must have a "local feel" and global providers must be good citizens everywhere they do business.

An executive at a U.S.-based manufacturer admits to the difficulty of this situation:

"We're not a global company. We're not as adaptive to local conditions as we would be if we became a global company. If you read any classic definition, we were multinational and acted that way in almost every case. What we're trying to do is take a multinational philosophy and our values/principles/systems in hand and move to be more customer focused . . . we're very functional and product focused and trying to be more accommodative.

"Today we're in between being multinational and global. We are trying to adjust our business to the countries we're in. We take a basic set of values, business principles, and systems, and tailor them to places we do business and try to be more accommodating to the local environment and still simplify."

What Do Your Global Customers Want?

To explore the global/local spectrum of demand for your company's products and services you must first understand your customer's demands for greater responsiveness and sensitivity. While every company today must pay rapt attention to the issues of features, cost, and quality, in the global arena the basis of competition is determined by a company's ability to provide highly differentiated services.

By understanding how your customers prefer the mix of global/local aspects of your products and services, your company can more accurately develop the variety of products and services to deliver what the customer wants, where they want it, ahead of the competition.

Jan Carlzon, CEO of Scandinavian Airlines System (SAS), speaks of the intersection between the process of delivering his company's service and the customer's experience as a "moment of truth."

For the traveler—especially the frequent business traveler—when the person at the check-in counter knows your name, seat, and meal preference and who you are traveling with, that's a pleasant experience. For the airline, it's a moment of truth.

For the traveler, when the cabin crew is friendly and realizes you are tired, that's a relief. For the airline, it's a moment of truth.

For the traveler, seat upgrades, bonus frequent-flyer miles, or a limousine to and from the airport are all extra incentives to remain a loyal customer. For the airline, these are more than just incentives; they are moments of truth.

Carlzon is gearing his whole airline to be responsive to the thousands of these moments that occur every day. For every business with a growing global-customer base, the total effect of these moments of truth is more than merely the sum of the individual moments. Global customers are gaining market power daily, and are increasingly able to exercise choice. These customers want global consistency, a high degree of integration within companies they do business with, and most of all a responsive relationship.

Global corporate customers are demanding more because they, like you, are competing in the global marketplace. They are under the same pressures to reduce "time to market" and to operate in an integrated way. They want not only to purchase your products and services wherever they are, but also to get information about these products and services to support their future purchase and design decisions.

On the other hand, local buyers—whether they are local customers or the local decision makers within global customers—are increasingly aware of and concerned with the image a company projects, its willingness to cooperate with communities, and its capacity to modify products and services to cater to local preferences. Local buyers want to know that your company will be there to service their needs, that your company considers their needs important, that you can adapt the product for the particular market, and that your company respects their community.

Global customers who see a product for the first time are most concerned with getting consistent information about and support for the product anywhere they choose to use it. Their next concern is with efficient delivery. Then comes quality.

Global customers want the time from purchase decision to delivery reduced. Today, many of these customers are willing to pay a premium for this quick delivery and consistent support. But this won't always be the case. In the future, speed will be one of the prerequisites to playing the global game.

Appealing to customers globally means forming a living relationship with them to develop an in-depth knowledge of how they think, dream, and communicate. Tom Peters describes how Nissan and Toyota explored their customer's lives and life-styles when trying to break into the high end of the U.S. car market.

"Toyota and Nissan sent their design teams to California to live with the people they were trying to design cars for: real people who treat cars as cars, not Detroit people for whom the car is by some way the most important thing in life, ranking significantly above spouse and children."* They made sure to join local clubs, to send their children to local schools, and to work to understand local issues and concerns.

Increasingly, a company's customers represent a mix of both global and local customers, with expectations ranging anywhere along this spectrum. Identifying significant clusters of global and local customer preferences today, and thinking about the future directions and trends of these preferences, is a first step in defining the parameters of your company's global product/service architecture.

Figure 3-1 lists key questions your company must address in exploring the global/local spectrum of demand.

Wherever customers fall on the global/local spectrum, they want to deal with a company that has the capability to adapt and deliver customized solutions that solve their problems and fulfill their needs, wherever and whenever they do business.

IBM is not only changing its orientation from a product-driven approach to a customer-driven approach in dealing with its 454 key global customers, but with every business customer. Ennio Presutti, head of IBM Italy, has worked since 1990 to align the company's efforts with his customers' desires by "creating a network of agents across the country who work with IBM to develop solutions for customers." David McKinney, former president of IBM Europe, used a great deal of this effort to create a blueprint for the way IBM should balance the desires of its local/regional/global customers with IBM resources.[†]

---

* Simon Caulkin, "Drucker, Ohmae, Porter & Peters," The Economist Publications, Management Briefings, Special Report, no. 1202: 73.

[†] Alan Cane, Ian Rodger, Roderick Oram, and Louise Kehoe, "IBM's worldwide lessons from Europe," *Financial Times* (May 2, 1990).

Questions a global company must answer:

- Who are our global customers? Local customers? Do we have clusters of customers which represent points between global and local on the spectrum, e.g., regional customers?

- What do the global customers want? Local customers? Regional, or other?

- How can the company provide these requirements?

- Where is the company positioned now?

- How does the company want to be positioned in the future?

- Can the company build scalable opportunities for customers, i.e., provide offerings which will build relationships with customers over the long-term?

Figure 3-1. Exploring the global/local spectrum of demand.

As we move from a product-driven to a customer-driven world, customer preference will change. Companies that up to now have competed based on specification, price, and quality will find that these attributes will become less important differentiators as all companies that survive and thrive learn to wrestle these issues to the ground. They will find that they must increasingly differentiate themselves with service to create competitive advantage.

Figure 3-2 offers some examples of how to differentiate your company for global and local customers.

An example of this kind of evolution of customer demands is found in the personal computer industry. As PCs began their rapid assent into the

Differentiations	Features	Cost	Quality	Service
Global	Consistent information about products to support purchase and use anywhere	Quick and efficient delivery of your products and services wherever customers desire	Zero defects; building a durable relationship with the customer	Consistency and integration; design, develop, and deliver customizations quickly
Significant clusters, regional or other	Reflect regional differences, e.g., multilingual instruction manuals	Packaged solutions which may vary to satisfy suitability to particular situations	High quality configurations of available products and services; presence to serve regional needs	Ability to flexibly customize configuration; responsive
Local	Observe local customs and regulations; communicate in local language	Willingness to deliver to local customers the best offerings available without charging a premium	Develop presence to service local needs quickly; local good citizenship	Sensitivity and capacity to modify and adapt products and services to cater to local preferences

Figure 3-2. Examples of the global/local spectrum of demand.

dual arenas of front-office business tool and consumer electronic, customers around the world wanted to get the machines. Sometimes the only available machines were those for English speakers—with English-language software and U.S.-denoted keyboards—English being the language of development.

Nevertheless, customers in France, Japan, Germany, Sweden, Korea, and elsewhere wanted PCs. Most assumed they would be able to adapt the product to their needs themselves, and they were willing to make the modifications.

Customers were willing to put up with delays of up to six months for deliveries. But as time became more of the basis of competition among suppliers, global customers wrote delivery times into contracts. Then, as products were delivered more quickly, customers turned their attention to the condition the products arrived in; they wanted perfect machines every time.

Finally, the competitive ground for many of these products has been what many call the "total systems approach." This approach adds service to the product, such as training, ideas on the implementation and usage within the company, and modifications for particular industries' uses.

Because local customers are first concerned that a company has complied with all of the local customs and regulations, many local PC customers were concerned with the safety standards of the screens used in the PCs, which delayed entry for some products in certain countries. They were also concerned that they receive the company's best offering, rather than older models.

Local customers tended to buy PCs from local dealers, many of whom formed strategic alliances with the major manufacturers. In fact, the network of local dealers and enthusiasts who shared the excitement of the product and its adaptation to individual cultures were responsible for the PCs initial market penetration. Without those dealers, PC manufacturers would have taken many more years to achieve the kind of penetration they have. The local dealers had a vested interest in providing high-quality service, and in participating in the community to get the products accepted. This product, since it represented a new technology that customers may at first have been wary of, depended on the smooth, steady introduction of innovation introduced by these dealers in an acculturated fashion.

Finally, local customers also wanted new products designed "just for them." Hence, some of the best designs for keyboards came from Sweden, some of the best games from France, and some of the best communication designs from Italy.

In order to better understand the future requirements of your global customer market segment, to anticipate demand, and to develop and deploy leading-edge services and strategies, you should follow a simple six-step plan:

- Segment the market and identify specific customers to study.

- Design and package a market-research program.

- Conduct customer visits and reviews on a pilot basis.

- Execute market research.

- Synthesize the results.

- Develop a global customer action strategy.

Bring the Company to the Customer

We have interviewed executives from over 100 companies and asked them if and how they think the basis of competing for customers globally is changing in their industries. Figure 3-3 shows the results of that survey. As Figure 3-3 indicates, the winning differentiators of the customer-driven company of tomorrow are those aspects that bring the company to the customer, focus resources on narrowly segmented markets, and provide high value-added services.

Today	Tomorrow
Price	Matching customer needs before he/she begins shopping
Specification	Differentiation through customer service
Quality	Bringing the company to the customer
Segmentation based on:	Depth of relationship and complex interdependencies
· Product ownership	Lifetime customer commitment
· Demographic subsets	Segmentation based on:
· Some psychographic/life-style and life-stage factors	· Attitudes (knowledge, feelings, action tendencies)
	· Images (attributes/characteristics)
Product image	· Decisions (evaluation process and dependence on preexisting knowledge)
Loyalty	
Delivery lead time	· Needs (desires, preferences, motives, goals)
Reliability	· Behavior (what, when, where, how often)
Cost of operation	· Life-style (activities, interests, opinions, possessions)
Product appeal	· Affiliations (formal/informal)
Residual values	Focussing resources to narrowly segmented market niches
After-market service	Corporate image
Matching needs and values	

Note: Listed in rank order

Figure 3-3. The basis of competing for global customers is changing.

Companies are focusing their efforts on understanding their customers' value systems, and how these values differ and are consistent in various countries. If a global company can understand the value system of its varied customers, it can develop products that complement the way these customers would like to live.

Although many companies are now focusing on the service end of the spectrum, the most immediate battle companies are engaged in is that of distance as a reflection of time.

Competitors from all over the world are trying to reach global customers with what they really want, and always faster. As the global economy becomes more and more connected, businesses will be faced increasingly with the problems of competing in time and space. Compressing time and crossing geographic space are two processes global companies must master in order to satisfy global customers and win market share. The customer does not care what the "time to market" from product development to delivery is; all the customer cares about is the part of the process visible to him or her—the time from order to delivery.

To explore the global/local spectrum of demand for your company's products and services, you must first understand your customer's demands for greater responsiveness and sensitivity. While every company today must pay rapt attention to the issues of features, cost, and quality, in the global arena of the future, the basis of competition will be determined by a company's ability to provide highly differentiated services.

By understanding how your customers prefer the mix of the global/local aspects of your service differentiation, your company can more accurately develop the variety of products and services to deliver what the customer wants, wherever it is desired, ahead of your competition.

The Customer's Culture

The more your business becomes customer driven, the more important it is that the business achieve a cultural fit with its customers.

Achieving cultural fit means more than delivering products and services to the market. It means understanding how the products and services appeal to the customer and his or her culture. To appeal to customers in a cultural context, a company may:

1. Adapt products and services and maximize global appeal.

2. Make an effort to fit in with cultural values.

3. Create a culture map of demand to guide business choices.

4. Invest in the culture to demonstrate commitment.

5. Promote the company's affinity with the culture.

Adapting Products and Services

Understanding the culture means understanding the country or cultural region and the values of customers who live there. Adapting or modifying products or services by local tailoring can include any action ranging from naming the products to designing the products to performing distribution in different ways.

Even when providing a universal product like Marlboro cigarettes, Sony Walkman radios, Mercedes-Benz cars, Perrier water, or McDonalds' fast food, successful global companies vary their offerings by incorporating local cultural aspects into the way they do business.

The Coca-Cola Company modifies the global appeal of Coke in different countries by building strong partnerships with local bottlers. These bottlers localize the way Coke gets distributed by "applying global concepts with native expertise" to influence the local soft drink market. Coke travels up and down the Amazon from nine local bottling plants on barges. In Maraba, "a sun-blasted outpost in Brazil's remote northeast," a distributor known as "Chico da Coca," Francisco Bezerra da Silva, scrambles Indiana Jones-style along perilous roads in the mountains to deliver Coke to the miners of the Pelada mine, the world's largest open-pit gold mine. Knowing the local terrain and the weather conditions, and understanding when deliveries will be most appreciated, Bezerra da Silva is able to link the customer with Coca-Cola company.*

Despite its rigorous standardization in terms of product, service, and quality, McDonalds allows local franchisees increasing leeway in connecting the company to the local culture. A McDonalds' outlet in Lyon, France, comes complete with hanging plants, softly playing music by Bach and Mozart, and a ban on smoking; in Stowe, Vermont, the McDonalds looks like a country inn. In Japan, Teriyaki beef is a special menu item, much as the "personal pizza" is in the United States.

McDonalds has been so successful in finding the global customer type and making each customer feel culturally comfortable that a Japanese boy scout returning from his first visit to the United States voiced surprise that "they even had McDonalds there."

Being culturally knowledgeable and culturally sensitive means offering newly industrializing countries (NICs) and less developed countries (LDCs) products that are appropriate to their population's needs and that will help the countries create the infrastructure and economy necessary to thrive and compete in the future.

---

* Coca-Cola Company, "Journey," vol. 3, no. 1 (May 1989).

Appealing to customers in a cultural context means taking a culture's concerns into account when determining how your company will act in each national or regional environment. While many customers want to share parts of the emerging global culture, they are also deeply concerned about preserving important aspects of their local cultures. While European business and political leaders are moving their countries toward greater economic union for the sake of speed, efficiency, and economic growth, they are also working hard to help each other maintain distinct cultural attributes.

Successful global companies will fit their products and services into these key cultural aspects so that local buyers adopt global products as their own without sacrificing their cultural identity. Appealing to customers in a cultural context allows companies to respond to one of the great intangible characteristics of demand, a characteristic that will never go away because the global customer is not without a home, a history, and a culture.

Having a good fit with each of the many cultural environments in your company's sphere of activity is a necessity in a global company. Customization is not always costly, but it takes an understanding of a market's culture and values to evaluate the possibilities. Exploring the cultural values that may influence how customers relate to your company's products and services is a valuable activity.

Fitting in with Cultural Values

Many countries and communities today are weighing the long-term effects of corporate activity and are trying to attract those companies that will be good corporate citizens. Having a good cultural fit means having a presence that customers recognize and value. More and more, countries are looking for companies that will "give back" to the countries in which they do business.

Until fairly recently, this contribution primarily meant the presence of assets, payment of taxes, and employment of citizens. But there are other options for emerging global corporations that move the company away from country relationships based on transactions to long-term relationships built on the development of mutual resources. Countries are more interested in developing relationships that will preserve their culture and contribute to their portfolio of business opportunities and economic infrastructure.

Creating a Cultural Map of Demand

Every company that wants to succeed in the new global environment needs to draw a map of activities and of the ways these activities interelate with cultures. Understanding the cultural characteristics of demand also requires an understanding of where a culture is in terms of development in ways that effect the desire for your product.

Malaysia and Thailand, for example, are rapidly developing industrial capability, and their citizens are developing new tastes for consumer goods. But not just any consumer goods.

Products entering NICs have sometimes caused great damage; remember the baby-formula problems in NICs in the 1970s. This was a classic example of how a company's product was treated as a substitute by the population and some authorities, in a way that was not suitable. Many mothers used the formula—which had to be mixed with water—to replace mothers' milk, even where the water supply was contaminated. The result was the deaths of many infants and loads of bad publicity for the company.

There is a growing awareness by NICs that they have often been treated as second-class consumers, and a growing resentment toward this treatment and toward Western companies, even if these companies themselves have never engaged in such practices. Companies must understand these feelings, and the determination by NICs to be the master of their own destinies.

Kukrit Pramjoj, a former prime minister of Thailand, points to an example of this kind of invasion of products and services to NIC's culture with fast food: "Mass-produced and without taste." He adds, with more than a touch of nostalgia, "As a Thai, I don't want to see that happening here. I want to live as I always have, without the need to hustle and bustle."*

With an economic growth rate of 10.3 percent in Thailand, companies that understand its market and its attitudes are doing well. Colgate Palmolive, in Thailand for 30 years, reported revenue growth of 30 percent each year for 1988 and 1989 in sales of soap, detergent, toothpaste, and shampoo. Scott Paper, with a long production history in Thailand, is doubling capacity to meet demand for toilet paper and other products.

But the old days of selling a product based purely on price are rapidly ending. Successful companies that sell or have activities in Thailand and other NICs are learning to be sensitive to the cultural environment. Like Colgate, they have learned which products will sell and which are a waste of time to introduce. They offer staple products the country needs, which will contribute to the country's infrastructure and development, rather than luxury products that take a disproportionate part of the country's spending.

When Akio Morita of Sony entered the U.S. market in the early 1960s, he "began to feel that to establish our company more firmly in the U.S., I had to get to know the country better. I felt I needed to know more about how

---

* Ford S. Worthy, "Asians Reluctant Growth Champs," *Fortune* (April 24, 1989).

Americans lived and how they thought. To make the company name more common in the U.S. was one thing, to understand Americans would be more difficult. But I realized that my future and the future of my company would depend a lot on the United States and on other international business. I was struck with the idea that our company had to become a citizen of the world, and a good citizen in each country we did business in.*

Global companies are recognizing the value of being a good corporate citizen in every country in which they do business. Investing in local cultural programs, developing a relationship with countries, regions, and communities based on an understanding of presence to provide knowledge transfer opportunities at the leading edge, focusing investments on local as well as global concerns, and emphasizing what your company does locally demonstrate good citizenship.

Whether the investment is little or great, the objective is to create a presence that enhances knowledge of the market, increases ability to attract highly skilled local employees, and creates stronger, more positive relationships between the company and the country's citizens. An astute company can develop an understanding of a local environment almost as well as the local citizens. This understanding enables companies to create features or options in its products and services that appear highly customized to the local culture.

Investing in the Culture

Nissan provides a good example of how a company has invested in local good citizenship and nurtured not only the local culture, but valuable business. Janet Leiker, a manager in California, explains:

"It's no good just talking about being a good citizen. We knew we had to demonstrate it. Illiteracy is a national issue in the U.S. we could help solve on a local level. We have formed 'Nissan Family Learning Centers,' which encourage young children and adults to learn how to read and write. We are trying to help adults overcome illiteracy and the children to learn how to begin to read. It's an issue that can be treated in a family way, which helps the community. Nissan also donates money to several charitable groups, but with the Family Learning Centers we can own the issue and try to really contribute to the solution. The business benefit to Nissan is that people view the company as a company that is here to stay and interested in the community."

Being a partner with the community may mean investing in the knowledge infrastructure in a variety of ways. In moving to a more integrated

* Akio Morita, *Made In Japan* (E.P. Dutton, 1986), 102 (paperback).

market, Europe is looking more and more to companies to provide knowledge transfer opportunities at the leading edge. Cross-country trade cooperation regions—such as those formed by northeastern Spain, southeastern France, and northwestern Italy—are creating fertile economic and employment climates to attract enterprise and industry and develop mutual interests. These regions and countries are building an interest in such intangibles as the value of research and development, and are looking for alliances built between local industries and their universities.

Some companies view this knowledge infrastructure investment as a more expensive way to develop a market than to invest in plant and machinery in the same way multinational companies have traditionally done. Actually, infrastructure is a better tailored investment. Development-keen countries offer subsidies and incentives focused on their concerns. The investment, ultimately, is more integrated with local and global concerns, in that there is a mutuality of interests and a level of commitment between the community and the company.

IBM's good corporate citizenship is legendary. It has long realized that investing in community interests and expressions of good will are powerful. But perhaps even more importantly, IBM has recognized the significance of building research and development alliances with local industries and universities. In addition to tapping into leading scientific communities all over the world, these investments help IBM establish a long-term image as being part of the fabric of the community.

As a result of years of such investments in Japan, IBM is not only the most successful American company in Japan, but also a formidable competitor to Fujitsu, Hitachi, and NEC. An organizational change inside IBM in the early 1990s gave IBM Japan worldwide responsibility for Entry Systems, from product design to service and support. With thousands of employees in Japan, IBM is regarded by many Japanese businessmen as "the" Japanese computer company.

Promoting the Company's Affinity with the Culture

Siemens, the medical and telecommunications equipment company headquartered in Germany, is also sensitive to the local buying environment. On January 1, 1990, during the Orange Bowl college football game in the United States, Siemens ran an advertisement showing American workers in the process of shipping Siemens goods from San Francisco to the world. The ad states that 35,000 people work for Siemens in the United States; that the U.S. business revenue is over $3 billion; and that 15 percent of U.S. sales are exports. Globally, Siemens 1988 sales were about the equivalent of $29.9 billion, and the company employed 364,000 people in 120 countries.

"We wanted to emphasize what we do locally," said Martin Weitzner, Siemens' director of public relations. "We export telecommunications to Japan and medical equipment to Germany from the U.S., and we wanted people to know about that.

"We have two major audiences. The first are hospitals to whom we sell CT (computerized tomography) systems, radiology and MRI (magnetic resonance imaging) equipment. Hospitals buy on quality and service. They like to buy from companies they know. We have a good reputation for quality. We wanted to let them know that we are a substantial local presence, that service can be done locally, and that parts are all available here.

"The second audience is in Washington, and is concerned about domestic and off-shore companies. We wanted to emphasize our presence here by demonstrating just how much business we do, people we employ, and amount we export. Over $3 billion sales, employing 35,000 people, and exporting 15 percent of sales, now that's presence."

Appealing to customers in a cultural context means taking a culture's concerns into account when determining how your company will act in a particular environment.

While many customers want to share parts of the emerging global culture, they are also deeply concerned about preserving important aspects of their local cultures. Many people predicted that the integration of Europe would result in a homogeneity of the cultures, but this isn't occurring. While there are many areas of sharing within the EEC, what is striking is the support each country is giving the others to preserve the distinct aspects of diverse cultures.

Successful global companies will fit their products and services into these key aspects of cultures so local customers adopt their products. By exploring the cultural values of your customers, your company can leverage local preferences to create a corporate presence that adds value for your customers and allows your company to be a good corporate citizen. Appealing to customers in a cultural context allows your company to respond to the intangible characteristics of demand.

Creating a Global Product/Service Architecture

Consistently delighting customers around the world rarely means providing 100 percent global consistency in everything a company does. Companies seeking to serve global customers frequently make the mistake of thinking that all resources must be replicated everywhere in a huge configuration to service global customers.

This isn't possible, and it isn't necessary. What companies must figure out is the optimal global configuration of capabilities. What has to be globally consistent is the way a company fulfills customer perceptions through its product quality and service standards.

The power of global consistency builds on both your company's core competencies and its diverse competencies. Blending these core and diverse competencies together is a complex balancing act.

Core competencies* are the fundamental strengths of a company that enable the company to be successful, such as the ability to get products to market quickly, the strength of a world-brand product, or outstanding customer service.

Diverse competencies are strengths the company must develop in dealing with change and differentiation, such as the variations of products and services your company provides its customers around the world. Frequently, providing this diversity results in new products or knowledge that appeals to a much broader customer constituency than you expect, such as what resulted from the development of the ergonomic keyboard for the Apple Corporation by its Swedish subsidiary.

Preparing for moments of truth for both global and local customers requires an understanding of both core and diverse competencies. Some companies demonstrate their global consistency in homogeneous products that can be marketed in many countries with few changes.

For products like Coca-Cola or Marlboro cigarettes this might be an appropriate strategy. But other companies, like Asea-Brown Boveri, one of the world's largest and most successful engineering companies, create unique services in almost every local market they serve.

By achieving their own particular balance, global companies create their real advantages. The other forms of international business—global exporter, multilocal, and multinational—all have tremendous difficulty achieving any part of this balance on a sustained basis. Figure 3-4 depicts the various forms attempting to achieve a balance, each in a different way.

The global exporter can appeal broadly to customers based on an outstanding ability to understand the least common cross-cultural denominator for its products. But it lacks the specific local presence and cultural knowledge to rapidly customize to microniches and individual needs. In a world moving toward "mass customization for markets of one"[†] such a homogeneous approach cannot be sustained.

Multilocals, on the other hand, may have the knowledge to tailor their products for each market. But many lack the necessary core of shared policies, knowledge, and expertise to support global customers consistently across borders. They cannot afford the administrative and other costs of

---

* Gary Hamel, "The Core Competence of the Corporation," *Harvard Business Review* 68, no. 3 (Boston, Mass., May–June 1990).

† Stanley M. Davis, *Future Perfect* (Addison-Wesley Publishing Company, Inc., 1987).

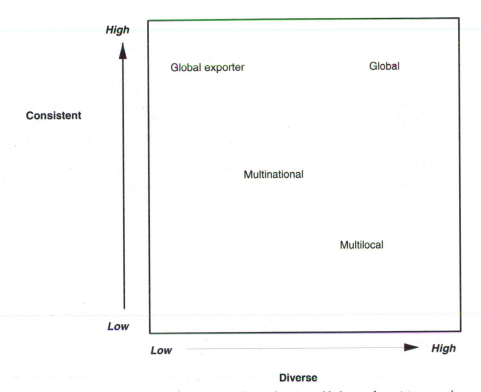

Figure 3-4. Positioning your company to achieve the optimal balance of consistency and diversity.

sharing management information for global customers. As a result, the proposition to support a global customer is something that rarely gets off the ground.

Multinationals are perhaps best positioned to appeal to both global and local customers. But, as a senior marketing executive of a major multinational said, "Every time we want to deal with a customer on a worldwide basis, we have to set up a virtual company within our company, organized around the customer." This activity is not only expensive, but also complex to orchestrate.

But a global company can create global/local balance because management starts out with a perspective of creating a spectrum of capabilities to be applied flexibly to respond to customer desires. By developing a global architecture of product and service offerings, and by mapping out the company's capabilities to provide this, your company can provide the optimal blend of what your customers want, both globally and locally.

A global product/service architecture is a dynamically changing map with three dimensions:

- Patterns and trends of customer demand
- The product and service offerings from design to delivery
- The company capabilities and flows of processes

It indicates common and diverse characteristics of demand, as well as how resources are shared across borders to develop products. It shows where products and services are sourced and delivered. It provides the blueprint for the optimal flow of the company's business processes. Figure 3-5 shows the elements of a global product/service architecture.

Let's illustrate what we mean by a product architecture by looking at a fairly universal product: bathroom plumbing.

First, customer demand: American Standard (Ideal Standard in Europe), as the world's largest supplier of bathroom suites and the only worldwide plumbing manufacturer, recognizes that customer demand varies because water pressure and pipe size varies in different parts of the world. While the outer casings of the bathtubs, bidets, and toilets can be consistent, the inside components vary by market.

Second, product offering: American Standard manufactures these products in Belgium, primarily for Europe, in Korea, primarily for the Far East, in the United States, for North America except Mexico, and in Mexico, for that country and the rest of Latin and South America. As the products are being assembled, the consistent outer casings need to be married with the diverse internal components. Furthermore, because the products are being delivered to different countries, the installation instructions and packaging have to be provided in the language of the intended destination.

Third, company capabilities and process flows: American Standard wants to respond as quickly as possible to changes in forecasted demand. Having a great distribution system is critical to the company's success. This means the plant in Belgium may be asked to supply customers in the Far East or South America, or the plant in Korea to supply Europe. The ability to be responsive to orders—to build to order rather than building to forecast—requires the global coordination of plant schedules and manufacturing processes.*

In a similar way, Benetton has developed global advantages through the consistency of having the same 3000 products worldwide, subcontracting methods, and advertising campaigns. The United Nations and United Colors of Benetton advertisements have become the company's holistic symbol. Benetton gets a high percentage of repeat business from traveling

---

* Gary Biddle, interview with author, Cambridge, Mass., June 1990.

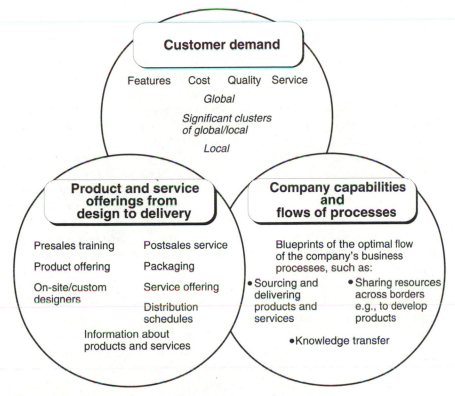

Figure 3-5. Elements of the global product/service architecture.

customers by positioning its 5000 stores in major shopping areas all over the world. Its customers have grown to expect a certain level of product consistency and quality wherever they are.

Yet the fashion industry is fickle, and styles and colors change quickly in different parts of the world. To cope with this diversity, Benetton shops now use graphic images to test market designs with customers and retail shop license owners; they then place orders to the company's flexible factories, which can manufacture and deliver to any store within three days.

Ford of Europe is attacking from a different point. In the late 1980s, the company developed a strategy to improve customer loyalty by dramatically compressing the time from vehicle order to delivery, and at the same time overhauled its parts and service logistics activities to provide improved parts availability and consistently higher levels of service. Ford wanted to serve regional and local customers in the best possible way. Implementing the new strategy required installing a common information technology platform in almost every one of its 7000 European dealerships. Cars ordered from anywhere in Europe will be delivered to the local customer's specifications, including local emissions standards and other local features, from the regional system.

As a customer itself, Ford is striving to do business efficiently on a regional basis in Europe by looking for a computer vendor with the ability to present a consistent offering to its dealers. When Ford went to the multilocal technology supplier of its previous dealership computer system, it found that the vendor wanted to have separate negotiations for product price and service standards in each of the 15 countries where Ford did business.

From the technology vendor's standpoint, supporting Ford's requirement would necessitate an extraordinary effort because its strong national organizations were unwilling to subsidize losses in countries where its position was weaker. In England, one of Ford's largest markets, price and service support for the vendor was not an issue, because of its large volume. But in Portugal, with small volume, not only was the price offered significantly higher, but the vendor was unwilling to commit to the same service and support conditions.

Ford found a different computer vendor. Its feeling was, "If we can develop global/local capability, so can our suppliers." More and more, companies are making the same kinds of decisions.

For companies dealing with global business customers, creating a consistent business experience is becoming absolutely critical for success. As Debbi Biondello, an executive at Apple Computer, put it:

"Figuring out the key aspects of the business that have to be the same so that everything else can be different is a vital step in architecting our global capability to meet our customers' needs. Building this flexibility into our product and service architecture helps us to manage the complexity of dealing in many markets without going through the expense of building physical assets everywhere. We can manage and combine our resources to produce the optimal product and service offering when and where we need to for our customers. Instead of creating a virtual company every time we meet a different request, we have to create a living map of our global resources. We can then apply these resources when and where we need to, flexibly and quickly."

By figuring out what has to be consistent, your company is well down the path toward developing an idea of the key diversities it must offer to different parts of the market.

Low global barriers promote the sharing of key aspects of a business that have to be the same. By building the right blend of consistency and diversity into its products and services, a business takes advantage of a wide range of design criteria and achieves powerful economies of scale.

As companies become global, success is not just an issue of getting consistent products to market. Today, a global company must consider how its products will be perceived and used, and tailor those products—and especially the services that augment them—to meet local needs when required to by local custom, conditions, or taste.

By allowing for multicultural perspectives during product and service design and development, better positioning can be achieved. By providing key local variations, which bind a customer to a particular aspect of a business' products and services, and which differentiate a business from its competitors, the power of diversity in a company's products and services will contribute to added value and competitive edge.

When Peat Marwick merged with Klynveld Main Goerdeler in 1987 to create KPMG, the world's largest public accounting firm, the first order of business was to create an audit manual for auditors around the world,* so the company could better serve globe-spanning clients like Citicorp, Honda, and Philips in a consistent way. If it had failed to develop a consistent set of worldwide procedures, KPMG would have lost some of its most import clients. By adopting the new manual, KPMG created a global edge every place it operated, since no other accounting firm had so broad a geographic reach.

To be global, a company must deliver the products and services it develops anywhere the company's management chooses to sell products. It does a company no good if it has great products and services that employees, business partners, and customers can not obtain, understand, and use. Consequently, global companies must create mechanisms to aggressively transfer product, service, and operating knowledge globally. Companies must learn how to continuously improve by leveraging their existing global knowledge bases.

To dramatically improve customer satisfaction, companies must provide globally consistent and profitable prepurchase and postpurchase support on a local basis to global customers. This implies that the company must define and implement a minimum level of service and support that is "globally" consistent, which global customers can expect locally in countries where the company commits to do business with them. At first, companies should be highly selective in whom they identify as "global customers;" companies should ensure that the commitment to these customers does not outstrip their ability to deliver.

The diverse aspects of local demand must be well understood. The identification of key differences in markets is an essential ingredient in understanding the perceived value of products and services delivered to local customers. By analyzing the cultural characteristics of demand, a company can develop a plan for customization that creates balance. Local variations,

* Larry Horner (chairman KPMG), interview with author, 1988.

dependent on local cultural traits, can be analyzed to see whether the local market responds to the particular customization.

The blending of a business' core and diverse competencies depends on identifying the appropriate resources to share—such as customer information—and integrating the use of these resources with the company's overall policies and culture. The global product/service architecture provides the glue for sustaining this global effort.

Understanding the Customer's Customer

In an increasingly global marketplace, it's not enough for industrial companies that sell to product-manufacturers merely to understand who their customers are; they must get a line on who their customer's customers—consumers—are, how their customers are reaching consumers, and how they can work more closely with their customers to project consistency of service and create relationships with the consumers for both companies.

Let's look at the car industry for a couple of good examples.

A U.S. consumer living in the northeast buys a European model car manufactured by a U.S. manufacturer. One of the features of this car is tires by a world-class, highly respected manufacturer of high-performance tires.

When the winter comes and the snow, freezing rain, and sleet begin to batter New England, the consumer realizes that his rear-wheel-drive car with high-class European tires is fishtailing all over the place. He goes to his dealer, who recommends snow tires and sells him a pair made by a U.S. manufacturer. For this driver, the tires by a well-known, respected European tire company were a "nice-to-have" for prestige reasons, but for safety in winter he's willing to take the dealer's recommendation.

Before three years are out, the consumer has driven about 35,000 miles and realizes that the four original tires from the European manufacturer are wearing down; a little early, he thinks, especially since he rotates the tires and uses his U.S.-made snow tires for a few months each winter. Again, he goes to his dealer. This time his dealer sells him a set of four replacements made by another European high-performance tire manufacturer.

The manufacturer of the original four tires has lost two sales it could have made: the sale for snow tires and the sale for replacement tires. Some of the blame rests on this manufacturer; it doesn't know and understand its customer's customers.

The tire manufacturer doesn't know that for the vast majority of Americans—even those who purchase European cars—the knowledge of tires and sense of the importance of brand loyalty to tires is small. Toughness—the ability to deal with an increasingly decrepit highway system—and long wear are of more importance to most Americans than name brand or the qualities high-performance tires add to the overall ride. To preempt that U.S. driver from taking his dealer's suggestion, or from driving to his nearest Firestone or Sears car-care center or nearest discount tire distributor, the manufacturer of high-performance tires needs to educate this consumer.

There needs to be literature in the car's owner packet that tells the buyer that high-performance tires are also temperamental. Because the tires are precision instruments designed to enhance the car's performance they are not imbued with some of the qualities of U.S.-made all-weather tires, so snow tires will be necessary in certain climates and driving conditions (the company has a full line of snow tires, which your dealer can supply.) Because they are designed to provide peak performance, they will withstand less wear than other tires before that performance falls off, so purchasers need to be aware that they will need to buy replacements sooner than with certain other tires (ask your dealer for the replacement tire that's right for you).

Of course, the tire manufacturer can't be held completely responsible. In the U.S., the independent dealer is a powerful entity, able to negotiate with any vendor of replacement parts, and increasingly respected more by many buyers for the quality of repair and maintenance work than for the good prices the dealer is willing to provide on new cars. In fact, manufacturers around the world sell most of their cars through independent dealers, and many manufacturers consider the dealer their customer and know less about their customer's customers—again, the car buyer—than one would think.

It wasn't until just a few years ago that a particular European car manufacturer decided it needed better information about individual customers to generate future sales. Since the company, like almost all other car manufacturers, does not deal directly with customers, it turned to independent dealers to try to create customer profiles and understand customer needs and desires. By taking this step, the company recognized the significance of local buying habits and how local customer preferences could have an impact on a global product.

Car dealers, who live around the world in the same communities their customers live in, know a lot about their customers based on personal contact. Some dealers keep sales records about customer ownership patterns. The best dealers keep a service history of the cars they sell, limited, of course, to customer visits to their own dealerships. They often use that information to check on customer satisfaction. These checks help build customer loyalty to that dealer, leading to repeat sales.

Manufacturers, however, do not receive any direct benefits from this information. Dealers are not in the habit of sharing records with manufacturers, nor do manufacturers ask to see them. In fact, dealers sometimes switch from selling one manufacturer's cars to the cars of another; when this happens there is often a conflict in customer loyalty, whether the customer is purchasing the manufacturer's product or the full range of dealer services, including a car.

Traditionally, to get customer information to its major functional areas like design and sales, the manufacturer relies almost entirely on warranty information sent by dealers who sell the cars, dealer councils, customer focus groups, and market research.

At the individual-owner level, the manufacturer usually knows only the names and addresses of car owners from their warranties and information about what is going wrong with these cars from dealers who submit claims against the warranties. The warranty claims, along with parts consumption, are valuable in correcting some design errors in the car models, but they are of almost no use in developing a real understanding of who buys a manufacturer's cars, of what that individual customer needs and desires, and of what the manufacturer could do to the product that would really delight that customer.

Dealer councils tend to illustrate customer problems by example and anecdote, but again are more indicative of trends in customer groups rather than individual requirements.

Similarly, the manufacturer resorts to customer focus groups and market research for much of its customer information. Focus groups are useful for getting customer reactions and suggestions of what they like and do not like about prototype cars, so company engineers can alter designs to fit these customer preferences more exactly. Market research provides demographic information for building better knowledge of the major market segments.

Of course, when a customer finances a car through one of the car company's captive financing arms, the amount of information obtained about that person becomes greater, but it is still statistical and only cursory in terms of obtaining a picture of a customer's life-style and possible future car needs.

The manufacturer recently came to the realization that to try to position its product at the top of current and potential customers' shopping lists the next time they go to buy a car, a much more detailed data base of customer information is necessary. The company would like to know things about its customers, such as when a city dweller moves to the suburbs or the country or vice versa, that currently gets lost.

If the dealer knows that a customer has moved, he currently has no inclination to share that information—indeed no way of sharing that information—with other dealers who sell the manufacturer's product. Because of this, the manufacturer is implementing an integrated information system based on individual customer relationships that captures information from the time of first customer purchase, includes financing information, tracks ownership through service history, and continues through the subsequent purchases.

In addition to providing better, more holistic, service to individual customers throughout a long-term relationship, such a knowledge base has internal ramifications. It can help the manufacturer do "quick-interest" marketing to target very specific customer sets rather than saturation marketing; it can facilitate customization of cars to match customer needs; it can produce more accurate sales forecasts; it can improve service because a record of engineering changes and service history stays with the customer wherever he or she travels; and it can provide faster feedback to the design, manufacturing, and quality functions, especially of items that do not cause warranty problems but are common later-stage problems.

Finally, because customer information will be shared with dealerships in 15 countries, dealers will be able to present a more consistent and integrated face to customers. The overall relationship will, the manufacturer hopes, be enhanced, and dealers may not switch manufacturer affiliations as often.

Summary

Every company that sells products or services on a worldwide basis has global customers. Few companies have a good understanding about the product and service requirements of these global customers. Global companies develop the ability to achieve cultural fit with the customers. A global product/service architecture provides a blueprint for the company's business processes. A global company develops valuable insights by focusing on the needs and wants of its customers' customers.

Action Checklist

1. Have you conducted market research on the product and service requirements of your global customers?

2. Have you built cultural maps to better understand the variety of demands?

3. Do you invest in and promote affinity with the various local cultures in which you operate?

4. Is your global product/service architecture kept dynamically up-to-date to reflect changing customer tastes and company capabilities?

4

Balance Global/Local Activities

Global/Local Markets

Edwards High Vacuum International,* a subsidiary of BOC, has recently reorganized to become more globally competitive. The company makes vacuums for a wide variety of purposes in industry, from pharmaceuticals to semiconductors. Organized into two units, the company addresses all types of vacuum technology needs in the world market. The systems unit creates complete system solutions such as a freeze-drying plant with all complementary equipment, while the components division provides vacuum parts of many sorts to complement the systems' business.

Edwards approaches the market on a regional basis, with three regions: Europe, North America, and the Pacific. As Dave Ringland, director of components, explains, sharing among regions of the company's key ingredients for success is absolutely necessary to be a world-class player.

To make the manufacturing activities in the United Kingdom more responsive to U.S. and Pacific customer requirements, channels of activity have been set up between the groups.

"We want them (the U.S. and Pacific operations) to tell us what the market needs in terms of products and specifications; also of niches and opportunities," Ringland says. "If we get that right, then we have got it right for at least 40 percent of the world market."

---

* Simon Holberton, "Corporate Restructuring: Esprit de corps: life-blood of the matrix," *Financial Times* (May 14, 1990), 13.

Getting the global business right is increasingly dependent on properly balancing the global and local aspects of customer desires, employees, and the business's processes themselves. In our last chapter, we focused on customers, and in our next chapter we will discuss human resource issues within the company. In this chapter, we will cover what we call the global/local balance of business activity—how to create, maintain, and continue to develop a worldwide sphere of influence that involves consistent internal business processes and processes that involve various forms of partnership. The issue of global/local balance involves:

- Dynamically monitoring global business activities, both outside the company and within, to keep from getting blindsided and to maximize opportunities

- Identifying which aspects of the corporation need to be globally planned for and managed on a worldwide basis

- Developing ways to carry out these global strategic initiatives; defining and obtaining the resources necessary to carry them out; determining when they can be done in-house and when a strategic alliance must be formed; creating and maintaining those alliances

At Edwards, employees from sales and marketing teams act as opportunity spotters for each other so that cross-geographic concerns are shared. Alex Mudge, director of systems, reinforces the idea when he says, "Dave and I act as a service to both sides of the business. We don't want both sides of the business going in opposite directions." This "identity of purpose," as Simon Holberton of the *Financial Times* calls it, illustrates the ability of world-class companies to share throughout the company.*

In order for these companies to take up the strenuous task of becoming global, striving to be low-cost and customer-driven, and plotting a course toward their global vision, they need to exploit relationships, capabilities, and information available on a global basis. For these companies to be able to keep to this course, agreement must be shared widely in the company as to the essential actions to be taken to achieve the global vision.

In order to manage global and local resources flexibly and effectively, management cannot merely refer to an organizational chart to figure out the best global process flow. Debating about whether to centralize or decentralize activities is largely a waste of time; since these are structural debates, they should follow rather than precede the discussion of the best global process flow.

The centralization/decentralization debate often swings on the argument that he/she who controls activities has increased importance. This

---

* Simon Holberton, "Corporate Restructuring: Esprit de corps: life-blood of the matrix," *Financial Times* (May 14, 1990), 13.

perspective creates limitations for thinking. Today and tomorrow the issue is not control; the issue is how to make resources available wherever they are needed to support the company's global product/service architecture and the company's business-process flow.

Plotting a global course, and adjusting the global/local balance, is a dynamic process that requires the complex coordination of many activities on an ongoing basis.

Richard Nolan, chairman of Nolan, Norton & Co., and Robert Eccles, a professor at the Harvard Business School, argue that the responsibility for creating the proper infrastructures under which this complex coordination takes place is the only responsibility of top management in the corporation of the twenty-first century; all other responsibilities—to conduct the day-to-day, anywhere, anytime business of the corporation—fall to employees throughout the organization, who are "networked" rather than functioning at one or another hierarchical level.

Nolan and Eccles believe top management creates a "superordinate" organizational design and has the responsibility to create seven organizational infrastructures:

1. Core competencies and expertise infrastructure

2. Shared knowledge and data bases infrastructure

3. Human assets and structural contour infrastructure

4. Project tasking and team assignment infrastructure

5. Performance measurement infrastructure

6. Resource allocation infrastructure

7. Information and telecommunications technology infrastructure.*

Core Competencies and Expertise Infrastructure

Senior management is responsible for identifying and articulating the core competencies of the organization—the diverse skills, knowledge, and technologies—and for ensuring that the skills and processes on which those competencies are based are continually developed and renewed. Continuous learning and innovation programs, up-to-date skills inventories, and targets for improvement are ways in which the superordinate design of core competencies takes place.

---

* Robert G. Eccles and Richard L. Nolan, "Framework for Design of the Emerging Global Organization Structure," Global Telecommunications Conference, Harvard Business School (May 1991). In a paper they delivered on globalization, Nolan and Eccles described these seven infrastructures in detail.

Shared Knowledge and Data Bases Infrastructure

Senior management needs to ensure that mechanisms exist for capturing and making knowledge available throughout the organization. While it is necessary to have particular data bases maintained in certain parts of the company to maintain data integrity, it is also necessary for many data bases to be available to the entire company. Therefore, common data base standards and communication protocols need to be established.

Human Assets and Structural Contour Infrastructure

Irrespective of technology, the knowledge that forms the basis of a company's competitive advantage ultimately resides in people. Therefore, a large part of senior management's superordinate design responsibility revolves around developing the company's human capital through recruiting, socialization, and training.

Project Tasking and Team Assignment Infrastructure

The company's human assets and structural contour are the "functional hierarchy," on top of which float the shifting networks of relationships that are formed to actually accomplish the company's work. While senior management is specifically not responsible for creating these networks, it is responsible for making the tools available so that people within the organization can continuously reconfigure the networks to accomplish work. People who are forming project teams need to know who is available when, and what particular skills each person can bring to the project.

Performance Measurement Infrastructure

Senior management is responsible for establishing performance measures for individuals, functions, divisions, and processes, in order to assess how effectively these assets are being utilized. In addition to traditional measures of financial performance, measures of quality, customer satisfaction, innovation, human capital development, and market share are necessary—the so-called balanced scorecard approach.

Resource Allocation Infrastructure

Resources, financial and otherwise, must be allocated to individuals, projects, functions, divisions, and businesses. Three of the most important examples of resource-allocation infrastructure are budgets, capital budgets, and compensation. While senior management may not make all of the specific decisions regarding allocation, it is responsible to establish the processes by which these decisions are made.

Information and Telecommunications Technology Infrastructure

The final part of the infrastructure of superordinate design is the information and telecommunications technology architecture that supports all of the applications and facilitates the other six infrastructure components. Senior management is responsible for establishing principles to serve as guides for the type of information technology resources available, where they are located and managed, and how they are developed and sourced.

In the rest of this chapter, we will show how companies are beginning to encounter and deal with the issues Eccles and Nolan raise, although few if any companies speak of their efforts within the confines of this framework. We will show how senior managements are beginning to adjust and balance the use and flow of resources, and how companies are looking to leverage their particular competencies with competencies of others through partnerships and joint ventures. In the next chapter, we will take a look at what Eccles and Nolan call self-design, the organizational design work that individuals throughout the company do as they constantly reconfigure task and project efforts.

Before designing and creating the superordinate infrastructures, senior management must first understand the lay of the global land.

Monitoring Global Business Activities

The global company must scan the environment and gather intelligence by investigating the company's wider business environment for information germane to global actions and strategies. Gaining knowledge about the global business environment and relating this to the company's global actions is continuous, since new information that could cause an essential reevaluation of global strategies could develop at any time.

Whether or not your company, business partners, and current customers carry out activities in a particular country, you need to keep keenly aware of key events around the world. A company needs to vigilantly consider the parties that create, provide, and deliver products and services in its business and related business areas.

Looking at what the company's network of business relationships is doing and planning to do keeps the management of the company aware and alert, continuously reviewing and seeking intelligence on global business operations. By communicating this knowledge throughout the company, management keeps all efforts geared toward acting with an informed and coordinated whole-world perspective. By exploring the sources of information and the dynamics of multidimensional business relationships, management can exploit the company's sphere of influence to better prepare their company to do business globally.

Alain Gomez, CEO of Thomson S.A., a worldwide electronics company home-based in France, looks at his own management role as one of connecting the company to its overall global business environment, and his business as a holistic entity. "An organization is neither an island nor inert," Gomez says. "It is a living system interrelated to a set of wider systems. The CEO's task is to monitor how the company is attuned to the outside world and how it is renewing itself internally."[*]

Scanning the environment means watching the activities of global, regional, and even local players in the same and related industries in order to better create global/local balance for your operations—and for your customers. Alain Gomez sites another source of opportunity: competitors.[†] Thomson keenly surveys the global environment for opportunities among competitors.

"Sometimes you can rejoin the first rank by being a shrewd follower," Gomez says. "The trick is being willing to learn from your competitors. Thomson Consumer Electronics (TCE) has done that twice in an important way: first with RCA in picture tubes, then with the Japanese in VCRs. Both times the reason was the same—we had no other option if we wanted to stay in the business.

"The picture tube accounts for about 30 percent of the cost of a TV. Less than 20 years ago, we did not know how to produce picture tubes. Now we are among the leaders. We had to learn how from RCA through a licensing

[*] Janice McCormick and Nan Stone, "From National Champion to Global Competitor: An Interview with Thomson's Alain Gomez," *Harvard Business Review* (May–June 1990), 127–135.

[†] McCormick and Stone, "Interview with Gomez."

agreement and a joint venture that lasted most of the 1970s. Finally, by the end of that decade, we were autonomous. Now, two years later, we've launched a new movie-screen format tube called the 16:9 that represents an important step on the road to high-definition TV. Other companies are making it too, but Thomson was the first to develop it and produce it."

Keeping keenly aware of key events may create an opportunity to exploit a global advantage or prevent the company from being blindsided from an unexpected source. Global companies like Thomson, British Telecom, and others have learned that they must quickly tack in response to unpredictable events. The best global companies develop global peripheral vision by acting in a wider environment and sharing knowledge gained. Taking notes, seeking explanations for successes and failures, sharing ideas with companies to gain insight, and exploring cross-geographic and cross-functional possibilities are ongoing activities within global companies.

The chairman of British Telecom, Ian Vallance, describes British Telecom's global business environment as one "exploding with new technologies, [experiencing] industry convergence [e.g., communications and information], global restructuring, and the transformation of customer needs."* Describing the company's intelligence gathering, he says, "The fast-growing customer requirement for seamless global communications networks is driving the structure of our industry. Customers simply do not want the hassle of trying to coordinate the activities of dozens of different national suppliers. They want an international supplier that can design and manage their networks for them, wherever they need to go. There are only a handful of major suppliers that have the skill and resource to do this. We are constantly challenged to think outside our current industry map, and we would make a serious mistake if we limited our definition of competitors to our rivals within the telecommunications sector."

Similarly, Sony has widened the scope of its activities from being in the business of providing consumer electronics products to being in the business of helping people communicate, be entertained, and be better informed: "Changing the way we see our world."† This new definition of its sphere of influence is allowing Sony to expand horizons ahead of competitors. By scanning the global environment for developments in communicating, entertaining, and informing, Sony is creating global strategic initiatives to serve customers in new ways.

Sony is positioning itself to satisfy the demands of future customers by assembling a powerful array of hardware and software capabilities from different corners of the world to offer integrated customer products and services. The acquisition of CBS Records and Columbia Pictures demon-

* Stockton Lecture, London Business School, 1990.

† "Sony . . . The Long View," Sony Corporation of America.

strates that Sony is moving toward a highly integrated global business vision. Sony attempts to draw upon the best resources in the world to provide for its customers.

For many years, managers in the U.S. computer industry felt safe from the strong competition Japanese companies offered in other electronics sectors such as machine tools, semiconductors, and consumer electronics. They felt no need to develop knowledge about Japanese competition. But feeling safe isolates companies from reality, supporting narrow-sighted actions, and stops them from scanning the global environment for important information. The results can be drastic.

Not only are the Japanese dominating the $9.2 billion world market for Dynamic Random Access Memories (D-RAMs), a key component for most types of computers, they practically held most American and European computer companies hostage in late 1988 when there was a major shortage outside Japan. IBM, with 22,000 employees in Japan, responded by forming a strategic alliance with Siemens to jointly develop and manufacture 64-megabit D-RAMs to increase their global capability and enhance their competitive position. Together, they are extending their capabilities and perspectives.*

From design to delivery, the global company must be in a position to anticipate new opportunities. Japanese and Dutch companies are well-known for what we call the "notebook approach," or what Sheridan Tatsuno calls the "global search" approach.[†] Rather than stay at home and create products and processes based entirely on domestic ideas, Japanese, Dutch, and even Korean companies have gone out to the rest of the world to seek knowledge to increase their products' creative applicability.

Ezra Vogel, a specialist on Japanese business practices, writes that "organizations send out observation teams and invite in experts. They gather information from classrooms and golf courses, from conferences and value-added resellers (vars), from think tanks and television. They gather it from professionals and amateurs, friends and foes. New friends are cultivated because they might provide access to information. Potential sources are carefully nurtured so that further queries can be processed as needed. New areas of knowledge are explored to provide new clues, and people are assigned to spend several years mastering potentially profitable specialties. The process is nothing if not thorough.[‡]

* Louise Kehoe, "Siemens and IBM forge powerful link to combat Japanese," *Financial Times* (January 26, 1990).

[†] Sheridan Tatsuno, *Created in Japan* (New York: Harper & Row, Publishers, 1990), 76–77.

[‡] Ezra Vogel, *Japan as Number One* (New York: Harper & Row, Publishers, 1980).

Building relationships and strategic alliances to gather intelligence in these areas is another important aspect of environmental scanning. As time-based competitors and mass customizers come to the fore, domestic barriers will succumb to global communicators who seek out and rapidly transfer this new-found knowledge. Sensitizing your business partners' global antennae to be able to identify information that would be useful to your company enlarges the company's global intelligence gathering net.

Having gathered information about the environment, sharing that knowledge widely across many areas of the business is important for at least two reasons. First, someone in the company may understand the relevance of the information in ways the collectors have overlooked. Second, by considering the knowledge cross-functionally and cross-geographically, a synergistic understanding of the environmental forces may be attained.

A company needs to carry out active processes to share the results of its global searches. These processes may be electronic, such as putting up-to-date information on electronic bulletin boards, or manual, such as the formation of brain-storming sessions to discuss gathered intelligence.

Ford schedules frequent trips to Japan to observe the flexible manufacturing methods of Japanese automobile manufacturers. Returning executives prepare briefing papers that are circulated throughout the company. Sharing this information at many levels generates ideas about process and quality improvements.

Citibank scans newspapers, magazines, and other periodicals for information on its competitors' use of information technology in banking and then provides clippings for its managers all over the world. This information serves to keep high visibility on their vision of "Global Electronic Banking."

Environmental scanning and examination of a company's global business relationships are a dynamic process. A company should continually be "looping" though the process, observing how and why situations change. By plotting the trajectory of a company's changing relationships and influences, management can begin to develop global peripheral vision on how the company is being affected by the repercussions of its own actions as well as by the resonance of the global business environment. Winning global companies will exercise global peripheral vision to rapidly deploy resources and outflank competitors. But it doesn't stop here; global companies must be dynamically monitoring inside the company as well.

Creating Resources on a Global Scale

In order to implement global strategic initiatives, every company needs to have what John Sculley calls "new enterprise thinking." Companies need to completely rethink what their key resources and capabilities have to be. Most companies today still think of their physical assets and their in-house staff as their key resources. But as you attempt to expand rapidly into parts of the world you currently are not in, you may find you can't create physical assets or staff fast enough.

We are moving to a world where time, the ability to eliminate the negative impacts created by distance, knowledge access, and capital deployment are the resource variables that will determine the winners and losers in global business. While information and decisions about how to deploy resources once obtained are gaining increasing importance, the source of raw materials and the location of physical assets are becoming less and less important.

As an executive at CSX told us, "We don't necessarily need or want the physical assets on a global scale, scattered about the world wherever we do business. We would prefer just to have a superior logistics capability and the systems to manage the assets owned by others. We are trying to achieve globalization by making connections between the assets across countries without putting assets on the ground."

This is a world where buying raw materials can be performed by almost anyone, but deploying resources effectively is accomplished by relatively few. It's what you do with resources, how quickly and flexibly you can transfer them into goods and services and deliver them any place your customers desire, that will win the day and differentiate your business globally.

There are new considerations for global companies regarding resources: (1) the development of resources to a greater level of global capability, and (2) a decision on the company's core activities and the formation of strategic alliances to fulfill certain other activities.

Coca-Cola's new mission statement sums up the first situation quite succinctly:

"To succeed in this global environment we will make effective use of our fundamental resources: Brands, Systems, Capital, and, most important, people. Because these resources are already available, one might assume we need only to draw on them for achieving our goal. Nothing could be more wrong. The challenge of the 1990s will be not only to use these resources, but to expand them . . . to adapt them . . . to reconfigure them in constantly new ways in order to bring about an ever renewed relationship between the Coca-Cola system and the consumers of the world . . ."*

If resourcefulness is "the pace at which new competitive advantages are being built,"† then finding new ways of carrying out global business is essential in creating global business advantage. By developing the management of resources to look for global economies of scale, companies can create a momentum to the business.

---

* Coca-Cola, "A Business System Toward 2000: Our Mission in the 1990s" (1989).

† Gary Hamel and C.K. Prahalad, "Strategic Intent," *Harvard Business Review* (May/June 1989).

Secondly, a company's core activities are those that the company must perform to retain control over essential business. Recently, the management of a bank that had created a superb multinational networking system realized that to control the business process of the network it did not have to control every piece of the cable in the network. The company decided that by controlling the switches—in effect the traffic-control devices—on the network, it could maintain control of the process. The company subsequently subcontracted the maintenance of cables, etc., to a high-technology company that provided the service at a lower cost, and at a much lower investment of the company's management skills.

Having assigned and decided what resources the company will use, the global strategic initiative team should consider what other resources it will use to accomplish its objectives. To do this it must (1) figure out what its core activities are and how to make effective use of them, (2) identify potential strategic alliances to fill in gaps in its base capabilities, and (3) look for opportunities to pool resources with business partners.

Today, sound management of a global company realizes that "no one goes it alone anymore; technically, politically, or economically."* It becomes harder and harder to draw the line around an enterprise. Points of contact that were once considered "outside" the company are now inside, such as customer-design teams and vice versa and such as engineers assigned to other companies for knowledge sharing.

A global company has the ability to utilize the most appropriate resources in the world, many of which may not be under its direct physical control, to please its individual customers, wherever they are located, in ways that maximize the realization of the company's long-term objectives.

As the need for new-product introduction accelerates in almost every industry, we see strategic alliances taking place that may result in one company creating the product, another processing the transaction, and yet another selling and branding the product. These alliances are being formed to take advantage of diverse company strengths in various parts of the world's industry value chains. Today, not doing everything yourself enables companies shrewd enough to form intelligent ventures to narrow the gap between themselves and the world's leaders.

The Korean company Samsung has become a major contender in several world markets by forming joint ventures with American and Japanese companies. Integrating business processes with these partners has helped the company move much more rapidly up the global learning curve than it could have done on its own. "Samsung Corning hopes to produce 20 percent of the world's output of glass bulbs for TV tubes within five years. Samsung Medical Services makes diagnostic imaging products in league with

---

* Michael Spindler (Chief Operating Officer, Apple Computer, Inc.), conversation with author, 198.

General Electric. Ties have helped Samsung move into watchmaking through a joint venture with Seiko and into cameras with some initial help from Minolta."*

Pooling resources with other companies to create a team to solve an industry-wide global strategic initiative is also an approach worth considering. In the computer industry, technology development is becoming so complex that it seems more than any one company can handle. In the United States, Microelectronics and Computer Technology Corp. (MCC) is a consortium of 19 companies, including Boeing, Control Data, DEC, and 3M, formed in 1983 to "develop advanced computer and microelectronic technologies, including artificial intelligence." Another consortium, Sematech, was formed in 1987 and includes 14 companies, including Intel, IBM, and Motorola, "to improve semiconductor and manufacturing techniques."

In Japan, six companies, including NTT, Mitsubishi, and Matsushita, got together in 1976 to "produce the world's highest capacity memory chip." In 1981, nine companies, including Hitachi, Toshiba, and NEC, combined resources to "develop advanced computer technologies such as artificial intelligence and parallel processing."

Meanwhile, in Europe, ESPRIT is an EEC project to bring Europe into the competitive computer industry. An ongoing body of several research initiatives, its aim is also to further the development of computer-related industries.

As Robert N. Noyce, president of Sematech, says, "The first question a consortium has to ask itself is what can it do better than the individual members."†

In the financial community, where customers have long relied on the strengths of financial syndicates (consortiums) to bring out new issues of equity and debt, the benefits to the members include a lower risk and lower cost of implementation, while at the same time allowing them to gain a share of the action. The same was true for the underwriters who began meeting in Lloyd's coffeehouse several hundred years ago and spreading the financial risk of merchant shippers seeking to expand England's markets.

Consortiums, experiencing varying degrees of success, are examples of companies reaching far beyond their traditional enterprise boundaries to develop capabilities that might otherwise be impossible to realize because of the scale of resources or depth of experience required. This practice of putting together a consortium of investors to meet a particular need is increasing as even the biggest and best companies recognize they can't go it alone.

* Louis Kaar, "The Tigers Behind Korea's Prowess," *Fortune* (Fall 1989).

† Lee Smith, "Can Consortiums Defeat Japan?" *Fortune* (June 5, 1989).

Flexible resource management involves a certain amount of planning and a certain amount of guesswork. You must not only supply what you need today, but also prepare for the future. You must prepare today's resources to develop into the resources you will need tomorrow.

Resources should be viewed as a dynamic system. People, information, time, financial capital, and raw materials must be constantly combined and recombined with various management tools, frameworks, and technologies to achieve world-class quality in how you build relationships with your customers and treat your business partners. Each of these inputs has a dynamic effect on the others that can be exploited.

One of the primary objectives of achieving economies of scale is to reduce cost by combining resources. If you can figure out how to follow through on your company's global vision and global strategic initiatives by creating access to and support of the customer, when and where the customer desires, before the competition has a chance to get there, your company will be a global winner.

In this section of the chapter, we describe a number of things you can do in creating your company's global resources, and encourage you to leverage knowledge as the most important economy of scale your business can take advantage of.

Creating a Means to Transfer Knowledge

We talked to an executive team of a manufacturing company in Europe who said:

"The way we transfer knowledge in this company today is by transferring people. Transferring people may be a key way for us to share our culture, values, and beliefs; it may be a useful way for us to seed the start-up of a new location; it may be an expedient way to balance resources. But it is not nearly responsive enough, in today's information-intensive market, to transfer our company's knowledge."

Nippon Electric Corporation considers knowledge transfer to be fundamental to success in the global business arena. The company has stated that knowledge transfer is a top corporate objective, and a champion has been found to manage this activity.

"Our globalization policy is to localize our operations and build an integrated worldwide network that responds more quickly and flexibly to environmental changes in the marketplace," a company statement says.

By identifying a champion for global knowledge transfer, NEC has assigned accountability for an important part of its globalization process.

By encouraging and coordinating multiple centers of expertise, creating knowledge repositories, and using multimedia technologies to aggressively break down barriers holding back knowledge transfer, global companies are beginning to explore the new economies of scale required for future survival.

Establishing several geographically dispersed centers for resource expertise allows the global company to keep an ear to the ground for new technologies and process methodologies. Several different locations should be given mandates to make decisions for particular technologies or processes.

Ed Artzt, chairman and CEO of Procter and Gamble and a proponent of developing multiple centers of expertise, says, "We want to make sure that we have the strongest possible infrastructure to market our world brands and exploit our world-class technology to enter new categories in all of the world's key markets. That effort is going well.

"Globalization means increasing the focus of research and development on technology that can be readily reapplied and tailored to fit our business needs everywhere. It also means globalizing our sources of innovation. We will soon be underway with the construction of our new technical center in Japan, and this will give us a major capacity for product and packaging in the Far East, as well as the United States, the U.K., and continental Europe.*

P&G has over 6000 employees in research and development, representing more than 150 scientific and technical disciplines, with degrees from over 500 different universities in 50 different countries. The research, development, and engineering organization has more than 20 facilities around the world.

A global business is the ultimate embodiment of the networked organization, in that it has not one center, but multiple centers, located around expertise and competence. Having multiple centers of expertise enables a company to carry out simultaneous and concurrent development or products and resources.

The fundamental idea behind simultaneous development is that design does not have to be a serial process. Different teams can be at work on concept design and functional requirements, material selection and availability, manufacturing process, features and tolerances, commonality and simplification, quality, inspection and tooling, and assembly and systems—all at the same time.

For example, DEC has multiple centers carrying out simultaneous development of new computer products. Different labs work on different pieces of a tightly integrated product. The whole product-development process is coordinated globally, with different centers developing different parts of the product. The various components get pulled together at the final-assembly plants.

* Ed Artzt, "Ed Artzt Speaks to Employees," *Moonbeams* (Cincinnati, Ohio: The Procter & Gamble Company, December 1989), 4–6.

DEC also carries out concurrent development by setting two or more teams working on the same project separately. Different teams approach the problem with different perspectives, developing key problem-solving processes along the way. The company benefits as much from the development of the problem-solving processes as from development of the product. If breakthroughs achieved by either team are shared, a company can substantially cut down its product-development time. This might be called a "virtuous circle of knowledge."

A virtuous circle works like this: team A learns something and teaches it to team B; team B builds on this knowledge base, gains new knowledge team A lacks and teaches it, in turn, to team A. The process can cycle infinitely.

The virtuous circle phenomenon suggests that by sharing multiple perspectives and insights, a company gets better at activities and can perform them with more quality and efficiency, often allowing for the restructuring of the process. In this way, sharing knowledge gained globally can allow a company to achieve economies of scale of knowledge.

A primary obstacle to increasing global learning is that some individuals and business units are often sources of "not invented here" attitudes. Getting over the "if it isn't my/our idea, I'm not working on it" attitude is a major challenge for companies wishing to operate globally. Good ideas can come from the least expected places in a company or, for that matter, from the competition. Companies need to be willing to latch onto these ideas regardless of their source.

Centers of expertise are equally applicable to service companies and service activities. Some companies, for example, are effectively networking their in-house lawyers by making several locations centers for all real estate transactions and others for product litigation.

Global knowledge repositories make the experience of the company available on a broader scale. Key product and financial information is usually the starting point for creating knowledge repositories. They fulfill the need for ready-at-hand, accurate information about products and key financial performance. The real advantages, though, will accrue to those companies that can make knowledge about the customer available anywhere. Creating worldwide access, therefore, is a prerequisite for creating useful global knowledge repositories. It does no good if all the company's ideas are locked away at headquarters.

A company can have the best technology in the world for sharing its knowledge and still fall flat on its face. One of the keys to making knowledge repositories work is to figure out how to capture useful knowledge in the first place.

At Bain and Company, one of the most successful strategic planning consulting firms, a central project database can be accessed by any consultant in the firm, no matter where he or she works. According to Bill Bain, the company's chairman, this "experience store" provides one of the firm's competitive advantages. Many other consulting firms have tried to create "experience stores," but have failed because they could never figure out how to properly capture and share experiences. Consultants have little incentive to do the extra work of summarizing the key knowledge gained for others to use if this work isn't built into the original project fee or time estimate.

Bain's answer is to assign a "librarian" independent of the project team to follow projects around. A librarian might book a several-hour plane flight just to travel with a project manager so he/she can conduct an interview to capture and properly catalog the right ideas. Like NEC and IBM, Bain is an example of top management at a company recognizing that knowledge transfer is a key global success factor and doing something about it.

Video is becoming an increasingly popular medium for transferring knowledge. Companies like IBM, DEC, and EDS have established satellite facilities to broadcast training materials, product announcements, and news items to a broad cross-section of their employees. Perhaps the greatest technical advance to date in knowledge transfer can be found in multimedia workstations that incorporate interactive video disk. These systems, with their self-paced instruction, are allowing companies to update thousands of workers on a monthly, weekly, and even daily basis on changes in products, services, and systems.

Promoting Creativity and Problem Solving

In an Operations Management course at Harvard Business School, students are learning an important lesson about overcoming pride of authorship. The students are split into a number of teams, then compete in a semester-long project to see which can first complete the construction of a computer-simulated robot that can execute a required series of tasks.

As Professor Jai Jaikumar describes the game, he delights in saying that the assignment is so difficult that no team has ever been able to successfully finish the project by isolating themselves from their classmate competitors. To further complicate the exercise, he passes out a fixed amount of fake money to each team and encourages the competing teams to sell their innovations to each other.*

As the game progresses, important lessons emerge. Teams that get behind begin to realize that by forming a strategic alliance to acquire new knowledge they can improve their position, albeit at the cost of important

* Professor Jai Jaikumar, conversation with author, 1989.

scarce monetary assets or by giving up some aspect of their own proprietary intellectual capital. As a result of the development of a rapidly expanding market for new ideas, teams that were once ahead soon find that competitors, and sometimes consortiums of competitors, catch up to them or even pass them by.

The initial leaders often find they can't continue going it alone and remain competitive by developing everything themselves. One major aspect of the game, therefore, as teams learn to establish the value of their own as well as their competitors' intellectual capital, is the importance of collaborating and creating partnerships to push the frontiers of a company's knowledge.

In 1984, as the microcomputer market was taking off in Europe, several companies spotted the global opportunity and began to rapidly expand marketing operations by forming alliances with distributors and major retailers. In France, where the major consumer-electronics retailers were highly concentrated, supplier competition was fierce from day one. If one of the best retailers took a product on early, the market was virtually made for a supplier. However, since microcomputer products were relatively new and varied, the major retailers only wanted to take on a few. The competition among suppliers was intense. One marketing manager recounts:

"We were just beginning our growth period in international sales, and we had a lot to learn, but we knew we had to move fast in France before the market was saturated. We were close to securing a deal with one of the best retailers when they asked us if we would participate in initial promotional activities to introduce the product. Of course, we said yes. They then suggested that a live broadcast demonstration from the Eiffel Tower would be the most effective way to take the customer's breath away. It took our breath away too. We had no idea what technical complications we would hit, broadcasting and demonstrating halfway up the tower. Minutes before the broadcast, our technicians were still working at it. At 30 seconds to go, suddenly the large screens lit up and there was a big beautiful color display: on-line and live. What adrenalin. But we delivered and we got the contract."

Not all flexible global resource tactics are planned, but the sustainable best are. This company pulled together resources from all over the company to bring about a single event in an unusual location that was critical to its global strategy. It broke down organizational barriers to get the task done. Since it was a young and flexible company, people learned from this experience and others that followed with increasing frequency. The company is now finding, as it operates in over 25 countries and has quadrupled in size and revenues, that the challenge of one-of-a-kind location-oriented events involves many shared responses, and the company has developed an effective multidisciplinary response process to rapidly deal with special "anyplace" requests.

Every sizable company has created functional, divisional, or national barriers within its organization. Some of these barriers may have been created and fortified for valuable reasons, such as to keep certain resources focused on specific issues without being distracted. The value of barriers usually diminishes with time, and high barriers almost always hold a company—or country—back.

You need to look behind the barriers to see why they exist. Determine if the barriers are helpful or mere justifications of dysfunctional behavior. Reasons for the perpetuation of barriers are important to consider, evaluate, and probe. The Chief Information Officer of a European food manufacturing company told us, "If you want to know where we are adding people in this company, it's at the intersection between functions. It's symptomatic of our functional organization that our systems don't integrate."

By redesigning the business processes in just the distribution end of this business, the company was able to eliminate over 200 jobs and deliver its products in half the time from its factories to its customers.

Sharing Breakthroughs and Lessons Learned

A fast-growing American high-technology company originally took a multi-local approach as it attempted to rapidly develop national organizations across Europe in the early 1980s. In each country the company entered, it first established a marketing team, supported by a finance and administration structure. As business grew, it added additional functions: customer service, public relations, and technical departments.

The country manager, usually a local national hired away from a competitor, was given considerable leeway on how to approach the market as long as he/she achieved sales revenue and profit targets. In each country, widely differing approaches were taken with local distributors, and the president of the company soon realized that the country organizations were making many of the same mistakes over and over again.

Even though most national organizations were attaining their individual revenue targets, it soon became painfully obvious that the lack of a consistent framework in approaching the market cost many millions of dollars in lost revenue.

Sharing breakthroughs and lessons learned is impossible if there is strict adherence to hierarchic organizational principles. Cross-functional communication, facilitating process flow, is essential. As companies move away from following chains of command toward more networked management, we find more and more businesses becoming obsessed with a global strategic thrust of improving process effectiveness and efficiency.

In the process of becoming global, a company learns what type of approach to the market and what presence is needed in which countries. By combining lessons learned and talents across barriers, economies of scale in production, knowledge, and creativity can be gained; business processes can be streamlined.

Needless to say, companies attempting to become global that insist on creating physical presence everywhere are reinventing the wheel needlessly. But similarly, companies that insist on recreating intangible assets, such as information and decision making, everywhere are also reinventing the wheel needlessly.

For example, rather than making every decision, senior management should be concerned with seeing that timely decision making is occurring globally, throughout the organization, and that these decisions are related to the company's overall aims.

Management of relevant, up-to-date information and dynamic communications are needed to keep the global business moving. To be able to make and facilitate decisions, the global communications system must be the best a company can afford. One source of cost reduction relates to an enormous intangible cost that plagues virtually every company attempting to become global—that of information overload.

Many sales-field forces have learned to circumvent the lag time in hierarchical decision making. They have learned that they have to take action before getting the authorization from headquarters.

This predicament is exacerbated in the global business arena. If you are in the field and a customer wants something—something you may have just figured out your company can provide for this particular customer—and your competition is in the waiting room, you are not going to tell the customer that you cannot make an offer.

This predicament creates two kinds of risks.

The first is the customer uncertainty that each person faces in business; you make a decision about what to offer the customer based on the best information you have and trust your own judgment. The risk is that your customer may not like what you offer, or that the competition will beat your offer.

The second risk is the organizational uncertainty a person faces internally in his/her company; you make a decision based on the best information and wait for the staff person in headquarters to relate your decision to company policy or strategy by giving a thumbs up or a thumbs down.

When the first risk must be addressed more quickly than the second can be addressed, the result is what some managers call organizational ambiguity and what others call, more bluntly, being "caught between a rock and a hard place."

Another important lag on the momentum of a company's communications is caused by the additional control activities associated with the data collection demanded by the hierarchical company. In addition to the one-of-a-kind situations businesses face all the time, many business events are similar to those faced yesterday or last week. What frequently happens in a situation where a business event occurs regularly is that management begins to collect more and more information about the event so that they can prevent things from going wrong. Policies and control procedures are established, forms are filled out, files are created, data is classified and, it is hoped, analyzed, and more files are created. There is an abundance of information, a small percentage of which may actually be needed if one were just looking at a one-time event.

The purpose of building these files and classifying the information about these events, though, should be to learn what works well in the process and what needs to be improved. Some companies have effective continuous improvement processes. These companies tend to operate with global communications concepts in mind. The companies that don't constantly try to learn from their repeatable experiences might as well not collect the data.

But what happens when these business policies and procedures and the generated data change slightly or even disappear? A third lag is created by just wading through the information that is irrelevant to get to the relevant information. Because information needs change over time and the old information is not managed out of the business, wasted information lies awash in every organization. We've found in our studies of information usage in large organizations that at least 50 percent of all management information flowing within these organizations is obsolete.

Taking Advantage of Opportunities for Leading-edge Thinking

Making resources available where they are needed is a matter of considering your business system as a whole. But viewing the business system from anywhere within its sphere of influence will give you added advantages. As decision making gets spread throughout the globally networked company, having knowledge and resources at the point where decisions are made is of primary importance.

Knowledge from another company may also provide opportunities for knowledge transfer that will reduce investments. Many future global managers are now acting as researchers, transferring among countries to learn methodologies and processes.

Successful companies are developing the capability to share assets across borders. For example:

- DEC has 250 programmers working in India, assigned to a U.S. project, who use a satellite communications link paid for by the state of Massachusetts to transfer their new developments to their manager in Maynard, Massachusetts.

- New York Life flies insurance claims from New York to its office in Castle Island, Ireland, where they are entered into a computer for access back in the United States. By taking advantage of a large pool of well-educated young people who need jobs and are willing to work, New York Life has found a way to offset the lack of similar skills in New York City.

- In the education sector, we've seen a high school science class in Texas tell a robot submarine in the Mediterranean Sea where to point a television camera, while looking at the picture broadcast via satellite to high school classrooms throughout the United States.

The critical aspect of resource allocation is the ability to pull together resources wherever and whenever they are required across functions, and to be able to coordinate those resources around a particular decision to act quickly. Getting the right resources to the right place at the right time is enhanced by the ability to gain closer relationships throughout the sphere of influence, with customers and business partners.

When Pratt and Whitney, a major provider of jet engines, realized that its market share was being eroded by competitors such as General Electric and Rolls Royce, it sought and found the reasons: slow and inattentive customer service. Major customers such as the U.S. Air Force and Japan Air Lines had shifted significant orders amounting to billions of dollars.

Pratt turned the situation around by lowering external barriers between the company and its customers. This was accomplished by lowering barriers inside the company.

Pratt provided JAL with its own customer-service center near Tokyo. The company got closer to Northwest Airlines by providing it with engineers to work in its maintenance-engineering department.

Employees who have experience working on a customer's premises can be valuable resources. They have the opportunity to bring the inside information they gain into their company and share it with colleagues. The value created by sharing this close knowledge of the customer across functional or geographic boundaries may result in more "customer say" in the design of new products, better tailored distribution methods, and marketing techniques more responsive to current customer issues.

While Pratt and Whitney was lowering external barriers, it was also changing its internal structure. Previously, if a customer requested a change in engine specifications, the engineer involved would have to submit "mountains of paper" though nine departments and a weekly committee meeting for approval. Today, the engineer makes the decision and needs only three signatures. Average response time has been reduced from 82 days to 10 days, and the request backlog has been cut by about 95 percent. By cutting back on barriers and functional rigidity, Pratt and Whitney has allowed workers to get closer to the customer. Market share is moving up.*

In some cases, providing access to your company's information technology in a customer's office accomplishes the same objective as locating an employee there much less expensively. Federal Express now installs terminals in customer's offices that enable the customer to order a pickup, track a package throughout its journey, and get acknowledgment when the package is delivered. This lowered barrier enables customers to bypass Federal Express's own service representatives—as helpful as they might be—to immediately initiate a transaction or access needed information. Such barrier-busting links are becoming more common, resulting in quicker response and higher customer satisfaction.

In the late 1970s, however, when companies like American Hospital Supply first began installing order-entry terminals in customer offices, skeptics said, "You can't give the customer access to that kind of information; they'll see how messed up our records are." While many similar high-potential benefit information system projects in other companies were scuttled by such protectionist thinking, lowering this barrier enabled AHS to quickly jump to a dominant position in its industry. Not surprisingly, customers liked the easy access to a supplier that was easy to do business with, and the increased visibility of the formerly barricaded data caused many messes to be quickly cleaned up.

Firestone recently installed direct computer-aided design (CAD) links into General Motors, Chrysler, and Ford, so that its designers could rapidly transfer drawings with the automobile companies' designers. In addition to receiving higher customer-satisfaction ratings, this design partnership with automakers for tire and suspension design has enabled Firestone to become the 100 percent supplier of tires for a number of models.

---

* Jeffrey L. Funk, "How Does Japan Do It?" *Production* (Aug. 1988).

Creating Synergies
and Capturing the Benefits

Breakthroughs in one area of a business may create real opportunities for doing business in a new way for another part of the business, or for the business as a whole.

For instance, McDonalds learned "how to squeeze a kitchen into nearly any space by watching its Japanese affiliate build restaurants in Tokyo, where real estate is scarce and expensive."* McDonalds has successfully applied these design techniques in locations in many countries where space is at a premium.

On another front, when McDonalds opened its first retail outlet in Russia on February 1, 1990, it was absolutely uncompromising in its quest to provide a consistent management culture and quality control, lessons it had learned by serving global customers elsewhere around the world.

Normally McDonalds relies on local independent food suppliers in each country to deliver to local franchisees while meeting global quality standards. Developing and nurturing a network of local suppliers is very important to McDonalds' corporate philosophy of partnering, and with fitting into the local culture.

But in Russia, McDonalds had to largely start up the food-supplier industry, along with processing and distribution. McDonalds' unusual implementation had to be carefully planned and orchestrated by a multidisciplinary team of experts drawn from North America and Europe. The team had to teach Russian suppliers such diverse skills as state-of-the-art potato planting and harvesting techniques, and how to process beef to meet McDonalds' exacting quality standards.

McDonalds' blend of consistent product and tailored value-added services makes it a powerful global competitor. It builds consistent employee behavior and appeals to customers on a global basis by sharing information around the world, throughout its sphere of influence, with customers, suppliers, and would-be suppliers.

At McDonalds, global consistency is laid out in a phone-book-thick operating manual that covers such topics as how to greet the customer, how the bathrooms must be cleaned, and the temperature of the oil used to fry potatoes.

* Lisa Bertagnoli, "McDonalds: Company of the Quarter Century," *Restaurants & Institutions* (Cahners Publishing Company, 1989).

Local entrepreneurs from all over the world are taught McDonalds' product- and service-quality principles at one of four Hamburger University sites. Yet considerable latitude is given to the franchisees in determining how services are tailored to each local market. These entrepreneurs feel it is a "perfect partnership," to be allowed to run their own business, yet to do so within a highly successful management and value system.* Partnerships are also a good source of economies. In September 1989 Scandinavian Air Systems (SAS) and Swissair announced plans to collaborate. "The two companies intend to coordinate many of their activities—data telecommunications, hotels, catering, fleet planning, sales and marketing, as well as aircraft maintenance and staff training—to make both more cost effective through economies of scale." They will also be more effective in the strength of the routes each brings to the table.†

This kind of synergy can lead to important economies of scale that represent the efficient use of knowledge, and the effective combination of resources within a company. The potential benefits of creating synergies include:

- Finding new, more integrated, ways of doing business
- Being able to institute constant improvements in processes
- Involving employees in company objectives

Companies that can integrate internal processes, invest in a wider base of diversity, and optimize that diversity to please customers will gain a competitive edge.

Creating the Global Virtual
Corporation: Rosenbluth Travel‡

During the decade of the 1980s, a young executive in the travel industry named Hal Rosenbluth had a vision. The fourth generation of Rosenbluths to head up the family-run business, Hal Rosenbluth believed it was possible to leverage information technology, personal service, concern for and listening to employees, and cooperation with companies around the world, whose leaders believed as he did, to form a global travel alliance—a virtual global corporation.

Already by 1980 the company founded by Marcus Rosenbluth in 1892 was a $40 million a year business that had been built on trust and personal ser-

---

* Lisa Bertagnoli, "McDonalds: Company of the Quarter Century," *Restaurants & Institutions* (Cahners Publishing Company, 1989).

† Robert Taylor, "SAS-Swissair partnership takes off," *Financial Times* (September 29, 1989).

‡ David Miller (CIO Rosenbluth Travel), interview with author, June 1991.

vice. Marcus Rosenbluth had started his Philadelphia business so Eastern European immigrants could bring their families to the United States; he set up a lay-away plan so people could give him small sums each week or month until $50 had been accumulated to buy a relative a steamship ticket to New York and a train ticket to Philadelphia.

Until airline deregulation, beginning in 1978, the role of a travel agent was limited essentially to issuing tickets. Most automated agencies were tied to one airline's computerized reservation system, which gave that airline a natural advantage.

Hal Rosenbluth joined the family business just as deregulation began, and after a period of moving around the corporate offices in the typical family-business training program, he took a position "in the trenches" as a reservation clerk for two years.

He quickly determined that the travel agency business was a new game, one where an executive who took advantage of telecommunications and computer power could break the stranglehold of the airlines and truly add value for customers, a time when "the company that could gather information faster and turn it into knowledge would win."

In 1981, convinced of the value travel agents could add for corporate customers, Rosenbluth pulled all corporate travel agents from its eight offices around the Philadelphia region and created the country's first corporate reservation center.

At this time, Rosenbluth also began investing heavily in technology. The company developed the READOUT program, which displayed flights by fare cost instead of time of departure.

Deregulation had put pressure on travel agents to help corporate clients cut costs. At first this was done by many travel agents "rebating" a portion of the commission paid by the carrier to the customer, or essentially sharing the commission.

But Rosenbluth was among the first travel agencies to realize that with the information link between suppliers and corporate customers, they could help their customers cut costs more significantly by helping them actively manage their travel. READOUT was one way of doing this, allowing companies to be cost sensitive in flight selection as well as time sensitive. Another was negotiated fares; while travel providers began offering corporate-wide discounts for specific events or meetings in the early 1980s, Rosenbluth sought to extend those discounts for its corporate customers.

In 1984, DuPont became Rosenbluth's first national account, and Rosenbluth was able to help DuPont work out negotiated fares with a number of air carriers for the company's most heavily traveled routes. DuPont alone was a corporation with a $100 million annual travel budget.

In 1986, Rosenbluth took a major step toward client-travel management when its management information system (MIS) department developed the VISION system, which captured a record of every customer transaction and stored it in a data base. While carrier computerized reservation systems (CRS) were still used to make travel arrangements, the carriers were no longer the only party to be able to consolidate customer records. In time, Rosenbluth also developed the capability to link VISION records with customers' internal records, such as expense reconciliation and accounting, saving customers more time and money.

When the Apollo CRS system added scripting capability, Rosenbluth jumped on the opportunity to create numerous proprietary applications for front-office sales and reservation processes under the name PRECISION. Sales agents were able to call up detailed information on corporate travel policies, as well as profiles of individual customer preferences with regard to seating, meals, cars, hotel accommodations, etc.

By 1990, Rosenbluth had become a $1.1 billion company with 300 U.S. offices.

In the mid 1980s, as Rosenbluth was experiencing explosive growth and finding new ways to add value for its national accounts, it was forced to ask and answer the question, "How can this be duplicated on a worldwide scale; how can we make our national accounts our global accounts?" The company had to find a way to accommodate individual travelers worldwide in English, and a way to provide local nationals of its global accounts with service in their individual national and regional markets, and in their own languages. It had to find a way to provide global MIS, to establish baselines for accounting consolidation, and to provide the kind of statistics and negotiations worldwide that generated savings for its U.S. clients.

The company looked at three options:

1. Acquire or start up operations in selected key markets worldwide. Rosenbluth rejected it because of the local nature of so much of the travel industry. To do this requires heavy local presence and cultural feel. Even global customers want and need strong cultural affinity with their travel providers market by market.

2. Participate in worldwide travel management consortium(s). Rosenbluth rejected this also; the company had participated in consortiums before that didn't seem to work out.

3. Rosenbluth decided to create a global strategic business alliance, the Rosenbluth International Alliance (RIA). RIA is a virtual corporation, a group of philosophically attuned independent travel providers which pool their resources to provide global travel services to corporate accounts, while maintaining their unique local and cultural feel and their own client base for individual and family travel.

RIA met for the first time in London in 1988, and established a world-wide management headquarters there. The alliance has a staff, in London, Philadelphia, and Singapore, totaling less than ten people.

RIA's business principles include (1) strategy and plans established by the entire partnership, (2) decision making by consensus whenever possible, otherwise by majority, (3) one company, one vote regardless of size of company, (4) RIA budget funded by companies based on size of company, (5) aggressive cross-selling of services/products on a multilateral basis, and (6) local RIA company given right of first refusal on any multinational proposal sponsored by another partner company.

In addition, Rosenbluth *gave* each member all of its proprietary software.

Criteria for partnership in RIA includes a strong commitment to service, a long history of financial health, a well-trained and respected leadership and staff, a commitment to technology, and a general corporate-cultural compatibility.

In 1991 RIA had 34 partner companies with over 1100 offices in 37 countries, and gross sales of U.S. $5 billion.

The alliance offers a single contract worldwide, unified product definitions, and global forms of payment.

By creating a vision of product, service, commitment to employees and by the use of technology, Rosenbluth travel has been able to create the travel agency of the twenty-first century. And by realizing that, although the world is becoming ever smaller and the global business traveler becoming ever more universal in needs and desires, a single travel agency cannot provide everything for everyone, Rosenbluth has created a model for global service in the twenty-first century, the virtual corporation. The virtual corporation allows companies around the world to share ideas and knowledge, and to provide local feel and cultural context to their individual customers, while providing the critical mass to enjoy economy scales.

Product Development:
A Place to Begin

A company should begin to transform business functions to global business processes by focusing on product development. Companies that can manage their product-development effort globally have an advantage in carrying out global business.

First, the product-development team becomes energized by being more attuned to the market and more able to create and develop world-class products. Second, the rest of the organization will follow this process because product development has an effect on every function in the company, and can bring the rest of the functions closer to the customer. Further, employees can see the results of their efforts in the products and services developed, which creates a powerful organizational momentum.

Companies that share design and engineering information globally have begun to figure out what it takes to work as an integrated system. They are not only sharing ideas across the company, but also plan their worldwide development of products by looking at the whole of the company's capabilities. The stage of globalization of product-development is often a leading indicator of the fundamental switch from the company being a global exporter, multinational, or multilocal company to becoming a truly global corporation.

The benefits of global product development include:

1. Understanding more broadly what specific local market requirements need to be accommodated in the design

2. Having the ability to understand and test products globally or in different markets and under different conditions

3. Establishing much greater consistency and greater flexibility in the product/service architecture and business processes

4. Designing the product/service to be easier to support and enhance

5. Reducing product-development time by leveraging innovation in all parts of the company, from concept through market introduction to product enhancement

Summary

Achieving global/local balance requires the ability to dynamically monitor global business, to identify which aspects of the corporation need to be globally planned for and managed on a worldwide basis, and to develop ways to carry out global strategic initiatives. Top management has the responsibility to create this superordinate organizational design. Successful companies attempting to go global identify strategic alliance partners to fill in the gaps in their base capabilities and look for opportunities to pool resources with business partners. The ability to rapidly transfer knowledge is another critical success factor. A company can begin to transform traditional business functions into global business functions by focusing on product development.

Action Checklist

1. Is top management focusing efforts on creating the global organizational design?

2. How many means of monitoring global business activity does your firm have? How widely shared is this global intelligence information?

3. Have you defined your firm's core activities? Have you identified partners to perform noncore activities?

4. Does your firm have globally accessible knowledge repositories?

5. Do you create partnerships with other companies (perhaps even competitors) to push the frontiers of the company's knowledge?

6. How broadly do you leverage the value of breakthroughs in one part of the business elsewhere in the business?

5

Building Global Teams and Individuals

There is a stereotypical American manager of the postwar years who has since gone out of favor in Europe. He flies in from the United States on the red-eye, freshens up in his hotel for several hours, then holds his first European staff meeting.

"Tell me about your three top problems, and what you plan to do about them," he says, lighting up a cigar and putting his feet up on the conference table.

Each of the eight managers in the room presents his carefully prepared 20-minute briefing, which describes the situation in his or her country. When they are all done, the American sighs. "You know, I've seen this movie before, and I know how it ends," he says. "What you each are planning to do just isn't going to work. So let me tell you what I want you to do." Then he proceeds to present the action plan he developed at corporate headquarters the previous week.

Some managers have to overcome a handicap of inbred arrogance that leads to national chauvinism. They were brought up thinking that their countries, with the highest standard of living, and with the best colleges and graduate schools, must consequently have the brightest managers. They were brought up to believe that, while you might learn a lot about culture in other countries, there really isn't anything to learn from any other country about business. They were brought up in multinational companies to sell and control.

The problem is not unique to Americans, however. When you visit Japan today, you detect a similar underlying arrogance in many senior managers. It comes across as, "We're better than you, because we take quality and service seriously. We know how to work in cross-functional teams. We work harder and save more, and we don't waste our money buying frivolous things." Often, when Japanese global exporters move parts of their business to the United States or Europe, they keep a Japanese manager in charge to ensure their high standards are upheld and values instilled.

In Europe, hundreds of years of national rivalry and the development of separate languages and cultures make it difficult for people to expect cooperation across borders. The multilocal business form is, in part, an organizational response to minimize conflict. Only a few highly trusted managers, at the very top of each national organization, have to get together to sort out business issues and policy.

Before a company can become global, management's role must transform in significant ways. Essentially, global managers have to become connectors and facilitators rather than controllers; they must become part of a team that emphasizes cooperation across borders throughout the company, be sensitive to the cultural dynamics within the markets the company serves, and help the company cultivate a richer internal culture.

Possibly the most important aspect of a global manager's job is to instill in every employee he or she works with the desire to delight the customers and help the business prosper. This means treating employees with dignity and respect, allowing them to influence the work they do, really listening to them when they make suggestions, and taking their local cultural concerns into account.

As Hal Rosenbluth, president of Rosenbluth Travel says, "Clients can only be first to the associate employee if the associate is first to the company." Rosenbluth wants every employee in his company to constantly ask himself or herself the question, "How can this particular piece of work be done better?" And Rosenbluth demands that each manager listen closely and follow up on suggestions when associates come up with answers to that question.

A story about a match company in Europe illustrates this point beautifully.

The company, which made boxes of matches with strips of striking material on either side and a picture of some sort on the top, was so desperate to cut costs it offered a prize to any employee who could think of a major cost-cutting method.

At first, there were very few replies. Then, the vice president of marketing realized that to provide an incentive for this exercise in resourcefulness, the employees would have to have some idea that the prize was substantial. He issued a memo and had it tacked to every bulletin board. It read:

"The contributor of a substantial cost savings idea will be awarded 10 percent of the cost savings."

Simple, a soon-to-be rich employee said. Just coat one side of the box with the striking material instead of two. That change resulted in hundreds of thousands of dollars saved each year.

Putting aside the issue of how ideas and creativity are rewarded for a moment, employees must be made to feel that it is important to them to communicate improvements. Time after time, companies have found that if employees don't feel they will share in productivity gains and process improvements—either with greater pay or "gainsharing" of some kind, they will simply keep these improvements to themselves, making their work easier.

Managing individual knowledge contributions is especially important in the global corporation, where the reliance of various parts of the company on each individual for knowledge is high. The way employees in a global corporation communicate has a major effect on how knowledge is shared and resources are combined, and can have a substantial impact on business performance. Through better knowledge transfer, a proper system of incentives, and cross-functional integration, global companies can increase their value-adding potential among various activities.

Creating teams emphasizing process improvement helps to build bonds among employees from various positions in the global company. Japanese companies have an edge here on U.S. and European businesses because they tend to coordinate better cross-functionally. The Japanese companies' low functional barriers allow them to combine expertise to solve process issues. This coordination, along with direct communication, ultimately reduces the number of steps required to solve process issues and to take action.

This, in turn, reduces costs and increases revenues, since resources are more flexible and people react more quickly to changes in market conditions. Problem solving and innovation are cultivated, and ideas can be put into practice almost immediately. While Japanese companies continually attack functional barriers, many U.S. companies treat how the product is made or service is performed with secondary importance.

The global team comes together for the purpose of tapping specific expertise distributed around the company or its business partners, putting the product through its paces, identifying problems, and finding solutions. People who work on these teams constantly remark about how much they learn through collaborating with colleagues and sharing information, as well as how much fun they have on these assignments. One described how she came to more fully understand the scope of what her company was trying to do when she worked on a specific project.

"There we were, engineers from five different locations scattered around the world, all working on the same project. It was a real global village. When we weren't physically located together, we found ways of communicating through teleconferencing, computer conferencing, fax, and phone. Over time, everyone on the team developed a deep appreciation for what the other players on the team could do, and whether we liked each other equally personally or not, I think all of us grew to realize that

every other person on the team shared a similar intense interest in our project's success."

Implementing cross-functional projects at every level of the organization
increases global learning rapidly. While today's communication networks
enable multidisciplinary representatives within a company to rapidly and
easily cross barriers whenever they need to discuss business issues, it takes a
shared mission and common experience to bind people together.

By creating cross-functional and cross-geographic task forces that meet
for a specific purpose within the overall strategic framework of the business,
companies can gain experience working toward lowering barriers. Executive, management, and operational workers gain expertise and experience
as the activities on which they work cross barriers. These experiences contribute to the creation of a new global culture within the company and
develop a wider breadth of peripheral vision in employees.

Richard Nolan and Robert Eccles of Harvard Business School call the
process by which nonmanagement employees constantly work to create better work processes and "do things better" self-design. Nolan and Eccles
comment:*

"The distinction between superordinate design and self-design should
not be confused with the concepts of centralization and decentralization.
Superordinate design is not the same thing as centralized decisions, despite
the fact that it is a senior management responsibility and some decisions
must be made in executing it. But the primary purpose of superordinate
design is to provide resources, tools, and processes which knowledge workers can use in making decisions.

"Nor is self-design decentralized decision making, even though knowledge workers are responsible for making an increasing number of decisions.
The purpose of self-design is to take action that shapes the organization in
whatever ways are necessary to take and execute decisions."

They break the self-design concept into three components: structure, systems, and strategy.

In terms of structure, Nolan and Eccles point out correctly that the "networked" organization we speak about so often in this book does not really
replace the hierarchical structure, but rather supplements it to accomplish
actual work processes. Superordinate design issues are dealt with at the
highest levels of the hierarchical structure, and there must be some reporting hierarchy to draw the boundaries of business. But within boundaries
the network takes over. The result, Eccles and Nolan point out, is "relationships which form and dissolve once the task or project is done. The
network structure is thus designed by anyone who needs to get things

* Eccles and Nolan, "Framework for Design."

done, whatever their level in the functional hierarchy. Because the overall network structure is an aggregation of many local networks, it is extremely complex and constantly shifting—a static hierarchical structure is not replaced by a static network structure. No one person, whatever their level in the organization, has a total picture of what the network structure looks like. And because it is constantly changing, it is as much a process as it is a structure."

While structures have always been fairly simple to change, the systems that reflected those structures were, until recently, cumbersome and slow to change. But today, with enhanced desktop computing, data base availability, and telecommunications, individuals within the network can recreate systems to provide useful business information almost at will, without the intervention of financial and systems analysts. The technology also makes it possible for individuals to share their newly created systems within the network if they have wider applicability.

Finally, in the networked organization with good superordinate design and vision from senior management, employees at every level of the organization have a new role to play in strategy. No longer do they merely implement a strategic plan worked out at the top; they can now create and implement microstrategies that help them perform their tasks, get and stay close to their customers and understand their customers' needs, and finally meet those needs.

As Eccles and Nolan write, "This 'grass-roots' strategy formulation process utilizes the core competencies and expertise, shared knowledge and data bases, and resource allocation components of the infrastructure. Thus, although senior management is responsible for establishing the broad parameters within which the strategy formulation process takes place, it is self-designed by the same people who implement it."*

Create and Nurture
a Shared Company Culture

In order to move a company from a set of discreet national parts to an integrated global business—in order for employees within the network to feel comfortable initiating self-design throughout the global organization—management needs to nurture a shared corporate culture. And in order to nurture a shared global culture, a company needs a shared global vision, as well as a sense of how that vision will be achieved from the company's current position.

* Eccles and Nolan, "Framework for Design."

A shared culture means that the organization has shared beliefs, attitudes, values, and expectations wherever it chooses to do business. As the corporate culture develops and strengthens on a global basis, the consistency of the many parts of the business will create a kind of corporate DNA that employees, business partners, and customers all will be able to identify, recognize, and relate to the company.

These expectations, shared among employees about what the business values and how it operates, drives the consistent way the company treats its customers, vendors, and other business partners.

To nurture a shared company culture, management needs to (1) keep mixing the cultural stew and (2) motivate positive cultural change.

Keep Mixing the Cultural Stew

A company that rarely rotates its staff tends to breed ethnocentric managers. The more rotation the more new cultural strains can be mixed into the overall corporate culture.

This rotation should be from any point within the network to any other point. It doesn't help global progress very much to just send Americans or Japanese overseas from headquarters.

Citibank's unique culture reflects the ethnic diversity that can be found in each of its major branches around the world. You are as likely to find an Argentine in London, Milan, or Singapore as you are to find an American.

If you are a Citibank employee providing a financial product for your customer and you are going to do business with another office, there is a shared understanding of how particular activities should occur. There is a well-worn cultural path for communicating, making decisions, and carrying them out.

If you are a Citibank customer, you have an expectation of a certain level of quality before you walk in the door. You also have an expectation of how the business will interact with you. As one corporate customer put it:

"When you walk into the London office of Citibank, you see a diverse cultural mix of employees that are working together on consistent Citibank products. The particular product offerings may be different from country to country, but the Citibank culture pervades all of the product offerings. It's the same in any of their international offices. It's a quality I've come to rely on. I don't have to relearn their business organization when I move from country to country, and that is of high value to me, especially when I want something done quickly."

Motivate Positive Cultural Change

Kyocera, widely respected for being one of Japan's most innovative and entrepreneurial companies, began operating in the United States in 1971.

From the outset, Kazuo Inamori, Kyocera's strong-willed chairman, insisted that every employee understand and practice the company's philosophy.

While regular exercise and Japanese uniforms are part of the cultural trimmings, the more fundamental aspects of the shared culture have to do with an individual's involvement with work and with his or her care for product quality.

Each individual is motivated with incentives to act as an incubator of the new ideas they have in order to make their work process better. The ability to generate these new ideas is linked with increasing job responsibility.

Mavericks are made at home in Kyocera. They point out the new directions, but are also responsible for communicating how these fit into, or change, the company's vision and objectives for the better.

Finding the true economies of scale in your business requires imagination. For example, the way resources are combined affects the attitude or spirit of the company, an invaluable asset. If a company tampers with employees' attitudes, it may fail to motivate each individual to contribute to the business' overall performance, and thus fail to capture important economies of scale.

A leading paper-producing company decided to move all production of its leading-edge product line to one factory in one country, grouping all of the declining and outmoded product production to another country. Management did its sums, and decided that using each plant consistently to produce one product line would enhance productivity.

Although the older products were in decline, they still contributed in a very substantial way to the company's revenues. The change, as perceived by employees, created a detrimental barrier between the two production teams. Employees put on the old-product plant felt demotivated, while employees on the new-product plant felt cut off from the company's historical experience.

While in the past the company could rely on the production teams' flexibility in developing new world-class process technologies and problem-solving techniques together, management now found a reluctance to cooperate, and production slowed in both plants.

The company had to take a step backward to improve morale by spreading the development of new product lines over the two plants so employees could again find their jobs interesting.

Create an Organization That Is Obsessed with Something

Goals can focus employees' attention on the shared aspects of the global corporate culture. At Federal Express, Fred Smith and his management team have created an organization that is obsessed with the timely delivery of packages. They have set a goal of achieving 100 percent service performance day-in and day-out, which helps define the company's globally customer-focused corporate culture.

Today, while delivering over one million packages a day in over 100 different countries, the company delivers over 98 percent on time. This far exceeds the service standard in Federal Express' industry, and is one of the reasons the company has gained over 45 percent of the domestic market in the United States and is aggressively moving into European and Asian markets.

Federal Express makes a commitment to its customers that if it hasn't been able to track a package through its entire journey, the customer gets his or her money back.

There is a story about a Federal Express communications technician working at the airport at the company's Memphis, Tennessee, hub, who realized in the middle of the night that a microwave relay tower, key to the company's communication network, had a defective part. Without checking for authorization, he used his own initiative to rent a helicopter so he could get to the remote location quickly and make the repair. Keeping the network up at any cost was part of the shared corporate culture nurtured in him by the formalized Federal Express quality-consciousness program. This employee was able to take an initiative because he could interpret how the company would want him to react in a situation for which there was no policy.

Federal Express makes a major commitment to keeping every employee "on-line" to meet customer- and employee-information needs by giving them all access to the company's worldwide computer network, and also keeps its employees up-to-date through an in-house television network. In addition, Federal Express has over 3000 state-of-the-art multimedia workstations installed for the purpose of providing interactive instruction to its employees on service and quality methods. This investment in information technology is part of the way Federal Express has built an organization that shares global values, and one in which each employee feels that he or she is a vital link in the overall global chain of business.

Build Trust, Build Trust, Build Trust

One of the benefits of establishing a shared global culture is that your company doesn't have to spend an excess amount of time achieving "buy-in" or agreement from every part of the organization that has to cooperate to perform a global activity.

Achieving buy-in is a time devourer. We've seen it over and over again, companies caught up in iterative loops of buy-in. Making a decision is a tough process, but it is tougher if you have to sell everyone in the company on what you are going to do every time you want to make a move.

A pan-European downstream division of a major international oil company with whom we worked is typical. It developed a strategy for the future that required a major restructuring of its business in retail outlets to reorient process to be more integrated, and to be much more customer focused. The team rearchitecting the business spent five months of well-coordinated hard work at the grass-roots level building new organizational blueprints, designing cross-functional processes, and developing plans for the implementation.

When the global roadmap was on the table, ready for implementation, management and operational-level employees who had participated in the project—about one-tenth of the company—were enthusiastic. The company's senior executive team considered this first phase of the project a major success in pointing the way toward the reorientation of perspectives and capabilities of the company, and gave the go-ahead for the next phase.

Then came the slowdown. The project champion, who was told to first sell the plan to each of the major functional departments on a country-by-country basis, found pockets of resistance cropping up all over the organization. "You don't understand, we're different here," was heard repeatedly. It was not until six months later that sufficient company-wide management buy-in had been achieved and the project could begin moving again.

A senior executive at the time expressed frustration when he said, "We are developing a global culture, but we are a consensus-driven organization. This means that we talk over everything we are going to do ad infinitum. Usually, after talking about it all, we lose the energy to do anything. It's a shame, because there's a lot of good thinking going on; but we don't do enough. Five months to define a new, more responsive organization, then six months to establish buy-in. We're drowning in consensus. Buy-in is killing us. Our major competitors started a similar design well after we did, but they may beat us on the implementation because they have the ability to act across boundaries."

Many multilocal companies are obsessed with establishing consensus within each management team of each country before taking action. While these companies experience delays caused by over-communicating issues, more centrally controlled global exporters and multinationals suffer from another form of delay. These companies, trying to enforce their global reach from their headquarters every time decisions are taken, are hidebound. Wasting time going back and forth from headquarters with plans and decisions when networks of competent decision makers reside locally is a foolish extravagance.

Trust has to exist on an individual level. It is not possible to pay lip service to trust, to say, "We will trust other nodes in our network," and then just expect the network to work. Each individual in a company has to believe that he or she is truly empowered to act. Similarly, each individual has to develop a sense of understanding and responsibility for the efforts of others and work with them to cooperatively produce results, rather than constantly sabotaging their efforts for the sake of parochial interests. Individuals who accept this responsibility are global individuals.

A company with networks built on a base of trust allows more people in the company to make decisions and does everything faster. Many companies now expanding their activities in Europe to take advantage of European Community 1992 developments, or into the Asia Pacific region to take advantage of rising affluence, are learning how to empower their executives on the scene so that they can make quick decisions on market and supply developments. There are a number of ways to build trust that will add value to your business processes, among them are the following five:

Push Down Decision Making

The image a company projects is a driving factor in establishing its global competitive edge. Part of this image is transmitted by a company's ability to delegate decisions making. More and more, companies are realizing they have to push down decision making and empower employees outside of headquarters' locations to make decisions that move their companies ahead.

One of the major issues preoccupying the senior executives of several high technology companies today is how to empower their sales managers in their local, regional, and national offices to make appropriate discounting decisions on bids. The corporate marketing plan carefully lays out overall pricing policy as, among other factors, a function of projected sales volume and profit targets.

Typically, a range of discounts will be available for a customer, depending on such tangible factors as the volume of product ordered, and intangible factors such as how competitive the situation is. Historically, these companies have found that their individual salespeople, who are usually rewarded by commissions on sales, always try to give the biggest possible discount so they can maximize the chance of getting the order. If every customer gets the biggest discount possible, however, major profit erosion takes place and volumes have to increase.

The challenge for these companies is to get the sales managers in the field to understand the rationale behind these tradeoffs and to act responsibly without constantly sending queries and decisions up and down the chain of command. Up to now, regional executives have been reluctant to delegate such decision making to lower levels because they don't believe "the local branch managers will understand the big picture."

Yet these same executives painfully realize that the up-and-down activity takes so much time it often makes their companies appear unresponsive to global customer requirements. One suggestion being tried by at least one company in the industry is to change the performance measurement system at the branch level from revenue generation to profit generation. Only time will tell if this is the right approach.

Every company that is trying to do business globally faces this issue of trust and empowerment. Companies have to find ways to encourage employees to make decisions, to rely on other employees in the company to exercise judgment, to represent the company positively, and to act in the company's best interests. Without trust, there can be no enterprise.

Once people are given responsibility and accountability for certain activities, organizations have to allow them to make decisions. In the global corporation, there will necessarily be many more decision makers.

"To build trust, we need to bring skill power, resource power, and decision power closer to the customer wherever we operate,"* observes David Hancock, a senior marketing executive of Apple Computer Corporation.

Building trust takes time and lots of practice. Top management must set the example at the highest levels of the organization by trusting each other and their direct subordinates. If they appear to be fighting, the rest of the organization will be fighting for the same issues as their champions.

Create Programs to Share
Experiences Cross-culturally

One company we work with has a unique initiation program for new managers from around the world. They are brought together for a week-long orientation. During the morning of the first day, each individual is given the Canadian Mountie Survival Examination. This written exam asks the person to imagine himself or herself as one of 12 survivors of a plane crash in the mountains of Canada.

It is cold and snowing. There are a number of objects around that one is able to use: a lighter, a flare, canned food, etc.

The question is, "Should you stay with the plane or try to walk to a settlement you are told is ten miles away in an unknown direction?" You have to choose whether to stay with the plane or, if you go, in which direction you should go, as well as which objects you consider the most important for survival. In a typical orientation, 120 managers take the test.

In the afternoon, teams of 12 people each are formed and the same questions are put to them. The team has to come up with a solution. People are

* David Hancock, interview with author, spring 1988.

told not to acquiesce, but to work through each issue. The ten teams debate the objects, and whether to stay with the plane or leave, for about three and one-half hours, after which there are some very tired people. It is a fascinating process.

At the end of the day, the managers break for cocktails before the results are announced. Conversation drifts around subjects such as the team, "natural leaders," changing opinions, and how the process allows people to get to know each other quickly. Then the results are shared.

Of the 120 people, not many survived successfully on their own, and not one of them had all of the correct answers. Yet of the 10 teams, nearly all survived. The test is coupled with talks about culture and job security, and two days in which the managers are asked to solve actual corporate problems together.

Many companies use Outward Bound or other shared experiences to build trust in management teams. Companies bring employees from many areas of the company to experience working together on cross-geographic and cross-functional issue. By building trust, employees form networks they will use in the course of business, and gain experience working on process issues. They also develop awareness of other employees and their capabilities, which enhances and speeds up the communication process.

Giving multiple geographic units responsibility for different aspects of a global project builds trust and nurtures the shared culture. KPMG has a unique structure, since every national organization is a separate firm. Its national partners-in-charge have to work hard to keep various worldwide practice and industry networks transferring information to each other. When client projects cross national borders, however, KPMG uses these opportunities to get various units working with each other, because these projects are vehicles for building cooperation and pride.

Bonds form through experience. The only person who can tell you to trust someone is someone with whom you already have a bond. An open mind and first-hand experience in trusted relationships are the essential ingredients individuals require to build a network of trust. Trust moves individuals away from the sole-survivor or pride-of-authorship approach to a more shared approach for doing business.

Create Mutuality of Interest

In most companies today, performance measurement systems inhibit global behavior rather than build trust. Many companies pay bonuses and commissions to their salespeople, based primarily on performance targets set for national profit centers. Often, when someone sells products and services outside his or her territory, it doesn't count for the unit's goals. And when someone outside the territory sells to a customer inside the territory, people in the territory don't want to service the account because they may not get any revenue credit for providing the service.

Royal Trust Company management uses a concept called "mutuality of interest" to motivate global behavior in all of its employees as it expands outside its Canadian base. Mutuality of interest means that every employee shares in the profits of the overall company as opposed to the profits of the specific operating or geographic unit they work in. Through this global incentive program, employees are encouraged to partner with each other to meet the needs of the company's clients instead of fighting over who gets what commissions.

Goodyear motivates global behavior in its employees by making 50 percent of each individual's personal performance plan dependent on global performance measures.

Encourage Worldwide Meetings

Pulling together a team around a strategic initiative allows people to work together in positive ways that build relationships throughout the company. Apple Computer has a tradition of holding a series of annual worldwide functional meetings in places like Hawaii and Palm Springs. These meetings bring together the top 150 people in manufacturing, finance, information systems, and human resources, and are designed to be a combination of a management development program, technical training program, and functional planning session.

They also serve the purpose of global team building. In addition to having plenty of time for small-group discussion and problem solving, every day of the three-day program emphasizes group recreational activities like volley ball, skin diving trips, and luaus, where people from different parts of the world can really get to know each other. Apple complements these functional sessions with annual cross-functional meetings for its top 200 managers.

While the cost of all these meetings is significant, it is one method Apple uses to keep fending off the encroaching bureaucracy of a large organization. These meetings help Apple managers better understand the various people in their network and encourage point-to-point communications.

Take Advantage of a Crisis
to Bring People Together

Crises in business sometimes serve the same end of bringing people together. During a strike in the early 1980s in Europe, the management of a manufacturing company took turns patrolling the grounds and securing the factory. Marketing and manufacturing managers alike were assigned in teams to patrol these areas for hours. The rivalry between the two divisions was well known. It was the first time these two sets of managers, aside from the heads of their departments, had had an opportunity to share issues by working together.

During the few weeks of the strike, however, they were able to share experiences about the company's processes, from sales orders to production and delivery, which they had previously viewed only from their narrow functional perspectives. A new appreciation of each other's viewpoint developed, and within days after the strike was over they began to coordinate their priority actions to deliver their product significantly more quickly.

Crises sometimes work so well in getting people to work together that some CEOs even invent a crisis when none exists and business is booming. Tom Watson, Sr., of IBM, was notorious for his effective use of this tactic. You can only cry wolf so often, however, and even the best managers should be wary before attempting this.

The bond created by shared team experience is not a contract laid down by decision makers upon doers; rather it grows out of relationships formed when people are actively involved in achieving common goals. Trust is more than a two-way street; it is more like the critical joining of a multi-boulevard complex toward which traffic rushes from many directions and then continues onward with hardly diminished flow.

Global Management

Managers who would prefer to control all of the activities of people working for them must change their orientation in the global company. As Shoshana Zuboff writes:

"The traditional system of imperative control, which was designed to maximize the relationship between commands and obedience, depended upon restricted hierarchical access to knowledge and nurtured the belief that those who were excluded from the organization's explicit knowledge base were intrinsically less capable of learning what it had to offer."*

The global company, designed to maximize relationships among workers, must have managers who encourage and facilitate the sharing of appropriate knowledge. The relationships among workers depend on cooperation and gaining access to each other's knowledge. Managers must ensure that the communication gateways are kept open to allow people to act. Managers must change their roles from controllers to connectors and facilitators.

Without exception, managers resist change more than operational workers. The reason for this is that managers feel threatened by a potential loss of status and control over the work environment. These values and percep-

---

* Shoshana Zuboff, *In the Age of the Smart Machine* (Basic Books, 1988), 394.

tions of managers must change. The way to accomplish this change is by creating a powerful set of learning experiences for managers that educates them on their new roles.

In the global company, the dependence on individual workers increases because the worker is a direct representative of the company in face-to-face situations with customers, business partners, and regulatory bodies. The company's reliance on any individual to make a decision and carry it out will be higher, while supervision will be less practical and affordable. In turn, the dependence of individuals on good managers will be higher because every employee will require more knowledge, more resources, and more coordination with other workers.

Key global connections that require management are (1) the company's global objectives and daily employee activity, (2) cross-cultural activity, (3) activities between multiple centers of expertise, and (4) understanding and exploring the effects that decisions will have on the global company as a whole.

Global managers must act as conduits through which the organization discovers its potential. While policies do not necessarily need to be set centrally, they do need to be well coordinated throughout the company. While any given policy is set by a few people, coordinating actions to get the job done involves almost everyone.

Building a better management climate takes time. A good management climate requires good leadership, clear objectives, excellent communication and information systems, shared performance incentives that gain employee commitment and reward problem solving, and a process focus. As competition increases for educated and highly skilled workers, these workers will less and less accept being treated as unfeeling commodities. Managers must win the loyalty of their employees by inspiring them, encouraging their willingness to find solutions, and providing meaningful work in a pleasant working environment.

Allocating adequate global resources to get the job done is a crucial management issue in global companies. It will be a challenge to cost-justify investments in such knowledge infrastructure resources as information technology workstations, research libraries, and training. It will not be good enough to merely get the least expensive resources to do the job. You will have to try to get resources that will motivate your employees to do the best job. If your employees are starved for adequate resources needed to do the job, they will know it, and the psychological contract between the company and the worker will go sour.

The human resource function in the global company is to become human-capital developers and process designers. Human resources is no longer an area for complacent managers who only want to count heads and describe benefits. Human resources' staff will have to understand the work processes of the business well enough to know the kinds of skills and judgment employees will need to carry out business.

Human resource managers must also be risk takers. They must cultivate people with diverse points of view and facilitate the cooperative process. There is no place in the global corporation for human resource people who have not had cross-disciplinary experience. In some ways, these people are barriers to progress, and to cultivating a leading-edge view of how people can work in creative and productive ways. Human resource managers must be knowledgeable in the work process flow and in how worker activity relates to process improvement.

Managers must also encourage informal communications and casual learning. Managers will have to know what the work process entails and support workers in their efforts to solve problems. In most companies, some of the most informative places in the work environment have tended to be hallways, parking lots, cafeterias, and restrooms. Informal communication abounds in such places.

In the global company, managers must create the same kind of informal communication environment for people working in different countries—the telecommunications equivalent of the water bubbler.

Ken Olsen, founder and former Chairman of DEC, likes to speak about the two communication networks within his company, the formal and the informal. In the formal network, official communications flow through the hierarchies of DEC just as they would in any other company. In the informal network, which incidentally uses the same physical communication facilities, employees are encouraged to communicate directly with any other employee. Olsen takes great pleasure in describing how he gets up to 20 informal messages a day from employees anyplace in the company, to whom he responds directly.

Empower Global
Knowledge Workers

Electrolux is a company reaching a critical juncture in global growth. After acquiring several businesses and diversifying in the late 1970s and throughout the 1980s, the company finds itself facing the decision of how to carry on growth at its high rate.

According to the Financial Times, two proposed alternatives are being offered: either the central staff is enlarged to allow close monitoring of each business area, or the business areas are given more autonomy to develop business as they see it.

Anders Scharp, Electrolux's CEO, wants to preserve a traditional principle of centralized strategy/decentralized operations, with strategic supervision in his hands and financial control in the hands of the CFO. However, the rapid pace of the business doesn't allow time for committee debates before each decision.*

Sooner or later, Electrolux will have to increase the autonomy of all employees, who will need to be able to make global decisions. Increasing the autonomy of global employees can enhance their motivation to constantly look to improve the business processes in which they participate. The old adage, "If you are not part of the solution you are part of the problem," is absolutely true in global companies today. Companies hoping to be global competitors will have to rely on a culture of commitment and cooperation to search for economies of scale.

Here are three key ways to give global knowledge workers more autonomy:

Allow More Employee Discretion in Decision Making

As the customer becomes the final arbiter of business activity, the ability to make discretionary decisions on the spot becomes an increasingly important competitive weapon. In the mid-1980s, when a new British Airways management team began to transform the stodgy government-controlled airline with an abysmal service reputation into one of the most customer-oriented airlines in the world, it conducted a passenger survey to determine what elements of quality service made a difference. One of the major findings was that British Airways passengers wanted service people to be able to take more discretion in decision making wherever they were.[†]

Mitsuya Goto, former head of Nissan Europe, believes that Nissan made an important transformation in the 1980s under the direction of the company's new president that moved the company to more of an anyplace perspective, by shifting its perspective from adhering to the proper internal hierarchy to one of "customer first."

"We used to have a company that had three strategic objectives: to become more international, to strengthen Japanese sales, and to invest more in R&D to produce timely products. But since all of the decisions were made centrally, the midlevel of management learned not to make decisions. We had a saying: 'Let the big man decide.' "

Under the new president, the company "became more of a family of people with distinctive personalities. Different people with bright new ideas were allowed to make important design decisions. Instead of being based

---

* *Financial Times,* June 26, 1989.

† Ron Zemke, and Dick Schaaf, *The Service Edge: 101 Companies that Profit from Customer Care* (New York: New American Library), 22.

only on price and volume, Nissan broadened its base of decision criteria. The development of the Maxima is a good example. The car has been a runaway success."*

Create Programs to Open Employees' Minds

One of a global manager's key responsibilities is to demonstrate that global behavior is valued in the company. Actively rewarding good ideas regardless of where they come from, valuing collaborative efforts and partnerships that push forward the frontiers of the company's knowledge, and giving top jobs in operations to employees from many cultures are examples of some of the ways the global company can demonstrate a commitment to being a global company.

Sony recruits executives, managers, and operational employees from many countries. The company encourages decision making by employees rather than usurping their influence. Owners outside of Japan have 23 percent of the company's stock, traded on 23 exchanges throughout the world. Of 7000 employees in the United States, only 150 are Japanese. Sony has tried to give the top job in each foreign operation to a local national, and in the early 1990s it became the first industrial company in Japan with a director from outside the country.

Actively Build the Global Portfolio of Skills

The ability to develop employee education programs and build a global portfolio of skills is as important as the ability to find new forms of financial capital. Finding and developing human skills is complex. It takes time to develop skills. Developing knowledge-transfer processes requires the ability to recognize when more learning is needed, to be inspired to seek out the knowledge, and to coordinate the use of the new knowledge in the right places.

Companies from all over the world are recognizing that developing human skills is a key ability of a global company. Since the supply of highly skilled people is increasing more slowly than global demand for them, many companies are making the recruitment and development of a highly skilled workforce one of their major strategic initiatives.

---

* These remarks were made at a lecture to London Business School students on Nov. 16, 1989. Mr. Goto is now Managing Director for Japan Center for International Exchange (JCIE) and is the Executive Secretary for the Ushiba Memorial Foundation. Tel. (446) 7781-6. 9-17 Minami-Azabu 4-Chome, Minato-Ku, Tokyo 106, Japan.

Summary

As a company transforms into a global organization, all employees are affected. Just as top management's role is organizational design, the knowledge worker's role is self-work design, i.e., constantly creating better work processes and doing things better. A global organization nurtures a shared global culture. One key aspect of the global culture is trust. It is not possible to pay lip service to trust and expect the global network to work. Global companies need to constantly create programs that encourage the sharing of cross-cultural experiences.

Action Checklist

1. Is work redesign encouraged in your company?

2. What kind of programs do you have to keep the cultural stew mixing?

3. Does the top management team set the example for the rest of the organization in terms of trusting their peers?

4. Do you have incentive systems that encourage global behavior?

5. Does your company manage its global skills' portfolio?

6
Global I.T.:
Connecting the World

If there is one absolute truth about globalization, it is that a company can't become truly global without making excellent use of a wide variety of information technologies (I.T.). Most importantly, using I.T. well allows you to minimize the negative impact of distance and time, and permits you to share your company's most valuable asset: the collective knowledge of employees. This connecting of the world through technology enables the adept corporation to operate as efficiently as if all its employees were in the same building, rather than widely dispersed around the world.

Senior executives of every one of the companies we spoke with in our research with IBM and on other projects identified I.T. as one of its top four or five global strategic imperatives. Following are some of the things they said.

Jacques Henri Wahl, President and Chief Operating Officer of Banque Nationale de Paris, links the strategic business and information technology imperatives: "We can't be a global company without global systems."

The managing director of Benetton, Dr. Palmeri agrees: "To be global, worldwide organizations will be dedicated to managing the flows of the business in terms of product flows (raw materials, semiproduced goods, and final products), financial flows, and information flows. A company's management should be able to see flows move from one side of the map of the world to the other as soon as possible. We can not become more global without innovative information systems."*

"We must operate our company as one optimized integrated system," said Yasutaka Obayashi, Deputy Senior General Manager Corporate Strategy

* Interview 1992.

125

and Development of Canon. "We must create an information-based organization so that we can be fast and flexible."

The management team of Waste Management, Inc. identifies information technology as part of the information highway necessary to link capabilities worldwide. "We must implement the capability to effectively transfer skills and know-how around the company."

Pirelli's senior management team stated, "We must reduce the negative impacts of time and distance. Specifically this means: *a*) we need to achieve complete transparency in our manufacturing operations, and *b*) we need closer links to our customers through improved logistics and improved telecommunications."

"We must build and maintain an infrastructure which will enable the group to realize its global vision," said Matz Aquren, senior vice-president administration, AB Electrolux. "Specifically this means we have to: define the communications services which will be made available on the communications network and a program for implementing those services; continue development and expansion of the corporate communications network; and develop a glossary of terms to be used as a common language across business operations."

A general manager of a parts and service division at a U.S.-based manufacturer said, "We must provide a base of common capability as a global system foundation, enable tailored local programs, and enable integration and information exchange."

The paramount theme across all corporations is the importance and necessity of strategic information technology as an enabler to achieving global business objectives. Managing essential flows of the business in an integrated way, sharing knowledge and transferring skills on a worldwide basis, and reducing the impacts of time and space by relying on an information technology infrastructure that delivers capability to the global corporation are vital components of the global corporation. Despite this perceived strategic importance, few companies have made real inroads in developing effective global I.T. capability, although the leaders are on their way.

In this chapter we will lay the necessary groundwork for understanding what we mean by global I.T., and why today's technologies offer us much more hope than we might have had even a few years ago. We will describe the transformation taking place within the fundamental information technologies and how I.T. capabilities get developed—the supply side of the equation. We will also discuss the major market segments (I.T. investment portfolios) for global I.T. that have emerged—the demand side. We will conclude this chapter with a discussion of some of the reasons why developing effective global I.T. capability is so incredibly difficult to do well. In the next chapter we will proscribe an action program for organizations to more effectively develop and use their I.T. capabilities in order to compete globally. First, a few words of caution.

I.T. Alone Does Not Assure Success

Information technology is not a silver bullet that will help any company cross the global frontier if considered on its own. We are convinced a successful globalization process is one which balances organizational and technological change. Figure 6-1 describes our view of this balancing act.

The vertical axis describes the change from old world organization to new world organization. The horizontal axis describes the change from old world technology to new world technology. In the lower left quadrant we find the industrial bureaucratic organization (this could be a global exporter, multinational, or multilocal company). These are the industrial organizations that are characterized by an organizational structure that has many vertical layers and functional stovepipes. Their technology systems reinforce the organizational structures in that they are typically central systems and almost always fragmented by function.

The lower right quadrant describes the gridlocked organization. This is a company that has attempted to superimpose information technology on an industrial organizational structure. Rather than change the business processes to take advantage of the capabilities of information technology, these companies have "paved the cowpaths." In other words, they have applied technology to the way business is carried out, rather than improve the processes. Typically the benefits (if any) of the new technology rarely exceed 10 percent return on investment.

The upper left quadrant represents the flexible organization. This is a company that has redesigned the way work is performed and, as a result,

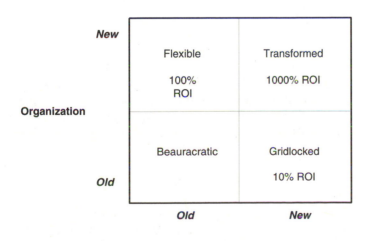

Figure 6-1. Balancing organization and technology.

reduced vertical layers, developed cross-functional processes, and instituted a bottoms-up people empowerment program. Typically the benefits of achieving flexibility might be measured as a 100 percent return on investment.

The upper right quadrant represents the global ideal: the technology leveraged organization. By integrating and superimposing new technology on a flexible organization, companies enable new organization effectiveness through such accomplishments as cross-functional processes, flexible manufacturing, customer/vendor linkage, and knowledge worker clusters. Typically the benefits of creating a technology leveraged organization might be measured as 1000 percent return on investment. Most organizations lack sufficient management discipline, however, to accomplish this delicate balancing act.

Implementing a Global I.T. Strategy Will Be Timely and Expensive

If you want to get to the twenty-first century as a viable global player, you better be prepared to stop at the bank on the way! The I.T. component of the investment alone, during the decade of the 90s, will be measured in multiples of the previous decade's. Three of the companies we visited with IBM, which had already developed their next five-year I.T. globalization architecture designs, were each going to spend in excess of $500 million on new development. Implementing a global I.T. strategy will take time.

Global Developments in Business Information Technology

Technologies are arriving daily that offer great potential. There has been a huge proliferation in the types and uses of I.T. Today, managers use the term "information technology" to reflect the convergence of multiple technologies dealing with information, from fax and cellular phone to video, in addition to the digital computer. Six themes emerge to describe the developments.

Price/Performance

I.T. has changed a lot in the thirty-five or so years since the first computers were used commercially. First, there has been a many orders-of-magnitude improvement in both cost/performance and size reduction, from the first electron-tube machines, which occupied whole floors of buildings, to today's computer on a chip, which fits between your fingertips.

Mobility

In just 10 years we've moved from mobile telephones to mobile facsimile and mobile videotext. In just a few more years we will have mobile videotelephones. From cars to cameras, products now have microchips imbedded to control some function of performance, efficiency, or user convenience.

I.T. Imbedded in Products and Services

A friend's five-year old car has 17 microprocessors in it. These chips help activities of the car like automatic fuel injection and antilock brakes perform better. Even in something as low-tech as a tire, Michelin is now implanting a microchip to check on pressure, temperature, and wear.

Today, for the most part, these chips are islands of technology, not integrated, but they do provide some driver signaling and can be accessed by technicians in the service bay to provide valuable diagnostic information. In a few years cars will have chips connected to the car's internal local-area network to provide integrated driver information and service-bay diagnostics. This step has global implications; plugging the car in the service bay also enables the car to be plugged into the manufacturer's central service data base. The step after that might see the car calling directly into the service data base (while it is in motion) and a whole worldwide integrated logistics chain being set into motion so that the required part will arrive at the service bay just as you bring your car in to get fixed.

Microcomputing and Communications

In the 1960s, companies went through some rudimentary stages of growth in their ability to adopt the mainframe computer to some basic clerical business applications, through the use of batch data processing techniques supplemented with remote job entry over low-speed data transmission lines. Few, if any, mainframe applications had a scope that crossed location boundaries, much less national borders.

In the 1970s, the improving mainframe and communication's technology, along with improving business knowledge on how to apply the computer, enabled companies to rapidly expand the functional scope of their applications, as well as to expand into on-line transaction processing, enabling "dumb" terminals installed on the desks of remote clerical workers to access simple data bases. Companies that effectively automated their basic operational transactions of payroll, order entry, inventory control, accounts receivable, accounts payable, and general ledger made their functional organizations much more efficient, leading to the ability of many organizations to begin the downsizing of administrative bureaucracies.

Since this highly cost justifiable operational automation took place at the bottom of the organization, however, few functional managers had the perspective (or requirement) to design systems that would work in more than one country. Planning for computers during this period was focused on how to support existing business functions in a better way. I.T. planning was treated as a tactical activity that should be performed within the business function (or national organization) by middle or junior managers, rather than by senior management.

By 1980 some strategic applications of mainframe computers had emerged that fundamentally changed the nature of a business or sometimes a whole industry (like automated teller machines in banking or computerized reservation systems in the airline industry). In most of these applications, strategic advantage appeared to come to those companies that extended the reach of their in-house applications to customers or significant third-party intermediaries with a range of services that were not readily duplicated. In all of the widely acclaimed "business use of computers for strategic advantage" cases, senior management played a significant role in championing the application of the technology.

During the 1980s, not only did the price/performance of mainframe computers and telecommunications bandwidth improve dramatically, but also the information systems organizations of most companies became more capable of efficiently building and running large-scale on-line systems, incorporating these improvements. On the other hand, these IS organizations became increasingly less creative in finding new "greenfield" applications to justify applying these technologies to produce tangible business benefits, partly as a result of another advance in technology—the emergence of the personal computer—a technology targeted at individual productivity and effectiveness.

PC technology penetrated almost every organization by going around the traditional Information Systems' organization and swept over companies in a very unplanned and uncontrolled way. Managers purchased their own PCs to get their own processing power, and reported the PC as part of their departmental material expense. As a result there were initially very lax standards on personal computer hardware and software selection, as well as understaffed or nonexistent support organizations. PCs were proliferating, and in many cases allowing individual users to become more productive and more creative. The net effect of having "thousands of flowers blooming" in a company in an unmanaged and unconnected way was that North American and European organizations actually suffered a net loss in productivity as a result of these islands of automation. The primary problem was lack of integration.

Most IS executives who grew up in mainframe environments were initially very apprehensive of the PC. They regarded them as if they were toys and referred to their applications as "underground" systems. Only reluctantly did they begin to seriously integrate PCs into their mainframe environments.

Most business executives in the 1980s, who were just beginning to get involved in the information systems planning game for mainframes, lacked the foresight or power to step back from the PC invasion, grasp its potential and focus it for organizational advantage by restructuring the way the company conducted its work. As a consequence, proposals for new or common mainframe systems that crossed borders were more often regarded as power play impositions from an unthinking headquarters organization, emphasizing minor efficiency improvements, rather than opportunities to make a more competitive international organization.

The days when most of our computing took place in the data processing "glass houses" we knew in the 1970s and 80s are rapidly passing. As businesses enter the global frontier, a vast array of emerging technologies, such as imaging, electronic data interchange (EDI), and the integration of voice and video into networks and workstations, will be commonly implemented and used broadly. The functionality and cost performance potential of these technologies often makes grown businesspeople drool. Surely it makes the new technologies' eventual use inevitable.

The cost of typical large mainframe hardware (circa 1989) capable of processing one million computer instructions per second (1 MIPS) was about $117,000. For a workstation utilizing microprocessing technology the hardware cost was $200! This amazing difference in cost performance is allowing companies to completely rethink the structure of their information technology. Tomorrow, instead of companies having terminals as peripheral devices to mainframes, they will have powerful desktop workstations working interdependently through a global network capable of accessing information utilities residing on mainframes.

Some companies that have already embraced microbased technology platforms—to perform advanced manufacturing requirements planning (MRPII), for example—are finding that they can get 80 percent of the features of the old mainframe systems at one-tenth of the cost, if they restructure the way work is performed to intelligently use the technology. ROIs on the same order of magnitude can be expected from companies that intelligently adopt these other new technologies.

There's a similar price/performance revolution going on in telecommunications. In 1988 a typical videoteleconferencing facility cost $200,000 a station. In July 1991, Picturetel announced it was offering videoteleconferencing transmission facilities for just $20,000. Today it is possible to rent by the hour for a few hundreds of dollars.

Since most of the existing technology structures in place today are incapable of supporting the integrated business strategies that many companies have on the drawing boards, such technological advances will only serve to complicate matters, unless a structured approach to assembling the new technologies, in concert with the multiple and incompatible technologies already installed in the various functions of the company, is used. The various technologies must coexist and support each other while maintaining their individual unique functions.

The relentless acquisition of personal computers and the application of microprocessor-based technologies at the intersection (or borders) between companies, their customers, and their business partners during the 1980s has already led many top executives to the conclusion that they should restructure the way business is performed from end to end. In the 1990s we see more and more leading-edge global process-support systems include the combination of tailored workstastions, supporting local customization, integrated with global server platforms, providing consistent data and communications. We see this trend continuing to gain momentum, as companies learn to form global alliances and capture the synergies of alliance process systems.

The Challenge of Integrating Desktops: Connectivity

Experts are saying that the required technologies have not sufficiently arrived to enable the envisioned global I.T. capabilities to be implemented rationally.

Bruce Rogow, a leading technology and strategy consultant in the United States, says, "We believe connectivity and ubiquity problems must be solved to enable the next generation of demand drivers. Vendor and user organizations are breaking into five camps, each of which believes it has a unique solution to the problems. Each group scampers forward at every investment decision point to plug its approach.

"1. *The open systems approach:* Proponents favor Unix, the Open Software foundation, Open Systems interconnection, Posix, X Windows, and SQL

"2. *The complete-connectivity vendor approach:* Examples are IBM's Systems Application Architecture, AT&T's Tuxedo, DEC's Network Applications Support, and NCR's Open Cooperative Computing, as well as solutions from Oracle and Microsoft

"3. *The CASE tools approach:* Examples include Texas Instruments' Information Engineering Facility (IEF), KnowledgeWare's Information Engineering Workbench (IEW) and Arthur Andersen's Foundation

"4. *The client/server architecture approach:* Proponents include IBM, DEC, Hewlett-Packard, Bull, NCR, and Apple Computer

"5. *The systems integrator approach:* Supporters include Electronic Data Systems, Boeing Computer, Andersen Consulting, Computer Sciences, IBM, and DEC

"As you can see the large vendors, wed to their existing base of clients or systems, are wrestling with four or five of the conceptual principals at the same time. That leads to massive complexity, turf battles, coordination problems and delays."*

Peter Keen, perhaps the most respected academic commentator on global telecommunications issues, remarks, "Telecommunications technology has overtaken the reaction times of the organizations that determine its use. The OSI model which is the globally accepted blueprint for open systems that are vendor-independent is just as obsolete as ISDN. In the United States, the TCP/IP communications protocol has been adopted by more and more firms as something that works in a computing environment built around the UNIX operation system for computers, even though it is totally incompatible with OSI. The OSI model is in turn built around UNIX as the essential "open" operating system. Meanwhile, the various UNIX committees fight each other as do the proponents of TCP/IP and OSI.

"For readers who are bewildered by these terms, think of this as 'Christianity' in the 1600s. Each of the zealots serves the True God. Each represents Truth. Each sees the rest as heretics. Each new technology creates an Anabaptist to rail against the forces of Catholicism (or, in the case of information technology, IBM)."†

Blake Ives and Sirkka Jarvenpaa, in a recent survey of 25 senior managers on global I.T. issues, found that "Our interviewees complained that equipping a local data center can be problematic because of high prices for local hardware, the lack of local service for products, the absence of an authorized distributor, and long lead times in acquiring both equipment and spare parts. Interviewees complained that in Japan, for instance, local distributors hold monopoly positions and charge rates nearly double the price of comparable products purchased in the U.S. Economic and technical barriers set by national governments include higher prices for computing equipment and communication lines, restrictions on the importation of equipment and services, and rigid hardware and software standards. Severe

---

* Bruce G. Rogow, *Directing Information Technologies into the 1990s,* Gartner Group Industry Service R-900-103 (Jan. 11, 1991).

† Peter G. W. Keen, "Telecommunication and Organizational Advantage" (Paper presented at a Harvard Business School Colloquium on Global Competition and Telecommunications, May 1, 1991).

import limitations on assembled hardware in countries such as Brazil forced one firm to enter the computer assembly business to outfit their foreign subsidiaries. Even in countries with open trade policies, new hardware models or software versions may take a year or two to be released to the market because the vendor may not have the resources available to quickly adapt the product, documentation, and support to local conditions. To support languages such as Japanese requires that a single character from the language be stored in two, rather than the customary one, bytes of computer storage, often necessitating vendors to make costly and time-consuming modifications to software packages."*

Despite these obstacles, each of the above authors concludes that companies cannot afford to wait for perfect technical solutions, but must forge ahead with eyes wide-open to the potential pitfalls that lie ahead.

Multimedia and Imaging

One of the major changes that has taken place in computing has been in the richness of its media. From the earliest computers in the mid-1950s until the 1980s, about the only way to communicate to or receive data from a computer was through alphanumeric characters on cards, paper, magnetic tape, and disk. We have been able to make great strides in our ability to manipulate numbers and text, but today, while Arabic numerals are almost universally used, we still are very much dependent on the local language of textual data.

Apple Computer changed the way the world thought about using computers during the 1980s. First, the company made it easy for an untrained person to draw and print pictures. Second, Apple changed the user interface from JCL to graphic symbols (ICONs). At first computer graphics were considered a niche, referred to as highly specialized activities such as computer aided design (CAD) or desktop publishing. Now every computer hardware vendor realizes that it needs to incorporate a graphic user interface (GUI) capability in its products for them to be acceptable.

Adding graphics to computers has had a powerful impact on the way we communicate, especially cross-culturally. Pictures really are worth a thousand words, and one of the main reasons is because they don't have to be translated into national languages.

An associated problem is the language required to invoke a computer instruction, such as saving a file or starting a program. The special notation, required by job control language (JCL) used by all mainframes and perpetuated in the IBM PC environment, meant that you needed specialized training in a JCL to become a computer operator or personal computer user. GUIs

---

* Blake Ives and Sirkka L. Jarvenpaa, *Applications of Global Information Technology: Key Issues for Management,* MIS Quarterly (March 1991).

opened up the PC to a much wider audience, including middle and senior managers who no longer had to fear that they would embarrass themselves in front of their colleagues by using JCL incorrectly. GUIs also enabled computer users traveling to different countries to click and point at an ICON or at a consistent location on a pull-down menu to invoke computer applications and tools without knowing the language displayed on the screen.

The ability to send pictures cheaply through facsimile transmission (fax) has revolutionized the way many companies communicate in just the last five years. Today, 50 percent of the communications traffic across the Pacific is fax. Fax, like electronic mail, is an island of technology that doesn't integrate into traditional applications. But now that people are seeing the communicating power of a fax image they are recognizing the potential of other "imaging" technologies more and more.

American Express was one of the early adopters to incorporate imaging technology into basic computer transactions. Any cardholder knows that their monthly statement contains images of AMEX transactions. What people may not know is that after American Express first scans a customer invoice received from a retail store, that document is stored away and only its electronic image is passed around the organization for processing. This is an example of a major step towards a paperless process that can make any aspiring global organization more efficient.

United Services Automobile Association (USAA), one of the most successful insurance companies in the world, has also achieved major productivity breakthroughs by imaging every piece of paper that comes into the organization.

If we illustrate our points with moving images we gain another order of magnitude in understanding. Anyone who has watched a film in a foreign language he or she doesn't speak can describe most of the action and emotion that takes place. (What doesn't come across is the precise meaning of what was said. In an action-packed film like *Raiders of the Lost Ark* this doesn't present much of a problem for the viewer; but in a film about an existential conversation, like *My Dinner With Andre,* we might get completely lost.)

We are rapidly reaching the stage in which moving images and sounds are being economically incorporated into the domain of computer media. The catch-phrase here is multimedia workstations. Multimedia, by combining the communicating ability of video and sound with computer logic, represents a major breakthrough in our ability to communicate ideas across borders and across cultures.

The American Airlines SABRE system is upgrading some of its travel agent terminals to multimedia workstations that have the ability to call up video clips of locations, like the various islands of the South Pacific, show local attractions and hotels a traveler might stay in, and then zoom into a selected hotel to display the ocean view or the mountain view. If a room style is selected, a reservation is made automatically.

Federal Express is using multimedia workstations for training its customer service representatives, to show them by example how to handle different kinds of customer requests. The system not only presents video clips of the right and wrong way to handle a variety of customer service situations, it also customizes the training program, allows individuals to perform self-testing, and keeps track of each representative's learning progress.

Club Med is introducing multimedia, *Bornes Interactives,* in areas to catch passersby with moving images illustrating their holiday villages. A person can select which activities and villages he/she would like to see a short film on, select a length of stay, and order the holiday. The tickets will be sent in the mail.

In stock brokerage firms around the world, multimedia systems deliver financial news from the Reuters wire, CNBC/FNN video, and other sources right to the desktop, along with a Dow Jones or *Financial Times* "ticker" running continuously at the bottom of the computer screen.

In Denmark, prospective home buyers use "HomeVision," a multimedia application that allows them to choose homes by location, price, type and to imagine how their living room and bedroom furniture will look, and if the yard is big enough for their children—all without ever setting foot outside the real estate office.

While we are just scratching the surface of the application of multimedia, we share Lucie Fjeldstad's (President of IBM's Multimedia and Education Division) belief that multimedia workstations will have a profound impact on a company's ability to share its knowledge globally over the next decade.

She says, "Multimedia is exactly the right technology at the right time, a time when communication among people of different countries and cultures needs to embrace many languages and to reach beyond the written word to a more universal language, the language of graphics, still photos, animation, full motion video, and music, a language that requires neither words nor alphabets. Multimedia combines the entertainment capability of television with the programming flexibility of personal computers in a way that energizes and engages the senses—sight, sound and touch. Multimedia encourages participation by breaking down language barriers, and permitting individuals to proceed at their own comfortable pace."*

Business Process Redesign

Figure 6-2 describes some of the fundamental changes in information technology over the last 30 years. Today's I.T. is allowing companies to communicate and share important customer, product, and process information

---

* Speech, Birmingham, England, May 1991.

	Application portfolios	Technologies	Software
1970s	• Transaction support	• Mainframes • Minis • Operational networks	• Stand alone programs • Alphanumeric
1980s*	• Functional support • Professional support	• +PCs • Delivery networks	• Separate programs from data • Graphics (desktop publishing)
1990s*	• Process support • Knowledge support • Embedded in products • Coordination/control	• Integration infrastructure • Client-server • Product networks • Information • networks	• Shared software objects • Compound documents • Sound • Moving images

Figure 6-2. Global I.T. environment.

when and where it is needed. As the environment for computing moves from the mainframe to the desktop, from alphanumeric textual information to media-rich information, incorporating graphics, moving pictures, and sound, and from unique, stand-alone software programs, developed in isolation, to the use of sharable software objects, developed by teams spread around the world, I.T. is allowing companies to cross the global frontier.

Richard Nolan writes, "Transformation involves not incremental change, but major changes on many levels at once."* This change on many levels is made possible because of connectivity, the convergence of communication and information in our daily business lives, which in turn is being made possible by rapid advances in I.T.

Exciting developments in how businesses view products and process change are being carried out by B. Joseph Pine, Andrew C. Boynton, and Bart Victor.† Stan Davis‡ has pointed out that firms attempting to become more flexible are attempting to *mass customize* product and service offerings for their customers. Put very simply, firms are trying to create products and services to suit particular customer's different requirements. For example, a car manufacturer may offer a different set of features on a newly

---

* Richard L. Nolan, "What Transformation Is," *Stage by Stage* 7, no. 5 (Sept./Oct. 1987).

† A.C. Boynton, B. Victor, and B.J. Pine II, "New competitive strategies: Challenges to organizations and information technology," *IBM Systems Journal* 32, no. 1 (1993), 40–64.

‡ Stanley M. Davis, *Future Perfect* (Reading, Massachusetts: Addison-Wesley Publishing Company, Inc.), 1987.

ordered car. This is an example of a mass customized product. The same car manufacturer may also offer delivery at the customer's choice of time and location. This is an example of a customized service.

As competition increases, the breadth of variations of product and service offerings will increase as well. Ultimately, companies may offer products and services customized to the unique customer, as is the case in tailored clothing.

The strategically compelling challenge here is for a company to offer customized products and services based on knowledge about individual customer's needs and wants in a flexible, economic way. Some car manufacturers are changing their business processes to enable the assembly of different cars on the same line of production. Conceivably, it is possible to create a string of different models of cars with different features and have each car that comes off the line consist of a different configuration.

Boynton, Victor, and Pine's work focuses on how firms can build business processes to create different products and services. Boynton and Victor call this capability *dynamic stability:*

"Firms faced with rapid, unpredictable market change are creating stable, long-term, yet flexible process capabilities that both decrease product time to market and increase product customization in a cost-efficient manner. These firms ... are managing these contradictory requirements by becoming "dynamically stable" organizations—firms designed to serve the widest range of customers and changing product demands ("dynamic") while building on existing process capabilities, experience, and knowledge ("stability")."*

Figure 6-3 illustrates this capability. Along one axis, *product* change can either be stable or dynamic, along the other *process* change. Invention firms are creating new products and processes and are the start-up ventures in business. Mass production firms hone their ability to make a product that has mass appeal in the market in a process that has also been stabilized. The conventional assembly line techniques that focus on creating efficiency of production would be an example. However, as time continues, many firms find that to maintain or improve production techniques, the process must be altered on a continuous basis for improvement. Quality circles and other dynamic process management techniques are used. In the mass customizing firm, the process of work is stable, yet has the capability to produce different products and services, as in the previous car manufacturing example.

Knowledge data bases as well as a set of performance indices need to be monitored to become a mass customizing company. On a global basis, this means creating knowledge about how customers' needs are changing, searching for the best products and services to fulfill those needs, and

---

* Andrew C. Boynton and Bart Victor, "Beyond Flexibility: Building and Managing the Dynamically Stable Organization," *California Management Review* (Fall 1991), 54.

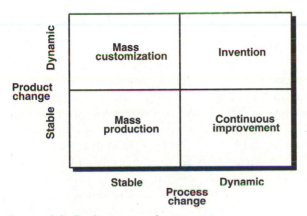

Figure 6-3. Product-process change matrix.

designing and implementing flexible processes to deliver to the market-place. The global information flows available often on an immediate basis are essential to enable management to make decisions about how best to design products and processes.

Business Process Redesign of the Management Process: Cross-functional and Process Management Information*

As corporations move to the Information Age, they are redesigning their businesses to better align activities with the processes of the business. They are moving from a functional orientation of the business to a process orientation.

Much of *business process redesign* focuses on redesigning the operational aspects of the business to align business and information technology strategies. By redesigning the business processes with an effective and efficient information flow of the business, operational activities are carried out in an improved way.

As companies move to a process orientation from a functional orientation, management activities, such as communication and decision making, must also change. Because management activities are more difficult to

* N. Caroline Daniels, "Bridging the Gap: The Use of Information Systems to Shorten the Design to Manufacturing Cycle in the U.K. Clothing Industry," Doctoral Thesis, London Business School (April 1992).

track, the change is difficult to put into redesign methodologies. The change can be characterized as the change from a functional management style to a cross-functional (or process-driven) management style.

As managers move from a functional (or sequential) orientation to a process orientation, management activities are overlapped. Instead of transferring information in "one shot," managers from upstream and downstream activities exchange information earlier in the business process (see Figure 6-4). Cross-functional management activities differ from functional activities in several fundamental ways, as seen in Figure 6-5.

Although it is possible to achieve some important business process redesign efforts by redefining the content and currency of activities, the significant strategic gains are achieved by redesigning business to achieve simultaneity of management processes with a consistent organizational language and culture.

Simultaneity, the Strategic Pivot Point for Redesign

Simultaneity necessitates management process redesign. An example will help make this point clear. In the clothing industry, a number of managers make decisions on a product as it passes from design to manufacturing (see Figure 6-6).

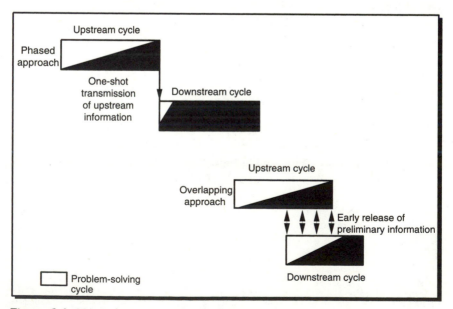

Figure 6-4. Moving from sequential to overlapping processes.

Description	Functional manager	Cross-functional manager
Cross-functional content relates to what managers are concerned about communicating with other managers from other functional areas, as well as how they go about determining what should be communicated successfully or unsuccessfully.	*What do I need to know?*	and who else needs to know?
Cross-functional currency relates to the timing of communication between (among) managers from different functional areas as well as how managers go about determining whether information should be communicated and when information actually is communicated in a timely or untimely fashion.	*When do I need to know and how current must the information be?*	and when do other managers need to know?
Cross-functional simultaneity relates to how managers consider decisions from two or more functional areas to be *associated, how mangers determine in what situations the interdependence of* decisions affects management decisions, and how the decisions actually do occur interdependently either successfully or unsuccessfully.	What do I need to know and when?	and who else needs to know, and when, so that we can make related, coordinated decisions at the same time?
Cross-functional cultural fit concerning management decision support relates to how managers communicate through the use of language to establish coherent methods of coordinating management decision making toward common corporate goals.	Function-specific language and objectives	Consideration of translation of language and objectives across functional boundaries

Figure 6-5. Cross-functional management concepts.

As one manager makes a decision, the product changes. The change in the product, in turn, affects other management decisions. For example, if the marketing manager and the customer decide that a change in the garment is necessary, the manufacturing manager must know in order to determine the best way to make the garment, which, in turn, alters the way the production manager plans production. Similarly, if a purchasing manager decides that a substitute component would fit the original customer and marketing specifications, and would reduce the cost of the garment, he/she may change the component. In each case, it is important for the managers to communicate the changes they are making to the product. Each manager's decision alters the product and the management decision process, thus the management decision making process becomes dynamic.

By enabling a company to change its management process to a simultaneous or dynamic process, time-to-market advantages can be gained. Since there is a limit to the amount of communication any human can manage,

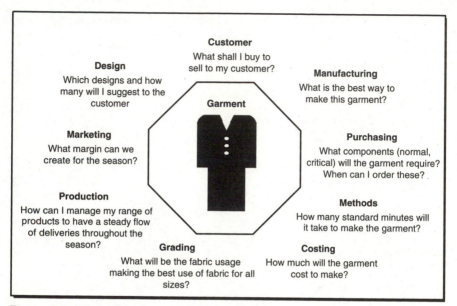

Figure 6-6. Who makes what management decision.

in large organizations, the use of management information systems is necessary.

Included in this illustration is the customer manager who is an important manager in the process. By dynamically altering the management decision process in the company to suit the changing customer preferences, mass customization can be achieved. Mass customization necessitates a change in the management processes, as well as in the strategic perspective and operational processes.

Figure 6-7 gives a high-level summary of the differences in functional and process management activities. The figure identifies the problems and objectives that organizations have that relate to the changing nature of management activities and to linking the new management activities to their strategic aims.

Global Applications Development

We believe the way a company's global I.T. applications are developed is at least as important a success factor as the technology on which the applications are developed. We've seen it over and over again; while some worldwide I.T. solutions attempted are wonderfully successful, most fail because

Description	Functional manager	Cross-functional manager	Problems	Objectives
Cross-functional content relates to what managers are concerned about communicating with other managers from other functional areas, as well as how they go about determining what should be communicated successfully or unsuccessfully.	*What do I need to know?*	and who else needs to know?	Bottlenecks, unclear responsibility, lack of a process perspective	Give access to those who need to know to benefit the overall corporate goals, reduce and resolve uncertainty and equivocality, assign clear responsibility, enable a shared management perspective of preproduction process to weigh costs, make tradeoffs, and learn to control and coordinate management decisions.
Cross-functional currency relates to the timing of communication between (among) managers from different functional areas as well as how managers go about determining whether information should be communicated and when information actually is communicated in a timely or untimely fashion.	*When do I need to know and how current must the information be?*	and when do other managers need to know?	Continuity, managing intensity, context of time	Share relevant and timely information to support the continuity of management decision making, manage the increased intensity of the management information responsibility, build an awareness of the importance of time in the cross-functional context.
Cross-functional simultaneity relates to how managers consider decisions from two or more functional areas to be associated, how managers determine in what *situations the interdependence of* decisions affects management decisions, and how the decisions *actually do occur interdependently* either successfully or unsuccessfully.	What do I need to know and when?	and who else needs to know, and when, so that we can make related, coordinated decisions at the same time?	Problem solving, decision interrelationships, management of interdependence	Allow managers to share a view of the work process, understand how various management decisions interrelate, and reorganize the management decision process to improve effectiveness.
Cross-functional cultural fit concerning management decision support relates to how managers communicate through the use of *language to establish coherent* methods of coordinating management decision making toward common corporate goals.	Function-specific language and objectives	Consideration of translation of language and objectives across functional boundaries	Organizational paradox, organized set of business practices based on intellectual assets, learning	Resolve the paradox between functional and process objectives with management commitment and involvement, develop a language and method to communicate ideas about how to create unique process strengths, and improve the social learning within the firm and importance of cross-functional communication valued in culture.

Figure 6-7. Concepts of cross-functional management information theory.

they are not conceived and developed with the whole business in mind. Systems well designed for one geographic location often are not readily transferable to other geographic locations. In the 1970s and 1980s many companies developed a system at home and tried to take the "core" of that system to another country and implement it with "local adaptations." Local variations usually must be taken into account in the design phase of potential global systems.

Our extensive database of corporate applications portfolios provides convincing proof of how systems designed without a global perspective up front are not only extremely expensive to roll out around the world, but also usually have ever-diminishing functional quality in each successive national implementation.

Here's a typical example of what goes wrong. A major European manufacturing company built an order-processing system in the United Kingdom in the mid-1970s and then decided to roll it out as a PanEuropean system. The second country in the "phased implementation" was France. The thought was that since there was already a system in the United Kingdom, why not capitalize on economies and use the "core system" developed in the United Kingdom and ask what the French office wanted to add on to that system. To be adapted to French needs, most of the United Kingdom system had to have functional modules rewritten or by-passed.

The third country to be implemented was Germany. France relayed accounts of the difficulties of implementation, and advised Germany to take their revised version. Germany, hoping to capitalize on the "learning in France" and in an effort to maintain company consistency toward the company's future hope of connecting, agreed to take the French version. Germany then called for extensive modifications to add on or bypass the French modules designed to bypass the United Kingdom modules. The systems-maintenance people soon developed long faces to match their long hours.

The gist is, as the system went from country to country, it had a cascading effect of lost functionality and quality. This is by no means a sequence of events that is limited to one company. This has been the typical multinational or multilocal approach (and result) to worldwide systems development. While the United Kingdom systems' degree of effective coverage of business functionality was relatively high, the French systems' was lower, and the Germans' still lower. No wonder worldwide systems get a bad name.

The next country to be implemented took a look at the experience of France and Germany and refused to be the next step of the phased implementation because "the system doesn't apply to our business. You don't understand, we're different," which translates into "I don't want to implement that system." The ultimate aim was to involve 15 countries. The painful process of rolling out a "centrally developed" system across Europe took seven years.

To date, some of the most successful worldwide systems have been developed by taking more of a global exporter approach. Systems developed with a global exporter approach permit little if any modification in other countries. They imply the ability to say "no changes" very loudly. In the quick change environment of the future, however, adaptability will be key.

One of the most impressive examples of using I.T. to share knowledge on a global basis can be found in the IBM RETAIN system, a system that provides anyplace, anytime technical support to people, primarily IBM customer engineers, who have to fix IBM hardware or software problems.

"Today, RETAIN has evolved into a network of 13 major IBM systems (3090/600's) installed around the world supporting 160,000 users. At any given moment, as many as 3200 users may be receiving information about how to fix a problem or give advice to a customer.

"The genesis of RETAIN,"* says Irv Schauer, Manager of IBM's Field Support Systems, "was in the early 1960s, when customer engineers, with a problem they couldn't readily resolve at a customer's site, were encouraged to telephone a buddy. In 1966 we decided to concentrate some technical specialists into support centers, and began building an information system to support them on a U.S. basis. This was actually one of the first significant on-line systems used inside IBM.

"And with the Remote Support Facility, added in the early 1980s, many problems can be diagnosed and fixed before a human knows about it. For example, an AS400 (one of our midrange computers) installed on the Fiji Islands may be running unattended at night and detect that it has some kind of intermittent failure. It can call up one of the major RETAIN nodes in Sydney, Australia and get checked out. If the Sydney machine recognizes the problem—let's say that the Fiji processor lacks the latest engineering change in its microcode—it can upload the new code and then create a notification for the customer and our local IBM support staff, that a problem has been fixed.

"But let's imagine the problem was a new one that hadn't been encountered before. Then within two, three minutes the same data examined in Sydney could be viewed in Osaka, Japan, Boulder Colorado, or Portsmouth, England by the appropriate specialist engineers who were notified to troubleshoot the problem. This ability to rapidly put our best experts, located anyplace in the world, to work on any customer problem, creates a powerful leveraging of knowledge and expertise for our service organization."

In fact it was the lack of its ability to leverage this multiplier effect outside the United States that was the driving force behind IBM turning RETAIN into a worldwide system. "In the mid-70s service managers outside the

---

* Irv Schauer, interview with author, spring 1990.

United States were really getting beaten up by IBM's top management," Schauer remarks. "Our mean time to repair the same problem in the United States versus the rest of the world was dramatically better. It was apparent to everyone that this difference in service quality was not in basic skills, training levels or physical tool kits, but in the information tools the engineer had at his or her disposal."

In 1975, after the US-initiated RETAIN had evolved through several generations of software (from RETAIN Under Coursewriter 1440—a primitive timesharing system—to RETAIN/360 under DOS to RETAIN/370 and then converted to OS/MVT), it was first made available in Portsmouth, England, using a fully mirrored data bank. By 1980, Tokyo and Uithoorn had also been brought on-line.

"In hindsight, we were very fortunate because we insisted on a no-compromises approach as we made the system available around the world," says Ray Garris, Manager of RETAIN Applications Development. "We told the locations that if they wanted the system they would have to take the whole package, with its core architecture principles not violated in any way, or don't play."

These core principles included:

1. Worldwide data mirroring

2. A proprietary common data base manager

3. A full text search engine

Of the three, the most interesting, from a global I.T. perspective, is data mirroring. IBM concluded, as RETAIN acquired more and more simultaneous users in the early 1970s, that it would have to create multiple copies of the data base in order to spread the load to provide adequate response time, and yet it was equally important to be able to keep the copies virtually identical so everyone could have access to the same information. By ensuring that any update to the data base is reflected on every RETAIN processor, typically within two to three minutes, they were able to create a capability that now synchronizes the 100 gigabytes of data stored at every node.

RETAIN proves an important point for global I.T. architects: that a very large data base can be distributed around the world and kept up to date if you insist on standards. In IBM's case there are some powerful business justifications that more than offset the expense involved.

RETAIN has been evolving for over 20 years, but it is not yet viewed as a fully global system. Its major global drawback is that it requires its users to interact with it using English, which is not so much a problem for internal use, but is increasingly becoming a challenge as IBM provides electronic access for its customers to solve their own problems. (Electronic customer support is available in the United States, for example, but it is not yet offered in Japan.) Also, "as a host-based dumb terminal system, it never quite meets the needs of everybody," admits Schauer. "The next generation of RETAIN, already well down the development pipeline, will allow users to better meet their own needs by further separating back-end data base power from applications developed on programmable workstations."

As Figure 6-2 shows, the application development environment today is much more complex than it was in the 1970s. Partly because of PC proliferation and partly because of the continuing desire of most companies to get I.T. application developers much closer to their customers, there are many more development "islands," making it difficult for businesses to rationalize and focus their I.T. investments. In addition, there is a much greater use of packaged software and third-party developers (often referred to as systems integrators). In a global world each one of these islands may need to be accommodated or reconciled.

The Global I.T. Portfolio

The ways in which the use of I.T. brings direct benefit to an organization vary widely. Today's major corporations typically have over 100,000 computer programs in operation or under development and scattered in various forms throughout the organization. These programs are typically aggregated into applications systems, products or tool sets for assignment of day-to-day support, accountability, and supervision. A portfolio-management approach that considers groups of these applications, products, or tool sets of similar type is a useful vehicle for sorting out the management complexities of linking the I.T. effort to business strategy, funding, setting of priorities, and harvesting of benefits.

We put every application in one of five global I.T. portfolios (see Figure 6-8): product-support systems, process-support systems, knowledge-support systems, control and coordination systems, and global I.T. infrastructure. We find this a useful way to describe the market for I.T. in an organization. In the next chapter, we will try to describe how companies that find themselves in different business situations might manage these various portfolios.

Global Product-support Systems

Products are getting smarter. As Professor James Cash of the Harvard Business School notes, "In just a few short years from now the amount of intelligence and communication an individual carries around on their *person* will increase dramatically."* Portable telephones embedded with chips that can take messages, notify the caller of your location, and hold replies are

---

* Professor James I. Cash (Professor of Business Administration, Harvard Business School), conversation with author, June 1990.

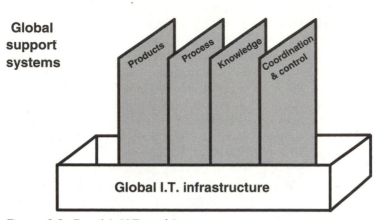

Figure 6-8. Five global I.T. portfolios.

rapidly entering the market. A camera that sets its focus and light requirements, stores a digital picture, fits in your pocket, and will display the picture on your television when you get home is available in Japan.

A chip in a car that controls an automatic function such as antilock
breaking can also provide service-diagnostic information. An elevator that
announces the floor with a spoken voice can also notify its service center
when problems are about to arise.

A cash-management account that consolidates the various financial transactions customers perform, regardless of where the customer is, is one
example of a product system offered by financial service companies. These
statements may include activity information about mutual funds, checking
accounts, credit cards, foreign exchange, and savings.

One of the advantages of imbedding intelligence in products is that it
makes it extremely easy to tailor products for particular markets or customers. Conner Peripherals differentiates disk drives made with similar
components for Compaq and Apple Computer by providing different software to control these components in ways that meet the different manufacturers specifications. Northern Telecom differentiates the electronic
switching equipment it provides to telephone companies through system
software.

Products with imbedded I.T. are important to a company trying to
become global because they can be easily adapted to diverse environments.
Product systems enable a high level of consistency within products while
providing alternatives for flexibility. Because these products are sold around
the world, the support for these products systems must be global in scope.

Using I.T. well enables you to emphasize the increasingly important
intangible aspects of your products and services that allow you to become
more customer driven. Walter Wriston, former CEO of CitiCorp, put his

finger on the value of information when he said, "The information about money is becoming more important than the money itself." In the same vein, we believe that, much more than the products or services themselves, what must be customized is the *information* about your products and services. This is true even for a commodity product such as a bottle of Coke. What's different in Indonesia and Indianapolis about Coca-Cola is the information that surrounds that bottle of Coke, i.e., different cultural messages that convey the consistent global message of enjoyment. Global companies that use I.T. well can surround physical products and services with customized information that can make the company appealing in any local environment.

Global Process-support Systems

Some pieces of the global process-support portfolio might include global customer management, global product development, global human-resource management, and global distribution management. The benefits of developing global process systems can be expressed in tangible measures (e.g., the number and frequency of repeat purchases by customers, who they are, and what they are inclined to buy, the time to market, and the organization's ability to respond to a customer's request).

Process systems are developed with a high degree of modularity so that local pieces can be flexibly integrated. Because of the requirements for consistency, global process systems have to be planned from a global perspective. Working with the design complexities from many diverse perspectives at an early stage of development, the global process design team can determine the system's overall logic, while still providing for local flexibility. That is, the team can decide the elements that have to be the same or similar so that the company can provide both consistent and customized support to its customers, suppliers, and other business partners.

Developing this perspective up front may seem expensive, but we contend that in the long term this is by far the lowest cost route. Companies that take a short-term, country-by-country approach to developing and implementing global systems incur higher costs due to redesign, reimplementation, and the costs associated with lost opportunities because "the system just wasn't there."

As business linkages are built that open the borders of business, global-process systems will be tied into your customers and suppliers, vertically and horizontally integrating market demand and supply.

An interesting development involves the rationalization, simplification, and rerouting of existing business processes with suppliers and customers. Extending global process integration of existing systems across company borders is a new threshold for global competition, enabled by I.T.

Electronic Data Interchange (EDI) is a capability with great global potential that emerged in the 1980s. On the surface, EDI seems little more than intercompany E-mail, a standard electronic way of communicating between buyers and suppliers. But the real power of EDI, because it represents a standard form of communicating, is that applications can be built to automatically receive or generate the interchange.

In the 1980s, companies like General Motors began specifying standard ways for vendors to electronically communicate an order or a drawing to their various departments. Seeing that some companies began to comply and that in so doing, the EDI communication process was a much more efficient and more effective process than the old manual ways, they then laid down the law that they would only do business with those suppliers that complied with their new EDI standard. Soon other companies in the industry, like Ford and Chrysler, followed suit and an industry standard for an EDI transaction was set.

Today global business wars are being fought by companies which want their EDI standards to become industry standards. Clearly being a first mover and having a lot of muscle helps.

Singapore's Tradenet is another example. As Ben Konsynski describes, "The Singapore government has spent a significant amount to link trade agents with relevant government agencies at the port, that is, linking freight forwarders, shipping companies, banks, and insurance companies with customs officials and immigration officials. Clearing the port, which used to take a vessel two to four days, now may take as little as 10 minutes. This startling reduction has more than halved the time any ship has to remain in port and is believed to be a key to ensuring that Singapore remains a port of choice in the Far East, where the competition is clearly growing."*

As one company develops a global order-entry system to reduce the time it takes to deliver parts to its customers by orders of magnitude, a partner company may develop a global-process system to supply these parts direct to the first company's customers, thereby creating an extra competitive advantage through the alliance. As each partner uses I.T. to compete on a global basis, the ability to integrate I.T. across these companies makes the alliance more powerful.

The point is that strategic advantage gained from connecting systems isn't limited to internal communications. In addition to connecting its employees, the company needs open gateways to its customers, suppliers, and alliance partners.

* B. R. Konsynski, "Strategic control in the extended enterprise," *IBM Systems Journal* 32, no. 1 (1993), 111–142.

In a global world a company needs to forge new kinds of connections with its customers. In moving from a production-oriented to a customer-oriented company, toward "mass customization in units of one,"* knowledge of individual customer needs becomes the focus of new business directions.

Global Knowledge-support Systems

To become global, a company needs to make fundamental I.T. investments to connect the knowledge within the organization. Bain's "experience store," described in Chapter 4, and IBM's RETAIN system are exemplars of global knowledge support systems. By developing the ability to connect its knowledge resources, a business can achieve its greatest economies of scale. To accomplish this, both a communications infrastructure and set of knowledge-management approaches must be in place so that there can be timely access to relevant information, regardless of where an individual is located.

One of the first new capabilities (with global potential) that allowed organizations to communicate more effectively across isolated automated desktops was electronic mail (E-mail). Organizations quickly discovered that the effectiveness of E-mail was directly proportional to the number of employees (as well as customers and suppliers) using the system. But, sadly, few organizations today have just one E-mail system. In fact most large organizations may have as many as 10 or 20 E-mail systems, most of which cannot easily interface with each other.

This situation occurred because E-mail systems developed around not only mainframes and minis (where each vendor had one or several offerings), but also word processing software and local area networks.

Another challenge with E-mail (as is the case with paper mail) is that it is not integrated into the normal business process. So if you receive E-mail and you need the information entered into a transaction-processing or management-information system (or vice versa), you need to perform manual activity to cut and paste or transfer the information from one medium to the other. And, unlike sending an envelope in which you can enclose pictures, most E-mail systems in the 1980s only allowed a user to send text or tables.

Knowledge-support systems are more a set of capabilities and tools than applications. As a prerequisite, a company needs to have a high-quality, point-to-point communications network available to ship needed knowledge around the globe in a "just in time" fashion. Without installing the capability to transport knowledge to every person in the company with a need to know, the company can never complete its globalization process. If the knowledge arrives too early it will be ignored and probably lost.

---

* Stanley M. Davis, *Future Perfect,* 169.

A company needs a robust capability to manage knowledge. This means having not only accessible repositories of internal knowledge, but also artificial intelligence to sift through massive amounts of project and customer data for relevant information. By automatically separating the wheat from the chaff, a company can save literally millions of hours. In addition, by installing multimedia workstations that can integrate moving color images, text, and audio messages, a great deal of depth will be added to assist the knowledge-transfer process.

Global Coordination and Control Systems

A top executive recently told us, "Global companies need coordination and control systems to amplify top management's capacity and ability. We can't be everywhere all of the time to supervise or facilitate work. It's almost impossible to understand the total global company from all aspects, but people must be able to manage day by day. We have to depend on the people and the systems to recognize irregularities in the flow of business. Management here must focus on managing the contingencies and the exceptions."

Executive-information systems give management the capability to monitor and coordinate the performance of the company's global processes. Coordination and control systems are based on the twin objectives of sharing resources and creating an optimal flow of processes. The systems have three key focuses: process-control information (sales and service, production, and development and design), external-management information (technology,economics, market trends, and customer needs), infrastructure-management information (administration, personnel, and finance).

A Chief Information Officer (CIO) of one of the most successful firms in Japan showed us his blueprint for a global executive support system. His plans included global management process simulation components for total optimization (for distribution of management resources and simulation of the appropriate scale of production and distribution), coexistence (with competitors, and for localization of management resources), and consolidated management (for analyzing the company organization of a global basis). As Takaho Kashihara, general manager of the business information processing division of Canon, described it to us, he said, "We need a completely different concept for systems by the end of the century. We need to climb a different mountain. And if we don't start building these systems today, we won't be there in time."

Many companies today are trying to tap into their management-information systems scattered around the world to create a global view of their activities and performance. While most companies today have difficulty gathering consistent global information, in the very near future the ability to count on reliable global information, particularly performance indicators, will be a competitive necessity.

Boynton, Victor, and Pine describe an interesting example at Asea Brown Boveri (ABB). "In 1988 ABB encompassed a geographically extensive enterprise of over 850 operating subsidiaries. The company set out on an international acquisition path that, by the end of the 1990, embodied over 1300 operating units. One of the most difficult problems facing senior managers was that of organizing these various worldwide businesses in order to centralize information accurately without stifling local initiative. The operating units had to remain responsive to their local market demands. The most significant operational effort to weave the ABB companies together at the top levels was the installation of a financial and managerial reporting system.

"To improve the organization's ability to provide central coordination and evaluation of product and process capabilities without interfering with local responsiveness, ABB designed a vertical information system called ABACUS (Asea Brown Boveri Accounting and Communication Systems). ABACUS was designed to be powerful in its simplicity, with each country transmitting its results by company and technological business area on an almost continuous basis across a proprietary teleprocessing network called the ABB Corporate Network. The system was specifically designed for use by the senior management of ABB and the business area managements. ABACUS was not intended to be an accounting and reporting instrument for needs of the individual companies. With such an information tool at their disposal, senior managers can discern regional trends, economic fluctuations, and internal managerial problems. ABACUS provides a universal language in that managers throughout ABB's global organization can understand the performance of any country or product group worldwide, thereby increasing the speed of decision making across products and process arenas. In short, ABACUS provides ABB's local companies and profit centers with independence. At the same time it ensures that the firm is taking advantage of the wealth of knowledge it accumulates about product and process performance and capabilities. The ABACUS systems gives ABB the capability to transmit information rapidly and accurately to senior managers. This allows the firm to maintain global operations that are dynamically responsive by company and by profit center to local needs."*

Apple's management decided that to augment the current, inadequate systems it had built for global management coordination, it would create an up-to-date database that included only the most highly critical performance

---

* A. C. Boynton, B. Victor, and B. J. Pine II, "New competitive strategies: Challenges to organizations and information technology," *IBM Systems Journal* 32, no. 1: 40–64.

indicators for its business. The company created data extraction and translation systems to gather pertinent global data from existing systems in over 20 countries, to circumvent the structure of systems it had in place that had been built on a country-by-country basis. The good news is that the company was able to accomplish creating this executive-information system capability in just 12 months. The bad news is that it cost millions of dollars, with plenty of outside help, to pull off.

This desire to create bridging systems for coordination and control is typical of companies that are attempting to speed up the evolution to global and have not kept pace with the investment and redesign of information systems to reflect new global processes. A key global issue is that coordination and control systems must keep up the pace with and reflect the capabilities of the new global processes.

Global I.T. Infrastructure: The Enabling Foundation

Defining the scope and nature of a base global I.T. capability will increase in importance as the implications of I.T.'s future role in global business strategy begins to clarify. For example, cross-functional flows of product information across organizational boundaries among the shop floor, engineering, and materials management is difficult because each organization is likely to have its own self-optimized communications, data and processing hardware, software, and protocols. A seamless, integrated environment that is flexible and malleable in the face of incessant business and technological change requires a set of data transport capabilities and data management interfaces usable by each function, but unique to and owned exclusively by none of them. The informational relationships among the business functions create a need for a shared I.T. infrastructure to enable certain capabilities within the organization that no one business function could afford or is interested in building.

One of the major challenges of infrastructure is that it doesn't come free. Indeed, infrastructure projects often tend to be expensive and require long lead times. Our research into the enabling I.T. infrastructure points to the need for companies to focus on the nature of the I.T. foundation on which their business will compete in the 1990s and to generate the initiative and consensus needed to build and manage it. A new way of looking at technology structures and the management approaches applied in their construction is required.

Much has been written on the role of infrastructure in the evolution of business and society. Our government and judiciary system can be considered part of our social infrastructure.

A closer analogy to I.T., however, would be the public-sector investment in roads, bridges, sewers, water, harbors and the like, or the public regulation of private providers in monopolies, such as cable and telecommunication services. All require large levels of capital investment, are built for the long term, and have a long life. All are managed in a fashion that allows the using communities to influence their construction and operation and are generally believed to add value to the community in a way that could not be achieved through individual private investment.

Recent investigations into the effects of public-sector infrastructure on economic success suggest that infrastructure investment:

- Increases the growth rate of a region as measured by personal income

- Increases manufacturing output in metropolitan areas

- Increases private investment

- Has a greater impact on net capital formation in distressed areas than in growing cities

Furthermore, experts often cite the declining levels of public investment devoted to expanding public infrastructure and the short-term nature of private capital investment as being two of the leading influences on the declining economic success of the North American economy.

With the analogy to the public sector as a backdrop, it is our belief that a basic global technology infrastructure is required in corporations for I.T. investments to be effective over time.

Recently the CIO of one of the largest energy companies in Europe told us how his Chairman had visited the General Manager of a new subsidiary in an Eastern European country. At the conclusion of the meeting the CEO said encouragingly, "Let's follow up on this conversation using the E-mail system," and was instantly struck by the disappointed look on the manager's face.

"You are on the network, aren't you?"

The manager replied, "No. In addition to the basic charge, your I.T. guys at headquarters wanted to saddle us, here, with all the additional costs of adding our 'outpost' to the network, and frankly his cost estimate would have sent our overhead costs way over spending guidelines, given our present transaction volume."

The CEO was unequivocal. "I really want to apologize to you for this bureaucratic thinking. I want to be able to have fast communication with all the key members of our organization, so that we can really make our strategy work. Having you bear all the incremental costs of our network is just stupid thinking. This kind of expense is clearly an infrastructure investment that supports all of us in the company in becoming a broad based European player. You're going to be on our network at the same rate as everyone else."

By investing in an I.T. infrastructure, direct-purpose investments in technology for traditional uses, or in the interest of cross-functional integration, should be more efficient, effective, flexible, and easier to bring to life, thereby making the I.T. infrastructure strategic in and of itself. If this is true, then several questions are raised: What is an I.T. infrastructure? What are its characteristics? How should the infrastructure be managed?

I.T. infrastructure is defined as *"the enabling foundation of shared I.T. capabilities upon which business depends."* I.T. infrastructure deals with the assembly of I.T. software and hardware components into a shared set of capabilities or services that are fundamental to the operation of the business, allows the "direct-purpose" uses of technology to be feasible, and allows the successful implementation of the I.T. architecture. It is the backbone of networks, databases, applications, and "groupware" that enables effective long-term use of I.T. by individuals, work groups, and ultimately the entire global organization.

These shared characteristics differentiate infrastructure from the other I.T. portfolio segments discussed previously. An analogy would be the difference between the electrical distribution infrastructure in a building and the direct purpose appliances that plug into the interface for service.

Developing Effective Global I.T. Capability

Most companies are not starting from a greenfields situation in designing global I.T. systems. The sad truth is that most companies have not managed I.T. well, even domestically, so raising the bar to advance rapidly on a global basis will require tremendous effort. Consider the remarks of the Deputy Chairman of a major European bank:

"Today our systems form a wall, a stone wall you cannot cross. What we need is something much more customer oriented. I can't say how to go from our actual systems to a future solution, there are such strong organizational and technical constraints.

"But putting those aside, the kind of systems we need are very much like your global attributes. We'll need to go from geographic to customer, from

* This definition and many of the ideas on infrastructure were drawn from recent research conducted by our colleagues David McKay, Douglas Brockway and Donald St. Clair, all partners at Nolan, Norton & Co. *The Managing the Technology Infrastructures in the 1990s Working Group* was a multiclient study involving Shell Canada, Mobil Corporation, The World Bank, Hughes Aircraft Company, Harvard University, AT&T, The Electronic Data Interchange Association, Eastman Kodak, IBM Corporation, and Dataquest.

centralized to decentralized, designing common elements in order to keep economies of scale. We'd have to go from production-oriented to marketing-oriented. The systems are mechanistic, and I'd like them to be holistic. Also they should go from isolationist to communicating, over low boundaries, so that anyone can get the system and answer his question—a common set of data that can be reached by anyone in the company feeling the need for it and who has been authorized to reach for it. New systems will make implementation of services possible for worldwide accounts. New global information systems are central to the vision of our company.

"We started too late, focusing on our systems. This should have been done 10 years ago. In the past, our systems were not well integrated. We have got the network now, but we don't have standardized data bases and software. There's too much heterogeneity in our hardware. Our systems should be transparent. Wherever the customer touches our product, it should have the same look and feel.

"I foresee I.T. expenditures rising as we acquire the workstations and software necessary to implement our network. But there is no question. We can't be global without a global system. This is a great impediment we have. We have relationships with over 2000 companies for intercompany services across the world, but if a customer requested even a listing of activity worldwide, I couldn't get it even in a single day. The system is not global."

One would think that companies would learn from their global success stories, but for every excellent example of a global I.T. system we find, we are astonished to find so little duplication of equivalent success in other parts of the business.

Consider the experience of Citicorp's global network evolution: Citicorp's international regions had developed networks independent from one another, and when the bank began to link the networks in the late 1970s, it found that it had different kinds of networks in each of the regions. It ultimately standardized on one specific vendor's multiplexers for the regional traffic, but then the bank began to look into a packet network to replace the store-and-forward network it had been using. It chose one vendor, but complications arose when some regions objected to a change. Ultimately, the regions agreed to use the packet network between the regions and rely upon the standardized multiplexers within the regions.

In the next chapter, we focus on tangible steps to build powerful global systems that align I.T. with the global business strategy.

Summary

Top management is convinced that you can't become global without making excellent use of a wide variety of information technology. Today information technologies offer great potential. Few companies have made real inroads in developing effective global information technology capability. New global I.T. should be implemented in conjunction with transformed business processes for maximum benefit. Five global I.T. portfolios help describe the market for I.T. in the global organization.

Action Checklist

1. Is I.T. one of your company's top global strategic imperatives?

2. When you implement a global I.T. change is it made in conjunction with some form of organization or process change?

3. Do your global I.T. initiatives align to your company's global business initiatives?

4. Do you have a way to sort out the wide variety of global I.T. investment opportunities into meaningful portfolios to facilitate decision making?

7

Taking Steps toward Creating Global Strategic Advantage with I.T.

Executives wishing to develop global I.T. capability must begin with the global business vision articulated by senior management, a vision, as we saw in Chapter 1, that grows out of executive deliberation of how the company should be run to survive and compete in the twenty-first century. The global vision leads to global strategy, through a more rigorous analytical process for determining key imperatives of global success—defining the activities that must be done well and the resources that must be allocated to achieve the desired results. Global strategy, in turn, leads to the formulation of global strategic initiatives—a finite set of programs packaged to achieve measurable progress toward the business vision. In most cases, I.T. will be integral to the accomplishment of these initiatives.

There are four major challenges to companies in building an organization that can leverage I.T. to compete globally:

1. Understanding the corporate global vision and where the company is today vis-à-vis that vision

2. Initiating global systems thinking

3. Developing a global I.T. architectural framework that aligns with the global vision

4. Developing global I.T. resource management and deployment capabilities for continuous improvement and change

This multistep process grounds the process with a thorough understanding of the company's vision, as well as a baseline assessment of where the company is today.

Global business tactics change quickly in reaction to the dynamic course of world events. Accomplishing a basic transformation to the new global business form, on the other hand, is a long-term process that may take at least 10 years. Quick strike I.T. developments must be delivered rapidly to support global business tactics, while the design and implementation of major global I.T. capabilities is usually a process that takes a minimum of four or five years. This is why it is so important to make distinctions between tactics and fundamental strategy and link the strategic direction of I.T. to the company's essential global strategy.

Understanding the Corporate Global Vision and Where the Company Is Today Vis-à-Vis that Vision

Just as the transformation from a given starting point on the globalization matrix (see Figure 2.1) into a global company is different depending on the starting point, so, too, the I.T. platform in support of these moves will be different. Managers in companies going global have to exploit their companies' strengths and focus on and shore up the weaknesses. They begin this process by understanding the company's global vision and position on the globalization matrix and relating it to the key areas where I.T. can add value. In many companies this positioning works at multiple levels. The global I.T. strategy must reflect the multiple positioning.

Let's consider two of Pirelli's major business sectors: tires and cables. The tire sector is a multinational with global products and is subject to fierce competition from three competitors, each three times its size. It projects a consistent image of innovation and quality which it needs to be able to exploit anywhere in the world. The tire sector's global strategy is closely tied to its ability to stay aligned to the strategy of its global customers. It tries to leverage central research with regional development or application centers. The tire sector has to be faster and more flexible than its larger competitors in order to survive. The tire sector's global I.T. strategy must support integrated activity and consistent high-quality delivery.

The cable sector, on the other hand, which is tied with Alcatel for first place in worldwide market share, operates as a multilocal and caters to very local markets with very local products. Its diversified products need extensive customization, consequently the role of central R&D is modified to take advantage of working with local R&D. It is also difficult to have focused factories in the cable sector, because of high transport costs relative to total product costs. In the cable sector, where integration is much less of an issue, the ability to develop and support common production processes to keep manufacturing costs down is a major global opportunity for I.T..

Because of their geographic coverage—143 factories in 17 countries—both Pirelli sectors stand to benefit from any I.T. support that reduces the negative impact of time and distance, assures better training of employees worldwide, or helps to better manage financial resources.

Simplistically, the global exporter's I.T. strategic challenge seems very much one of putting much greater flexibility into the user interfaces. The multilocal's challenge is in melding together disparate systems into a much more integrated central core.

The new global I.T. platform also requires sweeping changes to allow for (1) the coexistence of product, process, knowledge, and coordination support systems, (2) applications becoming much shorter-lived to meet fast-changing customer needs and unpredictable requirements, and (3) having modular, reusable I.T. components that can be rapidly assembled and disassembled which take advantage of a shared information and communication resource. All these changes will require a lot of investment, time, and new management skills and processes.

As Ives, Jarvenpaa, and Mason point out, "Without a shared business vision, developing global I.T. is costly and may be strongly resisted by country managers. . . . Even executives committed to globalize may be reluctant to approve such an investment without compelling understanding of how it will contribute to achieving global objectives."*

One CIO we worked with told his executive management team that the company needed a global telecommunications network to allow remote engineers (in Paris, Tokyo, and San Francisco) to send drawings to each other. When the network was considered on "its own" merits, without considering the added value that would be created in concert with other component programs from the various I.T. portfolios, the project failed to meet investment/return ratios that would satisfy executive management. The project was quickly shot down.

Six months later, after conducting a high-level global architecture study that more fully explored and developed the company's global vision, a much clearer set of justifications for the network was developed. These included

---

* B. Ives, S.L. Jarvenpaa, and R.O. Mason, "Global business drivers: Aligning information technology to global business strategy," *IBM Systems Journal* 32, no. 1 (1993), 143–161.

enabling new global processes such as global customer support, optimizing distribution activity, and coordinating worldwide manufacturing production schedules. This time the same proposal (in terms of technology and cost), now firmly anchored to the global vision, went flying through.

Peter Keen writes, "The key step in the business and technology dialog is to link business imperatives to I.T. imperatives. The linkage is based on the thought process that 'if this is a must for the business, it is vital to our I.T. strategy' . . . A business imperative may not have a corresponding I.T. imperative, but when it does, I.T. becomes a business priority, not a technical support function."*

Setting the Global Management Direction for I.T.

The Chief Information Officer (CIO) is a term we use to describe the senior person in the corporation with the responsibility for establishing and ensuring the direction of the firm's use of I.T. It's a tough, demanding job because the CIO's role is increasingly becoming one of influencing rather than managing a diverse set of technologies that are becoming more and more intertwined with the company's products and processes. Few CIOs directly manage more than 50 percent of the firm's I.T. resources, and many have no direct line operational responsibility. Yet the CIO is expected to be responsible for the strategic direction of I.T., as well as ensuring the alignment between I.T. strategy and the business strategy. The CIO is accountable for long-term progress and results.

In many companies, line responsibility for I.T. is devolving to the business units. As businesses decentralize, business managers want more control over their information assets. With I.T. as the fastest growing expense item in many corporation's budgets, line managers are attempting to take more responsibility over this investment affecting their bottom lines, often in direct conflict to the desires and strategies of the CIO. It's not surprising, therefore, that the half-life of most CIOs is less than five years.

In the past, most CIOs haven't had the time to treat anything outside the home country as anything other than a remote location. Today this is changing. Most have highly focused agendas. They are spending a great deal of time coping with increased requirements for integration while trying to accommodate the relentless quest for lowered costs and increased customer focus. As we have shown, these global objectives and national objectives are not necessarily incompatible. What is needed is the ability to step back and look at the problems from a broader perspective and with a global mindset.

---

* Peter G.W. Keen, "Information technology and the management difference: A fusion map," *IBM Systems Journal* 32, no. 1 (1993), 17–39.

While it's the CIO's job to oversee these programs, today's CIOs need to coopt every employee in the organization in order to be successful. Because successful implementations of I.T. are so integral to global success, it's every manager's job to understand the complexities and tradeoffs involved. Every manager must hold a piece of the I.T. solution. The most important success factors for any I.T. projects are commitment from the top and involvement of managers and employees.

Initiating Global Systems Thinking

Recently, while we were having dinner with the CEO of a major investment bank, we inquired about the relationship of I.T. to the bank's global strategy.

"Nobody can put it all together," he responded. "My I.T. people are very good at building computer systems, but they aren't bankers. My bankers are very good at defining problems, but they can only understand a narrow piece of the problem. I don't have anyone who can put it all together."

He then reflected on his professional upbringing. His academic degree is in operations research. He had been trained to think in terms of "systems," looking at the whole instead of the parts. He now found little of this systems thinking in his bank, nor in other organizations he was familiar with. His parting question was, "What ever happened to the systems approach?"

David Norton provides a plausible answer to this question. His basic contention is that the systems approach, which grew out of the operations research movement first observed in the United Kingdom during World War II and quickly picked up by the U.S. Army, can be applied to global information-systems planning. Such people as Tex Thornton (future founder of Litton Industries), Arjay Miller (future president of Ford), and Robert McNamera (future president of Ford and the World Bank, as well as U.S. Secretary of Defense), thought that the systems approach was "a good idea ahead of its time."

As Norton writes, "The underlying structural pressures faced by Western businesses between the 1950s and the 1980s did not require systemization. We witnessed the high point of the Industrial Era through the 1960s and its subsequent rationalization and decomposition in the 1970s and 1980s. The strategic paradigm was portfolio based; it accepted the operational structure of a business (a Strategic Business Unit or SBU) and dealt with the relationships among units. While this changed the financial foundations on which business operated, it did very little to change the operational structure. The systems approach was not needed.

"Today, as we enter the decade of the 1990s, we are searching for new fundamental organizational models; we are searching for paradigms that meet the needs of the emerging Information Age. The pressures of restructuring and resystemizing the basic operations of a business which were absent in the past 30 years are clearly present. It is time to bring back the systems approach!"*

Bringing back the systems approach involves three essential ingredients: a way of thinking, the use of models and dynamic simulation, and the use of multidisciplinary teams and processes.

The most important ingredient is the way of thinking about the whole system. Perhaps Jay Forrester summed up systems thinking best when he said, "Systems engineering is the formal awareness of the interactions between the parts of the system. . . . The interconnections, the compatibility, the effect of one on the other, the objectives of the whole, the relationship of the system to the uses, and the economic feasibility must receive ever more attention than the parts if the final result is to be effective."† If we think in terms of systems, everything else will fall into place.

Use Models, Simulations, and Systems Dynamics

Business today is in a state of transition, and we can count on transition as a permanent state for the foreseeable future. Thus any approach to organizational design that is static is inadequate. Global business design is a dynamic phenomenon that requires dynamic, time-variant approaches.

The concept of creating a dynamic global business architecture is drawn from process-control industries. These industries were very early users of simulation to model the flow of product through various stages of intermediate product processing and transportation. In the early days, the simulations were physical models that used fluid flowing through channels of different sizes.

While these abstract models were initially used for system design, over time we began to see the very same models on the walls of "control rooms," where the actual flow of material was being actively managed and controlled. In effect, the abstract simulation model had become a reality.

We believe that a similar approach to the design of more complex organizations is needed today. Dynamic simulation should become the fundamental tool of global business architects. The simulation should not be a one-shot effort to solve a single problem; it should be a living model of the business that is maintained as a point of reference for defining the business and information architecture. With such a dynamic approach, the abstract model should become a reality, allowing a company to quickly evaluate new directions and implement perpetual change.

* David P. Norton, *Stage-by-Stage* 9, no. 2 (1989).

† Jay W. Forrester, *Industrial Dynamics* (Cambridge: MIT Press, 1961), 6.

While some companies have converted their architectural blueprints into dynamic models on a local or regional scale, we don't know of any company which has implemented a dynamic enterprise model on a global basis. It is a concept that we've seen on the drawing boards of several leading companies, though, and it should give us all pause for thought.

Developing a Global I.T. Architectural Design Framework

We have been working with our colleagues and our research clients over the last 10 years to develop a strategic planning process for I.T. that incorporates these principles of systems thinking. We call this process I.T. architecture design. The term I.T. architecture refers to the structure of technology in the organization for carrying out business.* Today, we are firmly convinced that companies attempting to go global will have to incorporate some form of global system design processes or the various pieces of the organization can never be integrated. Orchestrating this process is the major job of the CIO.

After the global business vision has been developed, analysis can begin to determine the structural components of what we call global business design: global business processes, logical locations, and information. Senior management's validation of global business design is required to ensure that the attributes that can be created with I.T. are indeed the attributes most important to realizing the objectives of the global strategic initiatives.

Global I.T. architecture concerns itself with the relationships between business global design and the conceptual data, communications, and applications needed to enable that design. Because it is focused on the business vision three to five years out, global I.T. architecture describes the relationship between the business vision and the I.T. investments in much the same way that an artist's rendition, a model, and a set of blueprints describe a building that has yet to be built.

The conceptual global architecture can be derived from the global business design, linking executives with implementors further down in the organization. The conceptual global architecture is made up of high-level blueprints for key categories of I.T. (applications, data, and communications). See Figure 7-1. These blueprints can be conducted to assess the costs, benefits, time, and risk of building a target global architecture from a baseline global architecture.

* Richard Nolan first introduced this definition in a Nolan, Norton & Co. Research working group on I.T. architecture in 1985.

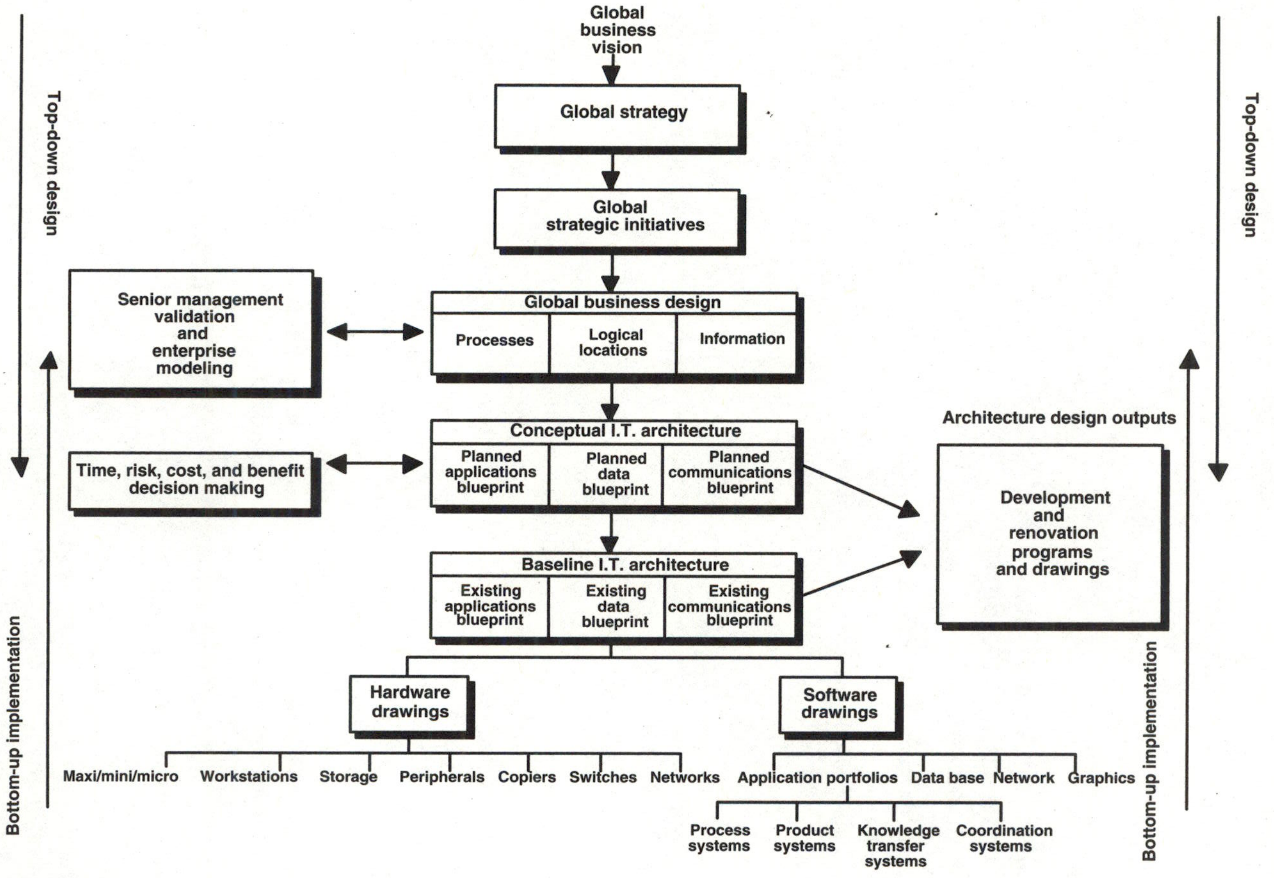

Figure 7-1. Global I.T. architecture design framework.

Global Business Design

Even the clearest global vision can be diluted as it diffuses through the organization, losing focus, and failing to bring about the many changes necessary to move the entire enterprise onto its chosen course. This dilution often results in fragmentation of the global vision, producing multiple interpretations and a state of organized confusion. Even a perfectly tuned global vision risks becoming just another slogan. The key is to translate the global vision into global business designs that embody three key business variables:

- Processes—The means by which an organization acts to accomplish its objectives.

- Locations—The places, both internal and external, where the business processes are performed.

- Information—The information required by the business processes at each location.

These three variables provide the necessary design platform for deriving the global I.T. architecture blueprints.

Processes.   The experience of one high-tech manufacturer illustrates how using an organizational or functional model for global I.T. design can result in a fragmented global I.T. architecture.

In response to declining customer satisfaction, the company recruited a new executive team and spun off the worldwide service function into a separate business unit, with its own IS organization. The strategy provided the needed focus on field service and resulted in greatly improved customer satisfaction. By making field service a separate, self-contained entity, with its own I.T. architecture, however, the company quickly noticed a great deal of inadvertent redundancy had been created which overlapped the I.T. architecture of the marketing, sales, and engineering functions. Soon the company found it couldn't combine data collected from field service with data from the other organizations. The sales force no longer had the information that gave early warning that existing customers were running out of capacity and might require an upgrade. And the design engineers could no longer analyze product-repair histories for ways to improve product quality. On top of it all, customers soon realized that they were dealing with two separate companies, neither knowing the full extent of the customer account activities.

The organizational split that created the separate field-service organization broke up the basic process flow by which the company delivered its goods and services. Creating a new I.T. architecture specifically oriented towards the functions of the new organization was like isolating the business in an island of concrete. Eventually the inability to communicate with the other parts of the business became a major competitive liability.

A process model of a business provides a much better description for designing global I.T. solutions than functional or organizational models. Since processes cross multiple organization boundaries, process models foster development of cross-organizational solutions and discourage duplication and fragmentation of activity and support. The scope of the process model need not be limited by corporate boundaries. Many companies are examining their customer's value chains and process flows, as well as those of their customers and other industry participants, as they seek to build alliances and lock in customer relationships.

American Airlines, for example, has reached beyond reservation and ticketing and is automating many other functions of a travel agency, thus insuring the institutionalization of its SABRE system in travel agents' businesses all over the world. Similarly, commercial banks are examining models of the cash-management functions within large corporations to find ways of embedding the bank's systems within the customer's business wherever they perform cash-management activities.

Business-process modelling is a useful tool for understanding the ways in which a company, its customers, and other industry participants add value. It is the marriage of this view with the information and location variables of business design that allows the facility to identify how I.T. will help achieve the goals set forth in the global business vision.

Locations.   Global businesses operate in a world that seems to be getting smaller. Securities firms, concerned with position exposure, are "passing the book" around the globe in 24-hour trading operations. Manufacturers are struggling to link up with offshore suppliers and domestic customers. Retailers are busy developing the sale's outlet of the future—in the customer's home.

Increasingly, managers in businesses are decoupling the logical view of their business from physical constraints and then rearranging the logic to best achieve the global vision. They are taking a fresh look at where they do business and how they might achieve competitive advantage by performing activities at locations ranging from corporate headquarters to their customer's wallet.

How do you unlock the latent potential of business locations? Begin by declaring all locations open territory for innovation and asking what might be gained by rearranging different parts of each process at different locations. Location analysis is greatly simplified through the technique of location modeling. Designing for each physical location becomes a nightmare when your scope includes 250 branch offices or 10,000 dealerships. We suggest you distill the basic location types into objects of design we call logical locations.

The logical location is a generic place for doing business, with a set of properties that achieve specific business objectives. Thus, 250 branch offices become three generic branch types and 10,000 dealerships become just two dealership types having several embedded locations such as a showroom, a parts' store, and repair bays. Each logical location is distinguished by its own unique properties such as a mix of business process, convenience, mobility, economics, and a number of physical occurrences.

These and other properties of the logical location work in concert to achieve the global business vision. Once defined, the logical locations become the basic unit of global architecture design, with each location having a unique architecture of data, applications, communications, technology, and associated cost and benefit. Each logical location can then be mapped to physical business locations, thereby achieving the translation of the "conceptual" global architecture into its real-world counterpart.

Information.   Dennis Mulryan, a former colleague at Nolan, Norton & Co., related a story that draws the fine line between information and data. The scene opens with the late Peter Sellers as Inspector Clouseau making his way to the front desk of his hotel. The Inspector is stopped short by a ferocious looking dog. Politely he asks the attendant, "Monsieur, does your dog bite?" The attendant replies "No" and Clouseau proceeds, only to be torn to shreds by the dog. Angrily, he says, "Monsieur, you said your dog does not bite!" to which the attendant replies, "That is not my dog!" Clearly the Inspector had some of the data, but no information.

This story illuminates the frustration felt today by many managers. They need only look at their in-baskets, either at the stacks of paper or electronic messages, to feel that they are drowning in a sea of data. The fundamental problem in distinguishing between "information" and "data" lies in your ability to draw upon the sea to assemble information useful to the business. This is like having all the parts to assemble a complex piece of machinery without having a picture or idea of what machine you are trying to build.

To ensure that the global I.T. architecture has the right set of data entities with the correct relationships to fit together into a valuable information product, it is necessary to capture the information requirements of the global business processes into a high-level bill of materials known as the global data entity model—the conceptual blueprint for global database construction.

Data entity models are extremely valuable tools for computer programmers. As conceptual I.T. architecture planning tools, however, the creation of these models can become so time consuming and costly that they usually have negative value for planning and decision making. Our advice to companies in the global business design phase is to first limit data entity modeling to *key* global business processes. Secondly, only work with high-level data entities such as "customer" or "supplier" (as opposed to "customer name" and "supplier address"). Then, since projects have been selected and sequenced for implementation, the models can be driven down from conceptual to logical and then physical levels.

Recently, the European manufacturing company described in the previous chapter desired to redesign and better integrate its 15 single country order-processing systems into the broader company business process. As a first step, a cross-functional, cross-geographic team of managers, who could each describe the various activities in their business locations, was created. At the beginning of the project, based on the team's collective experience, there was a general consensus that 20 percent of the functionality of the renewed systems could be the same and 80 percent would have to be different. The countries were adamant about this.

The often repeated comment was, "Forget building the intergalactic global system, what we need are basic local systems." As a result the team built separate process, location, and information-flow models for each country so they could clearly understand the basics and the opportunities.

Building the models in the same way, and with a common team, however, enabled senior management to see that what the countries did was much more similar than they had expected, even though various countries were at different stages of development. The team eventually reached the conclusion that over 80 percent of the studied activity was the same, and less than 20 percent different. They then developed the blueprints of the required applications, data, and communications, which provided consistency while allowing for diversity.

A global I.T. architecture is highly valuable because it serves as the master schedule for the complex integration required to tie together a wide variety of disparate projects into a unified conception that supports the global business vision and strategic initiatives. It not only provides the blueprints for integration, but it also establishes the required engineering sequence of activity (i.e., you can't start development of project C until project A is completed, but project E can begin at any time).

The global I.T. architecture is also of major value because it highlights the collective synergy between these projects and the business goals. While costs can be fairly easily associated with almost all of the specific projects contained in an architecture, the determination of benefits is often a more difficult challenge.

The global I.T. architecture requires executive sponsorship on an ongoing basis. A regular executive committee review can be an effective method of ensuring that the business strategy and global I.T. architecture are heading in the same direction. By establishing metrics of progress internally as well as versus the industry and competition, executives can monitor key business indicators. Throughout the design and implementation of the global

I.T. architecture, the executive team can keep exploring the idea of where and how the company has the capability and necessity to be global. Knowing where a company has to be more global helps to prioritize projects.

Developing Global I.T. Resource Management and Deployment Capabilities

Global I.T. resources are the technologies, people, and skills required to design, build, and operate global I.T. architectures. While allocating and managing I.T. resources and activities within borders has become a fairly well understood process, the problem is much more complex on a global scale. Because you can't develop global capability without first having a global mindset, the I.T. people resources must, as a first step, get deeply indoctrinated in and committed to the company's global vision and strategic initiatives. Competent I.T. staff will be the scarcest resource.

Secondly, the I.T. organization needs to be the exemplar in the use of global technologies as they point the way to the future. While we have seen many companies moving their business product development process to a distributed, around the world, 24-hour a day basis, we have seen only a few companies take a similar global approach to developing I.T. systems.

Ives, Jarvenpaa, and Mason write, "Successful global projects often employ an international design team. The international composition means that the team lives in a multicultural environment on a day-to-day basis, and reflects the environment that the resulting system must accommodate. For example, the design team for a worldwide logistics system included eight people located in two locations in the United States, six located in the Far East, and five others in France. The project manager worked in a location in France. The team met quarterly with their international executive steering committee. Between the meetings the design team made heavy use of information technology infrastructure to coordinate their activities. They used the same systems development methodology, computer-aided software engineering tools, and worldwide corporate data standards. Modules to be developed were assigned depending on the expertise within each country unit's systems development staff. Electronic mail was used extensively for daily communication among the team members. Electronic mail bridged the time zone differences and helped to maintain (but not necessarily create) personal relationships between the business and systems personnel."*

---

* B. Ives, S.L. Jarvenpaa, and R.O. Mason, "Global business drivers: Aligning information technology to global business strategy," *IBM Systems Journal* 32, no. 1 (1993), 143–161.

Since I.T. resources are scarce the world over, it will be an advantage to learn how to do concurrent design and development within the I.T. organization. AT&T, DEC, and CitiCorp are currently using teams of expert programmers in India to troubleshoot software bugs discovered in their U.S. operational systems. Other companies can develop similar capabilities. While today one of the main drivers behind such approaches is to take advantage of a lower-cost labor pool, this type of global resource sharing will in the future be used to leverage increasingly scarce expertise. And the more the I.T. organization develops the capability to work as a globally networked organization, the better able it will be to act as the change agent to help the business enter the global frontier.

Working together in the globally networked I.T. organization encompasses all the challenges we described in Chapter 5. Most importantly, concurrent and cooperative development requires the agreement to and adoption of certain common business processes and management practices (which might be embodied in a shared system development methodology for example), and common technical standards that facilitate interconnectivity.

Some differences in technical standards, such as those imposed by isolationist governmental practices, are extremely difficult to overcome, but more and more the vendor movement toward "open architectures" is allowing companies to overcome the old technical obstacles if they are disciplined and persistent in approach.

The up-front investment, particularly the infrastructure components, for rationalizing former incompatible technologies which allow the development of significant and valuable global I.T. capability, will be huge. Consequently, it is extremely important to thoroughly explore the potential added value created by broadly using such services and systems. A global I.T. architecture design process will prove invaluable in aggregating potential benefits, as well as in understanding the long-term cost advantages of taking a systematic global-development approach over patchwork incrementalism.

Developing global I.T. takes time, and the investment will be formidable. Managing the risk and complexity of the company's global I.T. architecture development, therefore, means that the company has to balance long-term investments with a regular stream of short-term deliverables. The value of going global will have to be continually reinforced and demonstrated to the company's managers.

Apple's executive information system referred to in Chapter 6 was designed very expediently. Rather than waiting for the "clean up" of each of the country systems that fed the global indicators, a multiyear undertaking, the data editing and translation was designed to occur after the source data was extracted and did not have an effect on any of the existing system functionality. These types of "quick-strike" global projects are allowing companies to become better coordinated without completely disrupting business. As long as the progressive benefits can be demonstrated on regular and frequent time intervals, the overall investment in the global I.T. architecture will proceed with greater commitment from the whole business.

Another method for managing the risk of a company's overall investment in global I.T. is to consider partnerships for outsourcing some of the global I.T. activities (like the provisioning of the global network). Increasingly, managers of global companies are realizing that no company can perform all of its global activities alone. The ability to do top-to-bottom integration is vastly too expensive. Many companies are concentrating on the core activities of their business. In this respect, I.T. is no different from any other management concern; developing your company's core and diverse competencies may entail outsourcing some activities to alliance companies which specialize in providing these services.

Outsourcing can be less expensive. The providing companies may have achieved economies of scale far greater than your company could achieve by performing these services for many companies, as well as developed far greater expertise. Providing companies may also be able to bring a far wider breadth of new technologies to bear on your issues, and may be more responsive to your company's needs since your company is their customer. By outsourcing, you acquire specialist services at commodity prices, while you focus on those activities that create competitive advantage.

Summary

A company's global I.T. strategy should reflect the company's position on the global matrix. Global I.T. architectural blueprints describe the alignment between the business vision and the I.T. investments. Three important business variables (processes, locations, and information) provide the necessary design platform for developing the global I.T. architecture blueprints. Dynamic simulation is a fundamental tool of global business architects. Managing global I.T. infrastructures is one of the key responsibilities of top management that cannot be delegated. The I.T. organization needs to be the exemplar in the use of global technologies as they point the way to the future.

Action Checklist

1. Does your global I.T. strategy reflect the company's position(s) on the globalization matrix?

2. Is global business process modeling an integral part of your global I.T. architecture activity?

3. Do your global I.T. architecture activities include the use of dynamic simulations?

4. Does your CIO take the lead in identifying key global I.T. infrastructure requirements and champion their funding and evolution? Do members of the executive team champion projects or play key roles?

8

Accelerating and Streamlining the Globalization Process

The Next Five Years in the Global Marketplace

For most companies with revenues of $100 million or more, becoming global is necessary for corporate survival. The global challenge for business is that globalization requires a fundamental structural change in business practices.

A number of executives' and managers' basic assumptions about work are being challenged. In this age of global business, managers will focus on how to build a consistent set of business practices, while balancing global and local customer demand, coordinating decentralized activities, and leveraging human, information, and financial resources.

Companies that are starting from different international orientations—the multinationals, global exporters, and multilocals—have different challenges to face. However, all companies face the same competitive environment, in which regulations and standards of trade are changing and major industries are integrating. The global shake-out of industries is occurring now. The race to build relationships with global customers and suppliers is on. The global challenge is here.

Throughout this time of change, one powerful influence on the global landscape of business will be information technology. Global information technology systems can inhibit or enable globalization. Information services, hardware, and software can help fulfill or deny the strategic direction of the business. The choice of direction is in the hands of business executives, managers, and teams. People can either choose to use tools effectively or disregard them. One vitally important point about information technology, however, is that the tool is not neutral.

Shoshana Zuboff, in her book about how information technology is changing the way we work,* states clearly that "computer-based technologies are not neutral; they embody essential characteristics that are bound to alter the nature of work within our factories and offices, and among workers, professionals, and managers. New choices are laid open by these technologies, and these choices are being confronted in the daily lives of men and women across the landscape of modern organizations."

These new choices offer an opportunity to link human effort in a new way, on a global scale, and to improve our lives and the environment. These new choices require executives and managers who have the courage to take up the global challenge. This book is a call to action, an attempt to decipher some of the changes that are occurring, and a guide through some of the exciting terrain of a compelling adventure.

This final chapter notes additional trends and influences on global business life, and synthesizes the initial steps to take to set companies in motion to take up the global business challenge.

Seven Key Trends

Going forward, companies will be focussing on seven major trends:

- Balancing technological and organizational change
- Opening up on-line communications and networks
- Building collaborative work
- Concentrating on core competencies and forming alliances for the non-core
- Creating the mass customization of product and process change
- Making knowledge data bases and performance indices available on a global basis
- Taking advantages in developments of microtechnology

* Shoshana Zuboff, "In the Age of the Smart Machine: the Future of Work and Power" (New York: Basic Books, Inc., Publishers), 1988.

Firms that build competence in these seven ways will have an advantage in the global business arena.

Balancing Technological and Organizational Change

As a whole, the organization has a learning curve to move up to acquire new skills to adapt technology to new business situations and to be able to cope with organizational change on an ongoing basis. Balancing technological and organizational change, therefore, is necessary to enable the organization to move up the learning curve. Professor Dorothy Leonard-Barton of the Harvard Business School has studied the effects of integrating technology and culture, and finds that the two can be managed in a simultaneous change process effectively.

"Successful new technology implementation is an interactive process of incrementally altering the technology to fit the organization and simultaneously shaping the user environment to exploit the potential of the technology. Thus it is a process of integration because technology managers must be concerned simultaneously with organizational and technical design."*

The integrative design approach supports organizational learning by addressing the strategic, organizational, and technological effects of change.

On-line Communications and Networks

The need for on-line information is increasing as companies seek to compress their design to manufacturing cycles and as the world becomes increasingly interdependent. Information intensive industries, such as energy, pharmaceuticals, travel, etc., are expanding their need for up-to-date market and economic data.

Industries that are concentrating on a global basis, such as steel, are also increasing their on-line information needs. James A. Rowe, an executive at the Iron and Steel Statistics Bureau in the United Kingdom, tells why.

"At the moment there is an overcapacity in the world steel industry. For example, in Europe, there are about 25 bulk steel producers at the same time market demand is equal to the output of perhaps 10 world-class producers. There is a downward pressure on the industry that creates an enormous demand for information. Both governments and companies need to stay in touch with production, delivery, energy, stocks, and raw material information on a regional and global basis.

* Dorothy Leonard-Barton, "The Role of Process Innovation and Adaptation in Attaining Strategic Technological Capability," Working Paper #91-029 (Boston, Massachusetts: Harvard Business School, Division of Research), Aug. 1990.

"Steel and steel products account for 10% in total of the number of headings for European tariffs. Our bureau monitors 25 leading countries around the world including the U.S., Japan, South Korea, South Africa, Australia, and all of the major European countries. The Eastern European countries do not publish their trade data as yet.

"The steel industry is, by tradition, an information intensive industry. We have developed a system based on a 4th generation language that has a good report generation facility. In the last ten years, there has been a tremendous shift to magnetic and electronic media and away from paper, to cope with the scale of data bases and volume of data transfers to update these. There has also been a dramatic increase in the number of people who understand information and technology."

In the future, there may hardly be an industry that could not benefit from tapping into the on-line networks of trade information to track the global information flows about raw materials, goods, and services.

Collaborative Work

Just as businesses are growing more interdependent, so workers themselves are learning to share knowledge across organizational boundaries. By understanding what others need to know, when they need to know, how a simultaneous decision process can work on a dynamic basis, and how to build a common language, managers and knowledge workers are building the foundation skills of the Information Age.

The management of information is a tool to enable flexible management decision making. Imai, Nonaka, and Takeuchi suggest that when companies attempt to overlap functions to improve time to market processes "information works to enhance flexibility." They found that managers introduced management control subtly developed from the cross-functional sharing of information from customers and competitors.[*]

"This sharing of information helps keep everyone up-to-date, build cohesion within the group, and act as a source of peer pressure. . . . Each member has to sharpen his/her own skills, and at the same time, mutually support the continuity of the network at large. Mutual support is enhanced through tightly knit interactions among members on a day-to-day basis to exchange relevant business information and ideas. Continuity is maintained by establishing a system of shared division of labor among the network members."[†]

---

[*] N. Caroline Daniels, "Bridging the Gap: The Use of Information Systems to Shorten the Design to Manufacturing Cycle in the U.K. Clothing Industry," Doctoral Thesis, London Business School (April 1992).

[†] Ken-ichi Imai, Ikujiro Nonaka, and Hirotaka Takeuchi, "Managing the New Product Development Process: How Japanese Companies Learn and Unlearn," *The Uneasy Alliance,* eds. Kim B.Clark; Hayes, Robert H.; Lorenz, and Christopher (Boston, Massachusetts: Harvard Business School Press, 1985), 337–375.

By sharing content cross-functionally, a shared basis of information provides a basis for continuity. This process of sharing content and building coherent business processes cross-functionally builds a management learning process.

As companies seek to become more customer focused and allow product differentiation in each stage of the production process, more and more workers will be involved in the ultimate design of the products and services offered to their customers. For example, the service employee who is able to change an arrangement to suit a customer, such as a British Airways employee changing a passenger's airline seat to allow the customer to enjoy the journey in more comfort, may be the decisive factor that determines whether a customer selects one company over another.

Dumas and Whitfield* discuss the need for cross-functional currency in communication throughout the design process. They suggest that because design activity is not a discrete activity, design decisions are made throughout the whole business process, and that "good communications and up-to-date information" are critical. They also suggest that any attempt at management control of the design process must take into account the whole of the company's operations, since "addressing only fragments of the design process can lead to overcontrol of the identified parts as a compensation for lack of control over the unidentified parts." Linking activities, such as design and manufacturing, through cross-functional information exchange on a current basis, enables the process to be more interactive.

Concentrating on Core Competencies and Forming Alliances for the Noncore

In the 1970s and 1980s, many companies experimented with diversification. There were some great successes, including Elf Acquitaine, one of the ten largest energy companies in the world. Elf has grown chemical and pharmaceutical businesses that now are top global contenders. Elf used its global reach, its knowledge of sourcing raw materials in several areas, and the knowledge developed in how to synthesize chemicals to develop these new areas. Elf has now decided to concentrate on these three businesses as core businesses.

Many companies have come back to focus on the basics of their businesses, to have a rethink on what the company is especially good at doing. In business jargon, this has been called "core competency." Companies are more precisely defining who they are, the resources they have, and what they can do.

* Angela Dumas and Alan Whitfield, "Why Design is Difficult to Manage: A Survey of Attitudes and Practices in British Industry," *European Management Journal* 7, no. 1 (1989), 50–56.

The need for alliances, not perhaps long-term joint ventures or mergers but alliances that are built on mutuality of competence and interest, is being created to forge new businesses across corporate borders.

Mass Customization Product and Process Change

Managing the dichotomy of being a low-cost producer while being responsive to local and global customers is the ultimate objective of the mass customization process. By focussing on creating an organization that has a stable process of teams coming together to solve problems, a company can address new markets and problems flexibly. By building a flexible, stable process, management teams can leverage their human and capital resources to customize products to customers' specifications.

Knowledge Data Bases and Performance Indices

Japanese companies have for many years developed research institutes in the markets they wish to penetrate to study customer purchase patterns and behavior. This is an especially effective technique in developing knowledge about customers on a global basis. Companies use local customer information to customize and match product and service offerings on a local basis.

Chris Samuels, CEO of the Center for Strategic Research in Boston, has developed a method to map customers' ideas onto a company's area of product and service offerings.

"Customer needs come first. The biggest investment a company will ever make is in its customers. Management's task is to understand and explain *why* customers become and remain customers. Demographics—type or size of business, for example—and behaviors—volume of business or channel—are never predictive of whether or why customers do business with particular companies. Using these indicators is like driving down the highway looking in the rearview mirror.

"But, knowing *why* customers do business with your company or with another company, now that information *is* predictive of whether these customers will be with you tomorrow. Knowing *why* gives management teams the decision model with which to focus resources—people, plant and money. This is a matter of logic and clear thinking.

"The process we have developed depends on being able to ask customers to share their best thinking about matters of critical interest to our clients. Think about these questions and the myriad answers that are possible: "Why do people do business with the ABC company? What does it mean for a supplier to be customer-focused? What frustrates you about doing business with the XYZ company?" To give customers permission to reply freely and then to transform their answers through coding into quantifiable data and from there into maps that reflect what customers need and expect from the products they buy and from the companies that supply them—now that is a true, customer-derived base for developing strategy.

"Everyday, we hear that price is a true driver. But, if it were true, then no one would buy from high priced competitors. Ah, you say, but those customers who buy the higher priced product are getting some things that other suppliers can't deliver. Precisely the point. Price being equal, what else do customers factor into the buying decision *and why?* These other things represent the added value that really drives the decision to buy.

"So, managers return again and again to the same question: How can we create products and services that customers really need, value and will buy? A good question that reminds me of the answer I saw posted in one client's office. It was a take-off on President Clinton's famous sign. It said: It's the customer, stupid!

"The Japanese are masters of incremental improvements. Once they believe they have a product with features that meet real needs, then they cascade these successful features (or value-added services) down onto products, creating a sense of continual improvements. Toyota has done this successfully with its best selling Lexus by streaming improvements that have proved their ability to drive sales and margins down to less expensive models. This process is based on excellent engineering, solid manufacturing *and* a solid lock on what customers need and expect from its automobiles.

"But, you don't have to be Toyota to get guidance from customers. What management teams need is a commitment to measuring things that matter to customers. It takes guts to ask and quantify the reasons *why* customers buy or reject a company's products and services. It's easier to lock on to information that reflects the past more than it reveals the future. I believe that the real challenge of this decade will be to hook each thing used to measure performance to money changing hands. Measures of satisfaction that don't reflect real increases in sales and that don't explain *why* customers are customers will reveal the real corporate dinosaurs in our midst. For those of us still seeking guidance in our decision making, the message is still: 'It's the customer, stupid!' "

Another type of knowledge data base that is shared within a firm is the skills data base. National Westminster Bank has created a product called ServiceLine that is a data base that helps to build employees' skills while linking the knowledge in the company. ServiceLine is a data base of answers to questions that customers and their own branches are likely to ask. Staff that work with the systems answer customer and branch service calls. They identify the problem and work through to a solution or take the problem as far as they can go. They have a very high problem resolution ratio. If the question cannot be answered, a specialist is contacted. By reserving the specialist for especially difficult questions, the company's scarce human resources are reserved and other staff members' skills are leveraged.

Data bases of development knowledge are shared between research and design teams. Sales and marketing teams share information on client development methods and global accounts. Management teams are sharing data bases on how the business is performing.

Executive information systems (EIS) were developed for high-level executives who wanted to have access to key performance indices of businesses. An EIS would extract vital information, such as sales by country, manufacturing output, and delivery times, and feed the information back to personal computer spreadsheets with user-friendly presentation capabilities located on senior executives' desks.

The EIS concept has worked successfully in a number of organizations and has been expanded into Strategic Performance Indicator Systems (SPIS) available to a wider range of managers. As companies decentralize decision making to cope with expanding global markets, SPIS will be used in most major companies to keep management teams in contact with how the company is performing.

Microtechnology

The microtechnology revolution is continuing to bring changes in price, performance, and power available on the desktop. Microtechnology allows the unbundling of the storage and processing of data. That is, executives and managers not only have access to data, but also interact with data to create new information.

Microtechnology is increasing the mobility of people and systems enabling the integration of power on the desktops, allowing multimedia and imaging to move from the mainframe to the desktop, and supporting the shift from alphanumeric to media-rich communications, and from stand-alone programs to sharable software developed by global teams.

Customers will have more access to data as microtechnology is imbedded in more products and services. In the near future, we will see more products and services offered by stand-alone multimedia workstations. The challenge of how to use microtechnology to reach customers in a new way is an interesting one.

An Action Plan

Measuring Today's Global Position and Establishing Priorities

Increasing volatility in economic conditions and competition have focused managers' attention on developing short-term plans to manage for quick results. A majority of business executives have said that they are looking for results from investment within one year for most projects, with many looking at time frames of three to six months.* Executives also state that they are conducting strategic planning on a one- to three-year basis, or, for a long-term plan, on a five-year basis, and more and more state that they are carrying out a long-term visioning program that covers strategic planning for 10 years and beyond.

Within this fast-paced managerial environment, one common strategic direction is that companies are attempting to integrate information flows. Some common first steps toward information integration include integrating order processing across regions, creating a common general ledger, and building cross-border information models of companies.

By assessing how the company is positioned vis-a-vis the global attributes (see Figure 2-8), management can get a feel for the international direction the company is currently heading in. By identifying which of the international models (multinational, global exporter, or multidomestic) most closely fits the company (or division), managers can come to grips with what it will take to turn the strategic direction of the company to become global.

Secondly, profiling global customers by collecting information on what global and local services they will want and separating fads from fundamentally different market demands will help management decide: What do I do differently tomorrow? Do we need partners or can we do it all alone? What product and service requirements will other companies that are attempting to become global have? How quickly are our domestic sales increasing vis-a-vis our international sales? What is the balance between global and local return on investment?

Finally, taking first steps on the global strategic initiatives will set a clear path for the firm's immediate future.

Step 1.   Develop a Global Vision and Mindset

A global vision is built with a cross-pollination of ideas. Ensuring that people understand and feel comfortable with the vision is a process of shaping the global vision. Henry Mintzberg calls this process "crafting strategy."[†]

---

* Ongoing research on "Global I.T. and Future Needs" carried out by Dr. N. Caroline Daniels at the European Institute for Advanced Studies in Management, Brussels, Belgium.

[†] Henry Mintizberg, "Crafting Strategy," *Harvard Business Review* (July–Aug. 1987), 66–72.

The world's leading companies will restructure their businesses to serve global market segments. The essential parts of a global vision are:

- Serving global and local customers

- Figuring out "what has to be the same in each location so that everything else can be different"; balancing global consistency with local diversity

- Positioning the firm as both a low-cost producer and customer driven

- Developing a flexible product and service architecture that allows for a high level of customization

- Connecting a highly coordinated value chain that utilizes multiple centers of excellence distributed throughout the world in the most appropriate locations

Whether the firm is a global exporter, multinational, or multilocal, executives cultivate the global vision process organically as well as directively. Creating global strategic action programs that get the right people involved up front and bringing more and more people into the process fuses the vision to the culture.

A global vision includes the company's approach to appealing to customers of the world; creating globally scalable resources; managing the connections; developing global leaders, teams, and individuals; leveraging I.T. to build global capability; and aligning the company with globalization stages.

However, the single most important step for a corporate culture attempting to become global is to create a global mindset.

Georges Vialle, Directeur de l'Informatique et des Telecommunications at Club Med, tells why the global mindset is so important as he describes Club Med's growing globalization. "We are a global company because we operate our operations centers on five continents in 40 countries and our customers come from 42 countries on five continents. The Belgian-French company began more than 40 years ago.

"Today no one can stay as a domestic company. 33% of our customers are French, 33% European, 20% from North America and 13% are Asian. The challenge is to have the same business concept all over the world, to sell the same product all over the world, and to be able to customize this concept to the habits of each country.

"If you decide to develop global systems, the big issue is the tradeoff between differentiation and integration. The value of global systems is economies of scale.

"We have gained economies of scale by sharing the development of our reservation system with the people in our operations all over the world. On the other hand, we have the advantage of having a global concept of the organization in the huge reservation system. The planning and development of the system takes place at a high level, so that we are able to integrate different countries needs into the system. We wanted to have their participation in the global systems. We had a lot of design stage specifications developed from feedback with all of the users all over the world. We wanted to see if we could design the system with all users in mind and then to see if users can adapt the way they are doing work to the system to get a good balance of global and local needs.

"To accomplish anything on a global basis, first of all, the mindset must be flexible. Different customers want different things, and the business systems must be flexible to manage this. For example, the Japanese like a fixed package for a holiday. Europeans tend to be more flexible and want more individual choice. The computer builds tailor-made solutions for the European and packages for the Japanese.

"There are other requirements that vary by country; for example, in Italy we have special country sales taxes. We have built a global system with adaptations for each country."

If employees have a global mindset, building global business processes is a company-wide activity that has a high degree of involvement and commitment throughout the organization.

Step 2. Know Your
Global Customer

At British Airways, John Watson, Director of Human Resources & Information Management, believes that the customer data base is one of the most valuable assets the airline is currently building.

"British Airways is becoming global. We have always been an international airline. It is essential for BA to have an information flow everywhere we operate.

"We create our competitive advantage by customer service, product differentiation, and keeping our cost structure flexible. All of this requires excellent information management.

"The analysis of data on customer preferences is fundamental to our decision-making process. Our customer data base is becoming more important. The more intelligence we can get out of the customer data base, the more we can feed the selling machine of British Airways.

"Building a customer data base is a sophisticated art. It is important to collect data at every point the customer contacts."

British Airways' strategy over the next years is to grow by acquisition to be the leading global airline. Currently, the airline is the world's largest international passenger airline, and the eighth largest in the world overall. BA has a flight taking off every two minutes, with 261,000 flights in 1992 carrying a total of 25 million passengers and 500,000 tonnes of cargo. Their differentiating factor in all of this is their customer service, adapting to customer needs and wants more quickly and, perhaps, more gracefully than any other airline.

Most companies are carrying out customer market research, but it is important to link this information to develop global customer action strategies. Ask the questions:

- How do your customers want greater responsiveness and sensitivity through highly differentiated services?
- What mix of products and services do they prefer?
- Can your company identify significant clusters of global and local preferences from your customer information?
- Do you understand the customer's company culture? How does your customer appeal to his/her customer?

By segmenting the market and identifying specific customers to study, companies can design and package a market research program which would include conducting customer visits and reviews on a pilot basis, executing market research data gathering, synthesizing the results, and developing a global customer action strategy.

Once market research information is available, it is important to make the information available throughout the company so that managers can adapt products and services and maximize global appeal, make an effort to fit in with customer cultural values, create a cultural map of demand to guide business choices, invest in the customer's culture to demonstrate commitment, promote the company's affinity with the customer's culture, fit products and services into the customer's culture to make adoption of products easy, and create a global product/service architecture to be consistent with the customer's perceptions of value.

Customers carry a holistic image of your company wherever they go.

Step 3. Understand the Global/Local Balance and Constantly Adjust It

To build an effective global infrastructure, companies concentrate on building core competencies and expertise, sharing knowledge and data bases, and developing human assets, in addition to project tasking and team assignment, performance measurement, resource allocation, and information and telecommunications technology to monitor global business activities and create resources on a global scale.

J.A. Collins, Chairman & Chief Executive of Shell U.K., assesses his company's global challenges: "Shell is in the risk business, a business entailing huge investments, often with long lead times and considerable uncertainties—political, technical and commercial." To manage these risks and uncertainties, managers will use information on a global basis to maintain what Mr. Collins calls "operational integrity" and we refer to as global consistency.

"For me, probably the greatest challenge for the energy industries, and the most potent influence of change, arises from the growing impact of human activity on the natural environment. The facts are stark. Postwar economic development has been fueled by a fivefold increase in the supply of energy and a corresponding burden on the environment, local, regional and global. Our consumption of natural resources continues to grow, driven by population increase and the material aspirations of those in the developing countries. Every day, the world population grows by about 220,000. UN projections expect the number of people in the world to top six billion at the end of this century and reach more than eight billion by 2025. Today the most affluent 20 percent of the world's population takes about 80 percent of the resources consumed. Modern communications and trade have created the understandable aspiration of the many to enjoy the same material standards of the few."

Rethinking key global resources and capabilities as the economic environment of the world changes involves rethinking the value of time, distance, knowledge, and capital to the business.

One of the ways companies are coping with environmental change is by creating a means to transfer knowledge and sharing breakthroughs across the company, taking advantage of opportunities for leading-edge thinking. Information technology plays a large part by conveying information about changing conditions and knowledge about how to manage them.

Les Alberthal, Jr., Chairman of the Board, President, and CEO of Electronic Data Systems (EDS),* describes the role information technology plays in the process of globalization.

"Winds of change are occurring all over the world, at different speeds, at various rates. They vary by country, by culture, by industry, and by company. Our challenge is to be flexible and visionary enough to stay a step ahead of the process whenever and however it occurs.

"All this change manifests itself in what's called globalization—a process with a different definition every week, every month, every year. In my opinion, a current definition of what it means to be a global corporation must include, in some form, these characteristics:

---

* Les Alberthal, Jr., "Creating an Impact in Today's Global Market Place," keynote address, Thirteenth International Conference on Information Systems (Dallas, Texas, December 1992).

- "The ability to serve global customers anywhere in the world,

- "The ability to gain access to markets anywhere in the world,

- "The ability to establish competitive advantages in those markets and, most importantly,

- "The ability to *leverage all the necessary resources* . . . to take advantage of the talents and skills in each component of the global marketplace.

"If we are going to win access and operate effectively on a global scale, we must acknowledge the emergence of the Triad—the Americas, Asia-Pacific, and the European Community—as the major economic forces in the world today and on into the future. Truly global companies will not only have to serve customers in these areas, but must, in addition, have a major presence and capability in all three areas.

"There's going to be an increased need to link information among all three of these parts of the world. As the interlinked economies of the Triad evolve, the implications for anyone dealing with information technology are clear: the demand from corporations and governments for timely access to information will skyrocket.

"Information technology is the key enabler that fuels globalization. And it's happening in two ways: push and pull. As I.T. evolves, it provides greater capability for businesses to increase their effectiveness. That's the push.

"And as markets change, businesses run into global competitors that increasingly look to I.T. for competitive advantage. There's the pull.

"This 'push and pull' process is propelling us toward the creation of an electronic highway system across the country.

"As far as technological change goes, there's no foreseeable end to the underlying innovation that's happening in our marketplace. If you look at the Research and Development facilities out there, it's clear that the generation of new inventions will continue on indefinitely.

"But you know, there's a bit of a problem with all of this innovation. Society has spent billions and billions of dollars in creating technology. That growth curve has increased tremendously with time. And we all become totally infatuated with these new inventions.

"However, we've spent far less time and money applying technology. This curve has had significantly less growth. The distance between our investment in technology and our ability to achieve a proper return on that investment represents a major gap in our ability to create competitive advantage.

"The next several decades will be heavily influenced by, and rapidly changed by, the new processes of leveraging the technology that has been and will be created. The rewards will go to those who achieve maximum impact from their investments.

"The four keys to global success are (1) focussing on the customer (2) committing to developing global leadership skills corporate-wide, (3) thriving on cultural diversity—attracting and retaining a variety of people from different countries who are team-focused and more results-oriented, and (4) leveraging resources including knowledge, expertise, and experience."

Step 4. Move from Isolation to Partnership

Years ago, most managers believed that each company should be vertically integrated from raw materials sourcing through product delivery. Today, as managers in companies attempt to compete in global marketplaces by focussing on their core competencies, they are building strategies that rely on partners for noncore activities.

Most major airlines, for example, have subcontracted food preparation and catering. Many companies have outsourced their payroll processing. Banks provide factoring and cash management services. The network and information management industries are growing at a rapid rate. Outsourcing is now moving into the managerial activities of the firm as well as growing in the operational tasks.

The ability to manage partnerships is a key global skill for the future. As customers increase their requests to suppliers to provide a *bundle* of products and services, it will be necessary for companies to form partnerships to meet the customers' expectations.

Step 5. Nurture Global Employees

A company's employees are its most valuable assets. Managing knowledge contributions is an important challenge to the global corporation. Shared missions and experiences bind people together. To create and nurture a shared company culture, companies are increasing involvement among management teams, creating a project or effort that people can be obsessed with or focus on, finding ways to build trust, pushing down decision making, creating programs to share experiences cross-culturally to create mutuality of interest, and encouraging worldwide meetings.

Mr. Lodewijk van Wachem, Chairman of the Supervisory Board of Royal Dutch Petroleum Company,* describes how Shell has striven to build a global culture: "A vital aspect of development is the experience brought to the individual by expatriate postings. They broaden professional compe-

* "Internationalization of business—a challenge to business and management," an address to the 46th German Society for Business Economics conference (Berlin, Oct., 1992).

tence, deepen understanding of our business, and increase personal versatility. Shell companies around the world actively cooperate to ensure a steady stream of development opportunities. Shell has some 5400 people of 76 nationalities currently working outside their own countries. We have Bruneians working in Oman and Omanis in the USA. We have Danes working in Nigeria and Nigerians in Malaysia. This reinforces our professional strength and gives us the flexibility to pursue business opportunities around the globe. But more to the point, it brings cohesion to the Group. It is comparatively rare for people to achieve senior positions in the Shell Group without having worked abroad and it is also unusual for the board of a Shell company not to have at least one expatriate on it. I, for example, spent over half my working life in Shell outside Europe, mainly in Venezuela, Nigeria and Brunei.

"This regular flow of people around the world is an important instrument for the transfer of values and standards. Any organization whatsoever which has an internally consistent set of values embedded in its operations has a head start in any sort of competition. In working abroad, an expatriate brings to the host country a set of values stemming in part from his/her upbringing, in part from his/her experience. Assimilating the values of the host country he/she achieves a synthesis of inestimable value to the business. And, in aggregate, the extent to which many of the senior managers in Shell are personally acquainted with one another is a source of great cohesion allowing many problems to be resolved more quickly and amicably than might otherwise be the case."

Global management of people empowers global knowledge workers, allows more employee decision making, creates programs to open employees' minds and actively build the global portfolio of skills.

Step 6.   Develop Global I.T.

Global I.T. is the necessary infrastructure for global business, however I.T. alone does not ensure success. As many firms turn to fiber optic infrastructures, the investment in I.T. can seem time-consuming and expensive. Some of the benefits include getting the most out of price/performance/power, increased mobility, new or more valuable products and services with information content, better communications, higher integration of capability on desktops for workers, and better matching of customer needs with the company's product and service offerings.

Balancing technological and organizational change is important. Professor Dorothy Leonard-Barton has studied the most effective ways to change work methods using I.T. She calls this "managing integrative innovation." Managing integrative (technology and organization) innovation requires, according to Leonard-Barton, attention to three management domains at once.

"Cultivating users as codevelopers; creating a support system, including a network of supporters and an adequate delivery system for users; and organizational prototyping (i.e., experimentation and planned learning about the integration of the new technology).

"To a degree not necessitated by the old hand-off model,* these three interactive streams require, housed in one person or one team, diverse skills such as an ability to manage differing perspectives and a capacity to design an organizational learning process."

Global applications development is a process involving both business people and people with I.T. skills. By designing global systems with local variations known in the beginning, a great deal of redesign effort and cost can be saved. The global I.T. portfolio includes global product, process, and knowledge-support, and communication systems for control and coordination.

Taking Steps to Accelerate the Globalization Process

The best way to accelerate the globalization process is to get the executives, managers, and employees of the company excited about global business opportunities. The more you can make the global vision meaningful and tangible to employees the better you will be able to energize the corporation in closing the gap between where you are today and where you want to be. You have to live in the future to get to the future.

By encouraging global systems thinking and using multidisciplinary teams to visualize and prototype new capabilities for the future, your company can launch sustainable change. Begin by focussing on the two or three business processes that will have the greatest impact on global customer delight such as improving customer service or producing more customized products.

Building the new models for the corporation of the future will tax your company's collective global imagination and depends on your ability to understand and leverage each others' unique strengths.

Envisioning and realizing the future with a global mindset are the leading challenges for executives and managers today.

Summary

As companies strive toward their global visions they will benefit from major trends which are making global visions more and more realizable. The

---

* Leonard-Barton is referring to the "sign-off" model of innovation where the business users describe their needs to the technical implementor, the implementor develops the system, and delivers the system to the user. The user then signs off on the acceptance of the system, and responsibility for its management and use is passed to the user.

frameworks presented in this book can serve as a useful starting point to help companies understand where they are today and where they need to get to if they are to realize their global visions. Six key steps should become incorporated in the globalization process: creating a clear global vision and mindset, knowing your global customer, understanding the global/local balance, moving from isolation to partnership, nurturing global employees, and developing global I.T.

Action Checklist

1. Use the global strategic ingredients checklist (see Figure P-2) to assess the status of your company (and its competitors). Plot today's position and where you need to be in five years' time.

2. Identify strategic actions which will move you to your desired position.

3. Measure progress on an on-going basis.

4. Bonne chance!!

Index

About the Authors

JOHN L. DANIELS is a vice president of the IBM Consulting Group and heads consulting for IBM Europe. Previously, he was a principal with Nolan, Norton & Co., an information technology firm of KPMG Peat Marwick.

N. CAROLINE DANIELS is a researcher at the London Business School, London, and a fellow at the European Institute for Advanced Studies in Management, Brussels. She has a Ph.D. in Information Management from the London Business School, a Masters from the Sloan School, MIT, and has authored several books on the strategic significance of information technology.